Dictionary
of
Economics

Mark Thompson

Andrew Betsis

Edited by

D.S. PAUL

GlobalELT

ENGLISH LANGUAGE TEACHING BOOKS

GLOBAL ELT LTD, 2015
www.globalelt.co.uk
email: orders@globalelt.co.uk

Dictionary of Economics *by Mark Thompson*
Copyright © 2014
Published by arrangement with Goodwill Publishing House, India
All rights reserved. First published by **Goodwill Publishing House, India**

● *Global ELT Dictionary of Economics* - ISBN: 9781781641163
Copyright for pages: 9 - 22: © Global ELT, 2015

Contents

PREFACE

Economics is the social science that analyses the production, distribution, and consumption of various types of goods and services. The current economic models emerged in the late 19th century, mainly due to a deep study and highly revealing findings by great economists like Adam Smith, David Ricardo, Alfred Marshall, John Stuart Mill and more recently, by John Maynard Keynes.

Publication of Adam Smith's The Wealth of Nations in 1776, has been described by Mark Blaug as "the effective birth of economics as a separate discipline". The book identified land, labour, and capital as the three factors of production and the major contributors to a nation's wealth. Smith discussed the benefits of the specialisation by division of labour. George J. Stingler describes Smith's concept that "the division of labour is limited by the extent of the market" which has been described as the core of the theory of functions of firm and industry, and a fundamental principle of economic organisation. To Smith has also been ascribed "the most important substantive proposition in all of economics" and foundation of resource allocation theory that, under competition, owners of resources, e.g. land, labour, and capital will use them most profitably, resulting in an equal rate of return in equilibrium for all uses.

While Adam Smith emphasised the production of income, David Ricardo focused on the distribution of income among landowners, workers, and capitalists. Ricardo saw an inherent conflict between landowners on the one hand, and labour and capital on the other. He posited that the growth of population and capital, pressing against a fixed supply of land, pushes up rents and holds down wages and profits. Value theory was important in classical theory. Smith wrote that the "real price of everything...is the toil and trouble of acquiring it" as influenced by its scarcity. Smith maintained that, with rent and profit, other costs besides wages, also enter the price of a commodity.

Coming at the end of the classical tradition, John Stuart Mill parted company with the earlier classical economists on the inevitability of the distribution of income produced by the market system. He pointed to a distinct difference between the market's two roles, viz. (i) allocation of resources, and (ii) distribution of income. According to him, the market might be efficient in allocating resources but not in distributing income, making it necessary for society to intervene.

T.R. Malthus used the idea of diminishing returns to explain low living standards. Human population, he felt, tended to increase geometrically, outstripping the production of food, which increased arithmetically. The force of a rapidly growing population against a limited amount of land meant diminishing returns to labour. The result, he claimed, was chronically low wages, which prevented the standard of living for most of the population from rising above the subsistence level.

Marxian economics descended from classical economics, and derived from the work of Karl Marx. The first volume of Marx's major work, *Das Kapital*, was published in German in 1867. In it, Marx focused on the labour theory of value and what he considered to be the exploitation of labour by capital. The labour theory of value held that the value of an exchanged commodity was determined by the labour that went into its production.

Keynesian economics derives from John Maynard Keynes, mainly from his treatise *The General Theory of Employment Interest and Money*, which ushered in contemporary macroeconomics as a distinct field. The book focused on determinants of national income in the short run when prices are relatively inflexible. Keynes attempted to explain in broad theoretical detail why high labour-market unemployment might not be self-correcting due to low "effective demand" and why even price flexibility and monetary policy might be unavailing.

The Chicago school of economics is best known for its free market advocacy and monetarist neo-classical economics systematised supply and demand as joint determinants of price and quantity in market equilibrium, affecting both the allocation of output and the distribution of income. According to Antonietta, it dispensed with the labour theory of value inherited from classical economics in favour of a marginal utility theory of value on the demand side, and a more general theory of costs on the supply side.

Development economics is a branch of economics which deals with various aspects of the development process in low-income countries. Its focus is not only on methods of promoting economic growth but also on improving the potential for the mass of the population.

International trade studies determinants of flows of goods and services across international boundaries. It also concerns the size and distribution of gains from trade. Policy applications include estimating the effects of changing tariff rates and trade quotas. International finance is a macroeconomic field which examines the flow of capital across international borders and the effects of these movements on exchange rate.

The study of factors that explain economic growth, i.e. the increase in output per capita of a country over a long period of time is known as growth economics. The same factors are used to explain differences in the level of output per capita between countries, why some countries grow faster than others and whether countries converge at the same rates of growth.

Public finance is the field of economics that deals with budgeting the revenues and expenditures of a public sector entity, usually government. The subject addresses such matters as incidence of tax, cost-benefit analysis of government programs, effects on economic efficiency and income distribution of different kinds of spending and taxes, and fiscal politics. The last one, an aspect of public choice theory, models, according to R.A. Musgrave, public-sector behaviour analogously to microeconomics.

Economic analysis is applied throughout society, in business, finance and not only the government's activities, but also in education, health, law, politics, social institutions, sports, showbiz besides a large number of other fields.

The *Dictionary of Economics* has been prepared including the main terms of all the above schools and thoughts of economics - from classical to neoclassical - right up to the modern. It is the result of an extensive information search of various sources, including standard textbooks on the subject, journals, academic papers, reports, data mines and sites, as well as interaction with experts in the field.

It contains simple terms, which provide basic information on the subject, as well as complex terms, which relate to the advanced applications of the principles of economics. Since it is a rapidly advancing field and one that is being applied to more and more activities as the human society is progressing further in all parts of the world, and is often faced with new challenges and difficult situations, leading to evolvement of new methods or better and modified applications of established norms, some new terms have emerged in recent times. The dictionary contains all such new terms. Many abbreviations and acronyms have also been included.

Each term has been explained in simple language and lucid manner for easy comprehension by the readers. Standard definitions have been given wherever necessary. Terms relating to all the sub-disciplines of economics have been provided to make it a complete treatise. Modern terminology has been included to keep the readers up to date on latest developments in the field. Another important feature of this dictionary is the inclusion of a large number of illustrations or diagrams to help in proper understanding of the related term. The editor and the publisher take this opportunity to thank all the sources which have been drawn upon to prepare this dictionary.

It is a work of enduring importance and will prove useful to students, teachers and researchers of economics as well as those preparing for UGC NET/SLET and other competitive examinations with economics as an option. It will also benefit businessmen, entrepreneurs and government officials dealing with various projects, making plans and doing some other related work. It will serve as an ideal reference source for schools, colleges and other educational institutes. It will also serve the information needs of a new generation of economists. To those who wish to know about the concepts of economics as defined through the terms, it will provide for a richly rewarding reading.

D.S. Paul

20 Major Stock Exchanges In The World

1. New York Stock Exchange (NYSE) - Headquartered in New York.

2. NASDAQ OMX - Headquartered in New York City.

3. Tokyo Stock Exchange - Headquartered in Tokyo.

4. London Stock Exchange - Headquartered in London.

5. Shanghai Stock Exchange - Headquartered in Shanghai.

6. Hong Kong Stock Exchange - Headquartered in Hong Kong.

7. Toronto Stock Exchange - Headquartered in Toronto.

8. BM&F Bovespa - Headquartered in Sao Paulo.

9. Australian Securities Exchange - Headquartered in Sydney

10. Deutsche Börse - Headquartered in Frankfurt.

11. NYSE Euronext, Europe - Headquartered in Brussels.

12. Bombay Stock Exchange - Headquartered in Mumbai, India.

13. BME Spanish Exchanges - Headquartered in Spain.

14. National Stock Exchange - Headquartered in Mumbai, India.

15. SIX Swiss Exchange - Headquartered in Switzerland.

16. Korea Exchange - Headquartered in Seoul.

17. Shenzhen Stock Exchange - Headquartered in Shenzhen, China

18. Milan Stock Exchange - Headquartered in Milan, Italy.

19. Nordic Stock Exchange Group - Headquartered in Stockholm.

20. Johannesburg Securities Exchange - Headquartered in South Africa.

The world's largest companies by Market Capitalisation (2013)

Name	Industry	Capitalization (USD billions)	Headquarters
Apple	Electronics	$510	United States
ExxonMobil	Oil and gas	$438	United States
Royal Dutch Shell	Oil and gas	$243	Netherlands UK
General Electric	Conglomerate	$212	United States
Chevron	Oil and gas	$211	United States
Nestle	Food processing	$207	Switzerland
Wal-Mart Stores, Inc	Retail	$203	United States
Berkshire Hathaway	Conglomerate	$201	United States
AT&T	Telecommunications	$185	United States
Samsung Electronics	Electronics	$181	South Korea
Petrobras	Oil and gas	$171	Brazil
Toyota	Automotive	$149	Japan
Gazprom	Oil and gas	$145	Russia
Total	Oil and gas	$120	France
Eni	Oil and gas	$94	Italy
Siemens	Conglomerate	$92	Germany
BP	Oil and gas	$89	United Kingdom
Statoil	Oil and gas	$86	Norway
BASF	Chemicals	$80	Germany
Volkswagen Group	Automotive	$77	Germany
Rosneft	Oil and gas	$75	Russia
Nippon Telegraph & Telephone	Telecommunications	$73	Japan
Honda	Automotive	$69	Japan
Daimler	Automotive	$64	Germany
UnitedHealth Group	Health care	$62	United States
CVS Health	Retail	$59	United States
GDF Suez	Electricity and gas utility	$58	France
Allianz	Financial services	$54	Germany
Verizon	Telecommunications	$53	United States
Lukoil	Oil and gas	$51	Russia
Hewlett-Packard	Information Technology	$47	United States
Ford Motor Company	Automotive	$47	United States
E.ON	Electric utility	$47	Germany

The world's largest companies by Market Capitalisation (2013)

Name	Industry	Capitalization (USD billions)	Headquarters
Tesco	Retail	$42	United Kingdom
Glencore Xstrata	Commodities	$42	Switzerland
Hon Hai Precision Industry	Electronics	$41	Taiwan
General Motors	Automotive	$40	United States
Phillips 66	Oil and gas	$39	United States
Costco	Retail	$39	United States
AXA	Financial services	$39	France
Enel	Electric utility	$34	Italy
Assicurazioni Generali	Financial services	$24	Italy
McKesson	Pharmaceuticals	$22	United States
Carrefour	Retail	$17	France
Valero Energy	Oil and gas	$16	United States
JX Holdings	Oil and gas	$16	Japan
Vitol	Commodities		Netherlands Switzerland
Trafigura	Commodities		Switzerland
State Grid Corporation of China	Electric utility		China
SK Group	Conglomerate		South Korea
Sinopec Group	Oil and gas		China
Saudi Aramco	Oil and gas		Saudi Arabia
Pemex	Oil and gas		Mexico
PDVSA	Oil and gas		Venezuela
National Iranian Oil Company	Oil and gas		Iran
Kuwait Petroleum Corporation	Oil and gas		Kuwait
Koch Industries	Conglomerate		United States
Japan Post Holdings	Conglomerate		Japan
Fiat Group	Automotive		Italy
China Railway Corporation	Transport		China
China National Petroleum Corp	Oil and gas		China
Cargill	Food processing		United States

Currency list

Country	Currency	Code
A		**A**
Afghanistan	Afghan Afghani	AFN
Albania	Albanian Lek	ALL
Algeria	Algerian Dinar	DZD
American Samoa	US Dollar	USD
Andorra	Euro	EUR
Angola	Angolan Kwanza	AOA
Anguilla	East Carribbean Dollar	XCD
Antigua and Barbuda	East Carribbean Dollar	XCD
Argentina	Argentine Peso	ARS
Armenia	Armenian Dram	AMD
Aruba	Aruban Florin	AWG
Australia	Australian Dollar	AUD
Austria	Euro	EUR
Azerbaijan	Azerbaijan Manat	AZN
B		
Bahamas	Bahamian Dollar	BSD
Bahrain	Bahraini Dinar	BHD
Bangladesh	Taka	BDT
Barbados	Barbados Dollar	BBD
Belarus	Belarussian Ruble	BYR
Belgium	Euro	EUR
Belize	Belize Dollar	BZD
Benin	West African CFA franc	XOF
Bermuda	Bermudian Dollar	BMD
Bhutan	Bhutanese Ngultrum	BTN
Bolivia	Bolivian Boliviano	BOB
Bosnia and Herzegovina	Convertible Mark	BAM
Botswana	Pula	BWP
Brazil	Brazilian Real	BRL
Brunei Darussalam	Brunei Dollar	BND
Bulgaria	Bulgarian Lev	BGN
Burkina Faso	West African CFA franc	XOF
Burundi	Burundian Franc	BIF
C		
Cambodia	Riel	KHR
Cameroon	Central African CFA franc	XAF
Canada	Canadian Dollar	CAD
Cape Verde	Cape Verdean Escudo	CVE
Cayman Islands	Cayman Islands Dollar	KYD

Central African Republic	Central African CFA franc	XAF
Chad	Central African CFA franc	XAF
Chile	Chilean Peso	CLP
China	Renminbi	CNY
Christmas Island	Australian Dollar	AUD
Cocos (Keeling) Islands	Australian Dollar	AUD
Colombia	Colombian Peso	COP
Comoros	Comorian Franc	KMF
Congo, Democratic Republic	Franc Congolese	CDF
Congo, Republic of	Central African CFA franc	XAF
Cook Islands	New Zealand Dollar	NZD
Costa Rica	Costa Rican Colon	CRC
Cote D'Ivoire	West African CFA franc	XOF
Croatia/Hrvatska	Croatian Kuna	HRK
Cuba	Cuban Peso	CUP
Cyprus	Euro	EUR
Czech Republic	Czech Koruna	CZK

D

Denmark	Danish Krone	DKK
Djibouti	Djiboutian Franc	DJF
Dominica	East Caribbean Dollar	XCD
Dominican Republic	Dominican Peso	DOP

E

Ecuador	US Dollar	USD
Egypt	Egyptian Pound	EGP
El Salvador	US Dollar	USD
Equatorial Guinea	Central African CFA franc	XAF
Eritrea	Nakfa	ERN
Estonia	Euro	EUR
Ethiopia	Ethiopian Birr	ETB

F

Falkland Islands (Malvinas)	Falkland Islands Pound	FKP
Faroe Islands	Danish Krone	DKK
Fiji	Fijian Dollar	FJD
Finland	Euro	EUR
France	Euro	EUR
French Guiana	Euro	EUR
French Polynesia	CFP Franc	XPF
FYR of Macedonia	Macedonian Denar	MKD
French Southern Territories	Euro	EUR

G

Gabon	Central African CFA franc	XAF
Gambia	Dalasi	GMD

Georgia	Lari	GEL
Germany	Euro	EUR
Ghana	Cedi	GHS
Gibraltar	Gibraltar Pound	GIP
Greece	Euro	EUR
Greenland	Danish Krone	DKK
Grenada	East Caribbean Dollar	XCD
Guadeloupe	Euro	EUR
Guam	US Dollar	USD
Guatemala	Quetzal	GTQ
Guinea	Guinean Franc	GNF
Guinea-Bissau	West African CFA franc	XOF
Guyana	Guyana Dollar	GYD

H

Haiti	Gourde	HTG
Honduras	Lempira	HNL
Hong Kong	Hong Kong Dollar	HKD
Hungary	Forint	HUF

I

Iceland	Icelandic Krona	ISK
India	Indian Rupee	INR
Indonesia	Rupiah	IDR
Iran	Iranian Rial	IRR
Iraq	Iraqi Dinar	IQD
Ireland	Euro	EUR
Israel	Shekel	ILS
Italy	Euro	EUR

J

Jamaica	Jamaican Dollar	JMD
Japan	Yen	JPY
Jordan	Jordanian Dinar	JOD

K

Kazakhstan	Tenge	KZT
Kenya	Kenyan Shilling	KES
Kiribati	Australian Dollar	AUD
Korea (North Korea)	North Korean Won	KPW
Korea (South Korea)	South Korean Won	KRW
Kuwait	Kuwaiti Dinar	KWD
Kyrgyzstan	Som	KGS

L

Laos	Lao Kip	LAK
Latvia	Euro	EUR
Lebanon	Lebanese Pound	LBP

Lesotho	Loti	LSL
Liberia	Liberian Dollar	LRD
Libya	Lybian Dinar	LYD
Liechtenstein	Swiss Franc	CHF
Lithuania	Lithuanian Litas	LTL
Luxembourg	Euro	EUR

M

Macau	Pataca	MOP
Madagascar	Malagasy Ariary	MGA
Malawi	Kwacha	MWK
Malaysia	Malaysian Ringgit	MYR
Maldives	Rufiyaa	MVR
Mali	West African CFA franc	XOF
Malta	Euro	EUR
Marshall Islands	US Dollar	USD
Martinique	Euro	EUR
Mauritania	Ouguiya	MRO
Mauritius	Mauritius Rupee	MUR
Mayotte	Euro	EUR
Mexico	Mexican Peso	MXN
Micronesia, Federal States of	US Dollar	USD
Moldova, Republic of	Moldovan Leu	MDL
Monaco	Euro	EUR
Mongolia	Tugrik (Tugrug)	MNT
Montenegro	Euro	EUR
Montserrat	East Caribbean Dollar	XCD
Morocco	Moroccan Dirham	MAD
Mozambique	Metical	MZM
Myanmar	Kyat	MMK

N

Namibia	Namibia Dollar	NAD
Nepal	Nepalese Rupee	NPR
Netherlands	Euro	EUR
Netherlands Antilles	Netherlands Antillan Guilder	ANG
New Caledonia	CFP Franc	XPF
New Zealand	New Zealand Dollar	NZD
Nicaragua	Cordoba	NIO
Niger	CFA Franc BCEAO	XOF
Nigeria	Naira	NGN
Niue	New Zealand Dollar	NZD
Northern Ireland	Pound Sterling	GBP
Northern Mariana Islands	US Dollar	USD
Norway	Norwegian Krone	NOK

O

Oman	Omani Rial	OMR

P

Pakistan	Pakistan Rupee	PKR
Palau	US Dollar	USD
Palestinian National Authority	Shekel, Jordanian dinars	ILS, JOD
Panama	Balboa, US Dollar	PAB, USD
Papua New Guinea	Kina	PGK
Paraguay	Guarani	PYG
Peru	Nuevo Sol	PEN
Philippines	Philippine Peso	PHP
Pitcairn Island	New Zealand Dollar	NZD
Poland	Zloty	PLN
Portugal	Euro	EUR
Puerto Rico	US Dollar	USD

Q

Qatar	Qatari Riyal	QAR

R

Reunion Island	Euro	EUR
Romania	Leu	RON
Russian Federation	Russian Ruble	RUB
Rwanda	Rwanda Franc	RWF

S

Saint Helena	Saint Helena Pound	SHP
Saint Kitts and Nevis	East Caribbean Dollar	XCD
Saint Lucia	East Caribbean Dollar	XCD
Saint Vincent and the Grenadines	East Caribbean Dollar	XCD
Samoa	Tala	WST
San Marino	Euro	EUR
Sao Tome and Principe	Dobra	STD
Saudi Arabia	Saudi Riyal	SAR
Scotland	Pound Sterling	GBP
Senegal	West African CFA franc	XOF
Serbia	Serbian Dinar	RSD
Seychelles	Seychelles Rupee	SCR
Sierra Leone	Leone	SLL
Singapore	Singapore Dollar	SGD
Slovakia (Slovak Republic)	Euro	EUR
Slovenia	Euro	EUR
Solomon Islands	Solomon Islands Dollar	SBD
Somalia	Somali Shilling	SOS
South Africa	Rand	ZAR
South Sudan	South Sudanese pound	SDG
Spain	Euro	EUR
Sri Lanka	Sri Lanka Rupee	LKR
Sudan	Sudanese Pound	SDG

Suriname	Suriname Dollar	SRD
Swaziland	Lilangeni	SZL
Sweden	Swedish Krona	SEK
Switzerland	Swiss Franc	CHF
Syrian Arab Republic	Syrian Pound	SYP

T

Taiwan	New Taiwan Dollar	TWD
Tajikistan	Somoni	TJS
Tanzania	Tanzanian Shilling	TZS
Thailand	Baht	THB
Timor Leste	US Dollar	USD
Togo	West African CFA franc	XOF
Tokelau	New Zealand Dollar	NZD
Tonga	Pa'anga	TOP
Trinidad and Tobago	Trinidad and Tobago Dollar	TTD
Tunisia	Tunisian Dinar	TND
Turkey	Turkish Lira	TRY
Turkmenistan	Manat	TMT
Turks and Caicos Islands	US Dollar	USD
Tuvalu	Australian Dollar	AUD

U

Uganda	Uganda Shilling	UGX
Ukraine	Hryvnia	UAH
United Arab Emirates	UAE Dirham	AED
United Kingdom	Pound Sterling	GBP
United States	US Dollar	USD
Uruguay	Uruguayan Peso	UYU
Uzbekistan	Uzbekistan Som	UZS

V

Vanuatu	Vatu	VUV
Vatican City State (Holy See)	Euro	EUR
Venezuela	Venezuelan bolívar	VEF
Viet Nam	Dong	VND
Virgin Islands (British)	US Dollar	USD
Virgin Islands (U.S.)	US Dollar	USD

W

Wales	Pound Sterling	GBP
Wallis and Futuna Islands	CFP Franc	XPF
Western Sahara	Moroccan Dirham	MAD

Y

Yemen	Yemeni Rial	YER

Z

Zambia	Kwacha	ZMK
Zimbabwe	Zimbabwe Dollar	ZWD

A

a/c. account

ADTV Average Daily Trading Volume. It is the average of the amount of stock traded during a certain amount of time during a day.

agcy. agency

agt. agent

AIR Assumed Interest Rate

AMEX American Stock Exchange. It is the third largest in the United States. It has more than 700 companies in it and is headquartered in New York City.

AP Accounts Payable

APR Annual Percentage Rate

ARM Adjustable Rate Mortgage

ARPU Average Revenue Per User

ASAP As Soon As Possible

ASP Average Selling Price

asst. assistant

B

B2B Business to Business

B2C Business to Consumer

BAS Business Activity Statement

BAU Business As Usual

BD Business Development

bldg. building

BRU Business Recovery Unit

BUSI Business

C

C&F Cost with Freight

CAGR Compound Annual Growth Rate

CAO Chief Accounting Officer

CAPEX Capital Expenditure

CAPM Capital Asset Pricing Model

CB Current Bid. It is the amount of the bids at the current time.

CDO Collateralized Debt Obligation

CDS Credit Default Swap

CEO Chief Executive Officer

CFA Chartered Financial Analyst

CFC Consumption of Fixed Capital

CFCT Cash Flow Cycle Time

CFD Contract For Difference

CFM Certified Financial Manager

CFO Chief Financial Officer

CFO PEX Capital Expenditures

CFS Consolidated Financial Statement

CIA Certified Internal Auditor

CIF Cost Insurance with Freight

CIMA Chartered Institute of Management Accountants

CIO Chief Information Officer or Chief Investment Officer

CISA Certified Information Systems Auditor

CMA Certified Management Accountant

CMO Chief Marketing Officer

CMP Current Market Price. It is the price at which the stock is currently being traded. This figure is between the asking price of the stock and the bidding price.

COA Chart Of Account

COB Close Of Business

COGS Cost Of Goods Sold

COO Chief Operating Officer

Corp. Corporation

CPA Certified Public Accountant

CPP Certified Payroll Professional

CPU Cost Per Unit

CRM Custome Relationship Management

CSO Chief Security Officer

CTO Chief Technology Officer

CVP Cost Volume Profit

CD Certificate of Deposit

Depreciation and Amortization

EDI Electronic Data Interchange

EFT Electronic Funds Transfer

EFTPOS Electronic Funds Transfer at Point Of Sale

EOB End Of the Business

EOD End Of the Day

EPS Earnings Per Share

ERP Enterprise Resource Planning

ETF Exchange Traded Funds

EXP Export

ETA Estimated Time of Arrival

ETD Estimated Time of Delivery

D

DDA Depletion Depreciation Amortization

dept. department

DI Dispatch Information

disc. discount

DJIA Dow Jones Industrial Average. The average is taken from 30 of the top traded securities. It was first calculated by the founder and editor of the Wall Street Journal Charles Dow.

DMA Direct Market Access

DSP Delivery Service Provider

F

FDIC Federal Deposit Insurance Corporation

FDP Finance Department

FIFO First In, First Out

FIX Financial Information Exchange

FL Financial Leverage

FOB Freight On Board

FOC Free Of Cost

FOREX Foreign Exchange

FP&A Financial Planning & Analysis

FPO Follow on Public Offer

FRB Federal Reserve Board

FX Foreign exchange market

FYI For Your Information

E

EACs Export Assistance Centers

EAR Effective Annual Rate

EAY Effective Annual Yield

EBIT Earnings Before Interest and Taxes

EBITDA Earnings Before Interest, Taxes,

G

GAAP Generally Accepted Accounting Principles

GAAS Generally Accepted Audit Standards

GDP Gross Domestic Product

GFCF Gross Fixed Capital Formation

GL General Ledger

GNP Gross National Product

GP Gross Profit

GPO Group Purchasing Organization

GRN Goods Receipt Note

GSV Gross Sales Value

H

HQ Headquarters

HR Human Resources

HRD Human Resource Development

I

IAS International Accounting Standards

ICB Industry Classification Benchmark

ICRM Innovative Customer Relationship Management

IE Interest Expense

IFRS International Financial Reporting Standard

ILCLP IdentLogic Systems Customer Loyalty Program

IMF International Monetary Fund

IMP Import

Inc. Incorporated

IPO Initial Public Offering. This occurs the first time a stock is offered to the public.

IR Interest Rate - typically referring to an IR derivative product

IRA Individual Retirement Account. It provides tax breaks for people who are saving for retirement and invests in the stock market.

ISM Institute of Supply Management

IYR In Year Revenue

J

J Journal

JIS Just In Sequence

JIT Just In Time

K

K It is used as an abbreviation for 1,000. For example $225K would be understood to mean $225,000, and $3.6K would be understood to mean $3,600. Multiple K's are not commonly used to represent larger numbers. In other words, it would look odd to use $1.2KK to represent $1,200,000.

KPI Key Performance Indicators. It refers to a type of performance measurement. An organization may use KPIs to evaluate its success, or to evaluate the success of a particular activity in which it is engaged.

KYC Know Your Customer. It refers to due diligence activities that financial institutions and other regulated companies must perform to ascertain relevant information.

L

LBO Leveraged BuyOut
LC Letter of Credit
LIBOR London InterBank Offered Rate
LIFO Last In, First Out
LLC Limited Liability Company
LOI Letter Of Intent
Ltd. Limited Company

M

mfg. manufacturing
MGMT Management
MMKT Money Market
MoM Month on Month / Month over Month
MOQ Minimum Order Quantity
MOU Memorandum Of Understanding
MPC Marginal Propensity to Consume
MRO Maintenance, Repair and Operations
MSOD Monthly Statement of select   Operational Data
MSRP Manufacturer's Suggested Retail Price
MTD Month To Date

N

NASDAQ National Association of Securities Dealers Automated Quotation. Over 3,000 companies are traded on it and it is the second largest in the United States.
NAV Net Asset Value
NCND Non-Circumvent and Non-Disclosure
NDA Non-Disclosure Agreement
NIM Net Interest Margin

NOA Net Operating Assets
NOI Net Operating Income
NOPAT Net Operating Profit After Tax
NPV Net Present Value
NTE Not To Exceed
NYSE New York Stock Exchange

O

OC Opportunity Cost
OCF Operating Cash Flow
OEM Original Equipment Manufacturer
OIBDA Operating Income Before Depreciation And Amortization
OPEX Operational Expenditures
OTC Over-the-counter (finance)

P

P&L Profit and Loss
P/E Price-to-Earnings ratio
PA Purchasing Agent
PAT Profit After Tax
PBT Profit Before Tax
PEG Price-to-Earnings Growth ratio
PFD Preferred stock.This is stock which has a higher priority than common stock.
PMAC Period Moving Average Cost
PO Profit Objective or Purchase Order
PP&E Property, Plant and Equipment
PPP Purchasing Power Parity
PR Purchase Requisition
PSP Profit Sharing Plan

Q

QC Quality Control
QTD Quarter-to-Date
QTE Quote. It refers to a stock's last price it was traded for on its exchange.

R

R&D Research and Development
RE Retained Earnings
REIT Real Estate Investment Trust
RFP Request for Proposal
ROA Return On Assets
ROCE Return On Capital Employed
ROE Return On Equity
ROI Return On Investment
ROIC Return On Invested Capital
RONA Return On Net Assets
ROS Return On Sales
RR Resource Rent
RSP Retail Selling Price

S

S&OP Sales and Operations Planning
SAAS Software-as-a-Service
SCBA Social Cost Benefit Analysis
SCM Supply Chain Management
SEBI Securities and Exchange Board of India
SEC Securities and Exchange Commission

SG&A Sales, General and Administrative expenses
SIOP Sales Inventory and Operations Plan
SIR Stores Issuance Requisition
SIV Structured investment vehicle
SKU Stock Keeping Unit
SME Small and Medium Enterprises
SOHO Small Office/Home Office
SOP Standard Operating Procedure
SOX Sarbanes-Oxley
SROI Social Return On Investment
St Sales, during time period t.

T

TB Transaction Banking
TBC To Be Completed
TBD To Be Defined
TCO Total Cost of Ownership
TCV Total Contract Value
TSA Tax-Sheltered Annuity
TSR Total Shareholder Return

U

USP Unique Selling Propositon

V

VAD Value-Added Distributor
VAR Value-Added Reseller
VAT Value-Added Tax

W

w.r.t with respect to
WACC Weighted Average Cost of Capital
wasp weighted average selling price
WC Working Capital
WFH Work From Home
WIGs Wildly Important Goals
wk week
WLL With Limited Liability
wo work order
wrk work
WVN Withdraw Voucher Note

Y

YOY Year-Over-Year
YTD Year-To-Date
YTG Year-To-Go
YTM Yield-To-Maturity

Z

zcyc zero coupon yield curve

A

a priori
It is a form of first principles. The assumptions of an a priori argument are axioms that have to be assumed, and cannot be derived from empirical evidence. Though it is not advisable in economics to base policy prescriptions on purely a priori arguments, yet all economic arguments necessarily contain some a priori elements.

A.A.A.
It refers to the highest possible rating which is given by rating agencies like CRISIL, Moody's, Standard and Poor's, etc. in respect of the credit standing of outstanding corporations and companies. It is an indication of considerable commercial integrity and minimal risk of default.

abandoned option
It is used to refer to the situation when a buyer does not exercise his share option because the valuation is not in his/her favour.

abatement cost
It is the cost incurred for mitigating a problem like pollution or congestion.

ability to pay
It is the taxation principle that any tax should fall on those who can afford to pay. Paying for public goods or income redistribution requires taxes. Making the ability to pay as the base means that taxes should increase with the income or assets of taxpayers, and as some minimum consumption is needed for subsistence, taxes should be progressive rather than proportional. It is also fair for equal distribution of income and wealth in society.

above-the-line
It refers to the part of the budget which shows the current government expenditure and income. This part is above the line of division.

abscissa
It refers to the value on the horizontal (or X) axis of a point on a two dimensional graph.

absenteeism
The term denotes the act of absenting oneself from work without giving any reasonable cause and without any prior intimation or consent of the employer.

absolute advantage
It can be defined as the use of less resources per unit of output than other producers. If a country has more labour than others do, it has an absolute advantage, taking other factors as equal. In a world with many factors of production, absolute advantage is often hard to measure.

absolute cost advantage
The term was given by David Ricardo. It refers to a situation when a nation holds an advantageous position to produce an article, as compared to another nation.

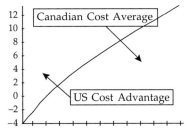

Absolute cost advantage

absolute difference in cost theory of international trade
It is a theory based on the absolute cost advantage principle where one nation has an absolute advantage in producing one good while the other nation has an absolute advantage in producing the another product. Such difference in cost leads to international trade.

absolute monopoly
The term is used for the control of the entire output of a commodity or service, for which there exists no substitute, by a single producer or supplier. Such kind of situation, however, rarely arises in real life. It is also called pure monopoly or perfect monopoly. The central idea is that the demand curve is perfectly inelastic.

absorption
It refers to the following:
1. It is the total expenditure on real goods, services, consumption, and investment by people and by the government.
2. Also the use of output; it excludes exports

and includes imports. This contrasts with production, which includes exports and excludes imports.

abundant
It means available in plentiful supply. It is meaningful only in relative terms, compared to demand and/or to supply at another place or time.

abundant factor
The term refers to the factor that is available in abundant supply in a country relative to other countries. It can be defined with respect to both the quantity and the price.

acceleration principle
It is a principle according to which autonomous investment always leads to a certain volume of induced investment that produces a further expansion of income. It points out the secondary effects on investment and incomes of the original autonomous investment. The basic fact is that the induced investment is a function of change in the level of output. This principle is also referred to as the Theory of Investment. To find the total effect of an increment in investment, multiplier and acceleration principles need to be combined.

accelerator
It is a model relating investment to change in output. The accelerator model states that firms invest more when output rises and less when it falls. This is quite reasonable because a rise in demand leads some firms to produce more, and makes them as well as other firms to expect that demand will rise further.

accelerator coefficient
It is a concept that implies that whenever output is to be increased, factors of production like capital and machinery have to be increased. The incremental capital/output ratio shows how much capital needs to be increased for raising an additional unit of output. If a plant worth $100,000 raises the output in a year by $20,000 the ICOR is 10:2 or 5:1. Accelerator principle depends on this ratio.

acceptance
It denotes to adding one's signature to a bill of exchange, thereby accepting liability to pay the bill at maturity if the original signatory fails to pay. Acceptance of a bill of exchange by an institution of high financial standing, as a merchant bank, makes the bill safer to hold and thus easier to negotiate in the market.

acceptance credit
It is the manner in which payment is done in international trade. In case the accepting house finds the credit of a foreign import merchant satisfactory, it may open an acceptance credit for him/her in a local bank branch.

accessions tax
In many countries, it is a tax which is levied on gifts and inherited property. Such receipts have not been normally classified as income but as they give spending the power, they are arguably a legitimate subject of taxation. An accession tax has been levied on the recipient, and, as it is related to a person's economic circumstances, it is superior, from an equity point of view, to the capital transfer tax where liability is on the donor.

accommodation bill
The term refers to the bill, which is drawn, accepted or endorsed with the sole aim of discounting it and thereby, making some money available for a short term, without receiving any goods in return.

accommodative monetary policy
It refers to a policy of allowing the money supply to expand in line with the demand for it. If the demand for money increases because of sustainable real growth in the economy, accommodative monetary policy is desirable, and failure to expand the money supply will hinder real growth. If, however, the cause of rising demand for money is a temporary phenomenon, money supply may prove counter productive.

account(s)
It is a statement about trade/financial activities over some period. For business houses/entrepreneurs, there is an obligation to produce such a statement. For example, the directors of companies are under an obligation to get the accounts prepared and put before the shareholders, etc. Accounts take various forms:
1. A systematic summary in money terms of the activities of a business over some period, usually a year. The two main statements in such accounts are the profit and loss account and the balance sheet. A profit and loss ac-

...pts and payments, and the ... during an accounting period. ... of the relations between two ... account records the deposits, ...als and interest entries. Firms ... ...ts of the goods and services provide... ...customers.
3. National income and expenditure accounts are surveys of the economic activities of a nation. These include analysis of the production of goods and services, the distribution of incomes, and the expenditure of investors, consumers, and the government.

accounting period
It is the period of time, normally a year, to which a set of company accounts refers. It starts, either from 1st January to 31st December, or, from 1st April to 31st March. In UK, accounting period refers to a period to which United Kingdom corporation tax is changed. It begins whenever a company is included in the corporation tax charge.

accounts payable
It is the amount that a business owes to its suppliers and other creditors, who give the customers a period of 10 to 90 days to pay for the goods already transported.

accounts receivable
It refers to the amount that a business is entitled to receive from its customers who are generally given a period of 10 to 90 days to pay for the goods already transported.

accrual basis
In accounting term, it is the method in which the income and expenses are not charged for the period in which they are actually received. Instead, they are charged for the period in which they are earned or incurred.

ACP countries
The term refers to the 63 African, Caribbean, and Pacific countries that had signed the Rome Convention with the European Economic Community.

acquisition
The term refers to the company expansion through the purchase of other business. If these are unincorporated, terms are agreed with the owners. If the other business is a company, its shares are bought.

active balance
It refers to a balance of payments that is favourable for a country, and which occurs when the revenue earned from exports is higher than the expenditure incurred on the import of goods and services.

actuary
It refers to the following:
1. An expert who uses statistical records to predict the future economic, financial and general conditions. An actuary uses records of the occurrence of uncertain events, such as death at given ages, fire, theft, and other accidents, to predict how frequently similar events are likely to occur in future.
2. A person whose job is to statistically calculate the risks, premiums, etc. for insurance.

Adam Smith
He was the first economist who discussed the problems of economics in a scientific manner in his book, The Wealth of Nations, published in 1776.

adaptive expectations
It is also called the model of expectations' formation in which expectations get adjusted gradually towards observed values of the variable concerned. At any given time, people hold expectations about the future values of economic variables, such as the changes in price, i.e., rate of inflation. Under adaptive expectations, if the level observed in the current period equals what was expected, the expectation does not undergo any significant change.

adjustable peg
It refers to a system where countries stabilise their exchange rates around par values, they retain in the right to change. Under this system, a country intervenes in the foreign exchange market to keep its currency within some margin.

adjustment costs
The term refers to the costs of making changes in the economic variables. Any economic agent, whether an individual, an institution, a firm, or a government, has a utility function which determines what the optimal levels of the variables they control would be, in case they were free to make a fresh start in setting them. When actual levels differ from these optimal levels, adjustment costs

must be considered.

adjustment lags
It denotes a time that a variable, like capital stock, takes to adjust to the changes in its determinants.

adjustment programme
It is a package of policy measures designed by the government or financial authority to cure balance of payments problems. Adoption of a satisfactory adjustment programme is frequently made a condition of assistance from the International Monetary Fund (IMF).

adjustment, price and quantity
The term refers to the relative timing of price and quantity adjustments. If in a market demand and supply conditions change, both price and quantity may need to be adjusted eventually. But the timing of price and quantity changes can vary. In some markets, a market maker sets the price. For example, in normal retail shops, the seller sets a price. In short run, any change in demand results in changes in the quantity sold.

administered price
1. It is a mark up price for a product fixed by a firm, producer or government and determined by an administrative rule, rather than by consideration of its marginal cost. It is done on the basis of the full cost theory of pricing. The seller adds a certain percentage or figure to the total cost and fixes the price.
2. It is a price set by some form of administrative process rather than being adjusted on the basis of market clearing. The levels of, and changes in, administered prices often require the consent of the government or regulatory body. Administered prices are often minima, as in the case of some agricultural policies and minimum wage laws, or maxima as in the case of rent controls.

ad valorem tax
It refers to a tax proportional to the price of the object being taxed. This is in contrast with a specific tax, at a rate per unit of quantity, independent of the price. Ad valorem taxes are often preferred to specific taxes because such taxes are considered unfair as they fall proportionally more heavily on poorer consumers who choose cheaper and lower quality goods.

advance funding
It is a prospect for the bondholders, whose bonds' expiry date is approaching, to exchange such bonds for new ones on some advantageous terms.

advances
The term refers to bank loans extended to their customers. These may be unsecured loans, but are often secured by the bank holding stocks and shares or life insurance unfavourable balance of payment and is characterised by an excess of aggregate imports of goods and services over the aggregate exports of goods and services of a country.

adverse balance of payment
It is also called an unfavourable balance of payment and is characterised by an excess of aggregate imports of goods and services over the aggregate exports of goods and services of a country.

adverse selection
It is the tendency for a contract offered to customers who are least profitable. For example, if an insurer offers medical insurance without any health examinations, the expectation is that people with poor health prospects are likely to accept it, while people with better health prospects, who can get better terms from a more selective insurer, will reject such a contract.

adverse supply shock
It is called a sudden reduction in the supply of an input necessary for an economy. It could result from natural disasters such as hurricanes, floods or earthquakes as well as from human, animal, or plant diseases. It may also result from major political upheavals such as war or revolution.

African Economic Community (AEC)
It refers to an organisation of African countries that aims to promote economic, cultural and social development among the African economies.

after-sales service
It is the provision of services after goods have been sold, which make them more useful to customers. This can include advice on the use of the product, routine maintenance, servicing and repairs in the event of breakdown,

provision of materials, etc., and spare parts replacement under warranty in case of failure of the goods supplied.

after-tax income
It refers to the income remaining with an individual or a company after direct taxes have been paid. It takes no account of liability to indirect taxes when the income is spent.

age-earnings profile
The term implies the relationship between earnings and age. A simple age-earnings profile is expected to be a horizontal line, which is stepping up from childhood at the age of leaving school with the size of the step being determined by the quantity of schooling number of years. The typical post-school age-earnings profile is more complex. The pattern for annual earnings shows a steep increase on leaving school followed by a lower increase until a plateau is reached in the mid-forties, after which a slow and then a faster descent follows.

agenda 21
It is a plan of action adopted at the Rio de Janeiro Summit in 1992 to promote sustainable development.

agglomeration
It refers to the following:
1. A geographical concentration of people and/or activities.
2. The phenomenon of economic activities congregating in or close to a single location rather than spreading out uniformly over the whole region or country.

agglomerationeconomies
The term refers to the following:
1. The external economies available to individuals or firms in large concentrations of population and economic activities. These economies arise because larger markets allow wider choice and a greater range of services. Agglomeration economies are believed to explain the tendency of conurbations to contain an increasing share of the population of many countries.
2. The savings in costs, which accrue to a firm as a result of expansion and concentration of industries in a region. Firms can enjoy three types of savings in cost due to such agglomeration: (i) the internal economies,

(ii) the external economies, and (iii) the locational economies.

aggregate demand
It is the total of intended or exante attempts to spend on final goods and services produced in a country. In a closed economy, aggregate demand is the sum of consumption, investment and government spending on goods and services. In an open economy, it also includes export demand and excludes imports. A rise in aggregate demand is a precondition for an increase in real output.

aggregate demand schedule
A diagram showing each level of national income for the total level of aggregate demand in an economy that would result from it. Internal balance in the economy requires that aggregate demand is equal to national output.

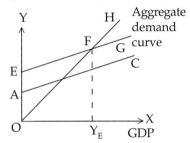

Aggregate demand schedule

aggregate expenditure
It refers to the sum total of nominal expenditures on goods and services in the economy, i.e., Consumption (C), Investment (I) and Government Expenditure (G) together with exports less imports. It can be expressed as: $Y = C + I + G (X - M)$. In the simple income expenditure model, the volume of aggregate expenditure ascertains the volume of output and employment. The volume of these expenditures could vary systematically with changes in the general price level.

aggregate supply
It is the total amount of real goods and services that the enterprises in an economy are willing to provide at any given ratio of prices to wages. It can be increased by rising productivity due to increases in the volume of production equipment or improvements in

technical knowledge, etc. Actual output equals aggregate supply-demands on two conditions: (i) there must be a sufficient aggregate demand to match the supply. (ii) there must be a sufficient supply of labour to satisfy firms' demand for it.

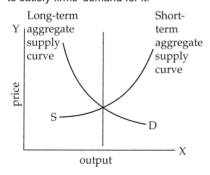

Aggregate supply

agio
It refers to the premium that is paid for exchanging one currency for another or for a foreign bill of exchange.

agio theory of interest
This theory states that interest is a payment for abstaining from current consumption. This is but a partial explanation as there have been other reasons for saving.

agricultural banks
The term refers to the banks that are specifically established to grant loans for the purchase of agricultural inputs.

agricultural goods
It refers to goods produced in the agricultural sector as compared to manufactured good.

agricultural marketing
Marketing is defined as a process of bringing together the producers and the buyers. Agricultural marketing refers to all those activities, which are necessary to carry the farm output from the producers to the consumers at the desired place and time. Marketing is the ultimate point and end of the production process and the marketing activities include the following: (i) Handling and manage ment of the produce in markets, (ii) Storing and warehousing, (iii) Grading and processing of the produce, (iv) Transporting and selling, etc.

agricultural protection
The term refers to the use of tariffs and trade controls on agricultural products to raise their prices in a country and thus to increase its farmers' income. In some countries, it is desirable to slow down the tendency for the share of agriculture in total income and employment to decrease. It may also aim at increasing self-sufficiency in foodstuffs and agricultural raw materials in the interests of national security.

agricultural subsidy
It is the amount paid by the government to the farmers to supplement their income and increase food production.

aid
It is an economic assistance from one country to another, the recipient typically being a least developed country (LDC) like Nepal, Pakistan and Bangladesh. Aid is usually intended either to provide humanitarian relief in emergencies, to promote economic development, or to finance military expenditure. Aid may take the form of outright gifts of money, which may be tied to purchases from the donor, or untied and available for expenditure anywhere.

Allen, Sir Roy George Douglas
Douglas was an economist who shot into fame by writing an article on the uses of indifference curves based on ordinal utility in 1934. He was a lecturer in London School of Economics. In 1944, he was appointed professor of statistics in London University, a post that he held till 1973 for a period of 3 decades. His publications include *Mathematical Economics* (1956), *Statistics for Economists* (1949), *Macroeconomic Theory* (1967) among others.

allocation
It refers to an assignment of economic resources to use. Thus, in general equilibrium, it denotes an assignment of factors to industries producing goods and services, together with the assignment of the resulting final goods and services to consumers.

allocative efficiency
It is a term used in contrast to the optimum functioning of the economy. Allocative efficiency is realised when the existing productive

resources of a country with the available know-how are put to maximum utilisation, leading to the highest level of production at the least average cost. It assumes that the factors of production are available at the least average cost and are mobile over place and purpose.

allotment
The term refers to the allotting of shares or debentures issued by a company to those applicants who have responded positively to a subscription offer.

allotment letter
It is a letter from a company that certifies the number of shares allotted to an applicant and also includes the information about the dates of payment and the manner in which due amounts need to be paid.

alpha stocks
The term refers to the most actively traded securities in the stock exchange. About 50 securities came into this category when it was in official use by the Bombay Stock Exchange. These were shares of companies with high turnover and high market capitalisation.

amalgamation
It is the union or merging of two independent firms or companies to form a single entity.

amber box
The term refers to the category of subsidies in the WTO Agriculture Agreement, the total value of which is to be reduced. It includes most domestic support measures that distort production and trade.

amortisation
The term is used in relation to the payment of a loan in advance. Such a fund can also be created when equated instalments are deposited at regular intervals of time, so as to accumulate an amount equivalent to the amount of debt including interest. It is the building up over a period of a fund to replace a productive asset at the end of its useful life, or to repay a loan. In the case of a loan, the amount required for amortisation depends on the interest rate, which can be earned on the accumulated fund.

analysis of variance
It is a statistical technique based on decomposing the overall variance of some characteristic of a population into parts correlated with other characteristics, and residual variation. The analysis of variance is particularly used to test whether sections of a population appear to differ significantly in some property. For example, if x is the personal income of an individual i, analysis of variance can be used to test whether there are significant regional differences in mean income.

announcement effect
The term, given by David Ricardo, refers to the effect of an announcement of a change in policy even before it is actually put into effect. For example, a promise by the government to increase taxes next year may lead to an immediate reduction in consumer spending, or an immediate rise in interest rates.

annual general meeting (AGM)
It is a meeting of the voting shareholders of a company, or the members of an association, in which the officers report on the last year's activities, and accounts are submitted for approval. Some important announcements relating to dividend, bonus, split, etc., are made in the AGMs.

annual percentage rate of interest
This term refers to the rate of interest on any loan calculated as interest paid per unit of the principal amount still outstanding.

annual report
This term refers to the statement of a company's finances and, often, prospects for the future.

annual report accounts
It is an annual report on a company's or other organisation's activities and accounts during the last financial year. The annual report is normally presented by the chairman at the annual general meeting of share-holders or members.

annuity
The term denotes the following:
1. A contract by which a financial institution such as an insurance company agrees to provide a regular income for life. The name annuity comes from annual payments, but

the payments can in fact be of any agreed frequency. The recipient will be a named person. There is also a provision to contract for full or reduced payments for life to surviving spouse or other dependents.

2. A type of life insurance contract that guarantees periodic payments to the insured at some future time, usually retirement. Thus there are two types of annuity: (i) *annuity certain*: It is annuity for some fixed period in which part of principal and interest are paid in equal instalments at fixed intervals and after the fixed period, the balance becomes nil. (ii) *annuity in perpetuity*: It yields only interest at fixed times and runs indefinitely.

anti-dumping action

It is the procedure by which complaints of dumping are investigated and the case for the imposition of anti dumping duties is assessed. Anti-dumping actions are processed by importing countries. Usually, a tariff commission investigates whether dumping has occurred, and whether it is causing injury to the domestic industry.

anti-dumping duty

It refers to the following:

1. A tariff levied on dumped imports. The threat of an anti-dumping duty can deter imports, even when it has not been used and anti-dumping is, therefore, a form of non-tariff barrier.

2. A tariff imposed to protect domestic producers of a good against competition from dumping of imports. Such duties are imposed only after investigation of complaints by domestic producers.

antitrust

It is a US term for policies designed to restrict monopoly and promote competition. The Antitrust Division of the US Department of Justice issues antitrust policies. The name comes from the US use of trusts to describe large firms formed by amalgamation. The US antitrust measures frequently work by making practices such as hoardings, monopoly and price discrimination illegal.

applied economics

It can be defined as a branch which is separate from the pure economics or economic theory. While economic theory is the scientific study of the economic generalisations,

the applied economics is the application of these laws in day-to-day solutions of the economic problems.

appraisal

It is an assessment of the worth, especially that of a property or business, for the determination of loans, insurances, taxes, tariffs, sale prices, etc.

appreciation

The term implies the following:

1. An increase in the value of something, particularly, in terms of value of shares or property, whose appreciation leads to the increase in their price.

2. A rise in the value of a country's currency on the exchange market, relative either to a particular other currency or to a weighed average of other currencies. The currency is said to appreciate.

apprenticeship

It denotes a system by which firms recruit workers, typically young ones, for an initial period of employment during which they are supposed to spend part of their time training. Training for apprentices may be provided either by formal instructional course within the firm or at outside institutions, or by learning on the job working under a supervisor.

appropriation account

It is an account which shows what has been done with the total funds available to a company, firm, enterprise or other organisation. It shows the division of total funds among tax payments, real investment, taking external loans or purchasing securities, retention of cash balance, and distribution to shareholders.

appropriation bill

The term refers to a US federal legislative bill authorising expenditure. This has to be approved by both houses of Congress before being passed.

arbitrage

The term refers to the following:

1. The simultaneous buying of currency, securities or goods from one market and selling them in another market at a higher price.

2. A combination of transactions designed to get profit from an existing discrepancy among

prices, exchange rates and/or interest rates in different markets without the risk of changing these.

3. Buying a good or asset in one market where price is low, and simultaneously selling it in another market where price is higher. For example, buying a particular share at NSE if the price is low and selling at BSE if price is high, thus making a profit. This does not involve taking any risks.

arbitrageur

The term denotes the following:
1. A person or company who/which undertakes a set of transactions involving buying in one market and selling in another, where the prices are known simultaneously.
2. It is also used to describe those who buy and sell companies or parts of companies at the pre-arranged prices, again taking very little risk.

arbitration

It defines a system for settling disputes by submitting them to the judgement of a mediator acceptable to both parties. An arbitrator may be an independent individual, or a committee, often containing nominees of both the parties with an independent person in the chair. Arbitration is often used in commercial and labour disputes, as it is usually quicker and cheaper than legal or industrial action. It is binding on the parties to accept the results.

arithmetic mean

It is called the sum of a set of N numbers a_1, a_2, ... a_n, divided by N, denoted by $(\Sigma_i a_i)/N$. This can be calculated for any set of finite numbers, whether positive, zero, or negative. The arithmetic mean, or unweighted average, is what is normally meant by the use of 'average' without further comment.

ASEAN

It is the acronym for Association of Southeast Asian Nations.

Asian Development Bank

It refers to a multilateral institution based in Manila, Philippines, that provides financing for development needs in countries of the Asia-Pacific region.

Asia-Pacific Economic Cooperation (APEC)

It is an association of nations around the Pacific Rim aiming at the creation of a Pacific free trade area. The body was set up in 1990 and has 18 members, including Australia, Canada, Chile, China, Indonesia, Japan, Malaysia, Mexico, New Zealand, Singapore, and the US. It aims at creating a free trade area for its industrialised members by 2010. It is devoted to promoting open trade and practical economic cooperation.

assembly line

It is a device used for moving a good being produced, for example, a bus or a car, past a sequence of workers or machines. As it passes each workstation, a particular task is performed. Tasks may include adding components, working on components already in place, or checking the work of earlier stages. This system of production allows economies of scale, by keeping down the time needed to move workers or machines from one task to another. It also leads to building teams of experts for different types of work in a manufacturing unit.

asset move

It refers to the incentive to hold money as a store of value. If prices are expected to be stable, money is a poor store of value as it earns little or no interest. When inflation is expected, money does even worse as a store of value. If prices fall, however, money is an attractive asset.

asset price

It is the price of assets, including land and building, or machinery owned. Financial assets include cash and securities as well as credit extended to customers. The assets side of a company's balance sheet includes both real and financial assets.

asset-stripping

It refers to a pejorative description of the process of dividing up the assets of a company in cases where the total value of the parts when separated is greater than their value when combined. Examples include selling off unused or underutilised land building, or activities where heavy investment carries tax allowances which the company cannot use, to other companies whose large present profits make the tax allowances valuable to them.

associated company

The term refers to an independent company that is connected or related to another independent company in a particular manner.

asymmetric information

It is a situation where economic agents do not have all the same information. This is, of course, the actual situation in any real economy. No economic agent has access to full information and each has some information that others do not. Information is available to some agents and not to others for various reasons. Some information is private, e.g. concerning the state of agent's own mind.

at par

It means at equality. Two currencies are said to be 'at par' if they are trading one-for-one.

at sight

It refers to the payment of a bill of exchange or promissory note when presented, i.e. on demand.

attrition

It is a term of labour economics, which refers to the waste of labour force that occurs naturally because of voluntary quits, retirements, discharges for cause, and deaths.

auction

It is a sale where the price is fixed by an auctioneer who invites bids, and awards the article being auctioned to the highest bidder. In an open auction, the highest bid is publicly announced at each stage, and other parties are given a chance to make higher bids. In a sealed-bid auction, the bids are not publicly announced. Each bid is submitted sealed, and a time limit is set at which the auctioneer opens the bids and awards the article to the highest bidder.

auctioneer

It denotes the following:
1. A representative of a seller, who is authorised to sell his goods at an auction.
2. An agent whose job is to bring about the fixing of a mutually acceptable price between buyer(s) and seller(s).

audit

It is the process of checking accounts. Auditors check whether the accounts of a company, private trader, or association are complete and consistent, whether they agree with other records of purchases, sales and inventories, and whether they comply with legal requirements and professional standards of accounts like GAAP. Companies are legally required to have their accounts externally audited, and many other bodies are required to do so by their own constitutions.

auditor

The term refers to a person or accountancy firm employed or hired to check the accounts of a company, private trader or association. Auditors check whether accounts are complete and consistent, and whether they are in agreement with other records of purchases, sales and inventories. They may certify that accounts present a 'true and fair view' of a company's finances, or they can 'qualify' the accounts, that is, add adverse comments.

auditor's report

It describes a report that a person who audits a company's accounts submits after examining the accounts and relevant records of the company.

autarchy

It is a situation when a country takes up the goal of complete self-sufficiency. At times, it was advocated on grounds of protection. In the present times of close interdependence and globalisation, the concept or maxim of self-sufficiency does not find any support in any part of the world, because it deprives us of the manifold benefits of the international trade. This, however, is not to deny the usefulness of self-sufficiency in essential economic overheads.

authorised capital

It is the nominal value of the shares a company is empowered to issue. Companies often extend their authorised capital in advance of the actual issue of new shares. It allows the timing of capital issues to be fixed in the light of the firm's need for new capital and the state of the capital market and allows sharing options to be exercised.

automation

The term refers to the following:
1. It is the mechanisation of the various operations of an economy.

2. The production by machinery, usually, computer-controlled, without the need for immediate human intervention. Automation is particularly useful where extreme accuracy is required, or in processing dangerous materials, where it may be difficult and expensive to protect the operators.

automatic stabilisers
These are factors that avoid extreme fluctuations in the functioning of an economy without any specific effort of the government, e.g. social security insurance, which has come to prevail in so many progressive parts of the world. When level of employment, output and income falls, it does not any longer proportionately reduce the aggregate effective demand as the unemployed persons receive from the public exchequer unemployment benefits.

autonomous consumption
It is that part of consumption which does not depend on current income. If aggregate consumption, C, is given by: $C = x + yY_z$, where Y_z is disposable income, a can be regarded as autonomous consumption, and $x>0$ because even those with no income need to consume to live, and can finance expenditure by running down assets or borrowing.

autonomous investment
It is that part of investment which is not explained by changes in the level of output. It includes investment in public services, which are determined by government policy, and investment to exploit new technical knowledge.

average
It refers to a statistical summary measure of size. The average of a set of numbers may be weighted. The unweighted average or arithmetic mean of a set of N numbers a_1, a_2, ...a_N is their sum divided by N, written $(\Sigma_i a_i)/N$. In an unweighted average, an equal weight is given to each number, which is often appropriate if the data concern individuals. A weighted average gives a 'weight' to each observation, denoted w_i; it is then the sum of the products of observations and their weights, $(a_i w_i)$, divided by the sum of the weights, written $(\Sigma_i a_i w_i)/(\Sigma_i w_i)$.

average cost
It refers to the following:
1. It is the total cost of production divided by the quantity produced. Average fixed cost invariably decreases with output. Average variable cost may decrease with output up to the point where the limits of capacity become a constraint, after which it tends to rise. If the average variable cost rises faster than the average fixed cost calls, this produces a U-shaped average cost curve.
2. Cost of statistical nature, rather than being an actual cost. It is obtained simply by dividing the total cost (TC) by the total output (Q), i.e., TC/Q = average cost.

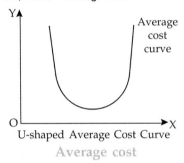

U-shaped Average Cost Curve

Average cost

Average total cost will be comprised of average fixed cost (AFC) and average variable cost (AVC).
Hence ATC = AFC + AVC.

average cost pricing
It refers to the policy of setting prices so as just to cover average costs, allowing the producer to break even. This is clearly not a wise policy for profit-maximising firm, but it may be so for a governmentcontrolled firm, or for a private but non-profitmaking body. The average cost pricing is distinct from marginal cost pricing, which is sometimes argued to be the first best pricing policy for a producer operating in the public interest.

average fixed cost (AFC)
It refers to the following:
1. The total fixed cost divided by the output. The average fixed cost will decline as the output increases. This is because as output increases the fixed costs are spread further and further.
2. In the theory of the firm, fixed costs are the costs of production, which are constant, whatever the level of output.

averaging

It denotes purchasing more of a security in the event of a decrease in its price so as to lower the average cost of a holding.

average total cost (ATC)

It refers to the amount spent on producing each unit of output. The average cost is obtained by dividing the total cost by the number of units produced. The average total cost is made up of two elements, the average fixed cost and the average variable.

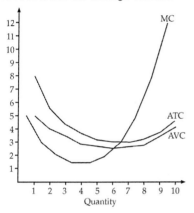

Average total cost

average variable cost (AVC)

It is the total variable cost divided by the number of units of output produced. Therefore, average variable cost is the variable cost per unit of output.

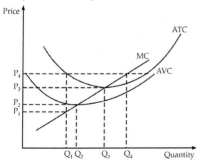

Average variable cost

avoidable cost

It refers to the part of the cost of any output that could be saved by not producing it. Some costs are clearly not avoidable, for example, capital costs. Other costs might appear to be avoidable at first hand, but may actually not be.

axioms

In economics, these are propositions, which form a set of relationships (which are specific in terms of the direction of the relationship and are assumed to be true as a basis for argument or inference but may not be true in actuality.

axis

It is a line in a graph along which one variable is held constant, often at zero, while only the other varies. Axes are normally drawn at right angles. Each axis of a graph is clearly labelled to show what is being measured along it, and the scale and units of measurement in use.

B

back door
It refers to the system by which the Bank of England changes the UK money supply by dealing in treasury bills on its own initiative at the market rate. This system is distinguished from the front door, when it lends to discount houses at their initiative, as a lender of the last resort.

backward-bending supply curve
It refers to a graph that illustrates the theory that when the wages of people increase, they start to spend more of their time on leisure instead of on working. In other words, it is a labour supply curve that is positively sloped for relatively small wages and negatively sloped for large wages.

backward integration
The term refers to the expansion of a firm's activities to include the production of inputs already bought from outside. Examples include a firm manufacturing its own components, mining its own mineral requirements, generating its own power supplies, among other things.

backwash effect
Its states that the economic growth in one region of an economy brings adverse effects on the growth of other regions. Such effects are said to be principally of flows of factors of production (generally labour and capital) from slow growing to fast growing region.

bad debt provision
It is a statement in the accounts of a creditor to write off bad debts, i.e., to cease to record them as assets in accounts. A firm with bad debts must, at some stage, decide to write them off. If it has numerous debtors, each of doubtful solvency, it is possible to make in the account books, a 'bad debt provision'.

bad debt
It is the debt whose repayment is known to be impossible or unlikely. Failure of the borrower to make payments of principal or interest on the due dates is a clear evidence that a debt should be suspect. A debt can become bad even before the payments are actually due if the debtor is known or believed to be insolvent.

balance budget
It refers to equality between total government receipts and expenditure. There is thus no need to borrow and thereby increase the government debt. In a fluctuating economy, it is neither possible nor desirable to have the budget exactly balanced each year. Some economists believe, however, that the budget should be balanced on average over a trade cycle. Others argue that there is no point in balancing the budget, and state that there is in any case so much scope for dispute over the definition of the budget deficit that the argument is pointless.

balanced budget multiplier
The term refers to the argument found in Keynesian economic model. It states that a rise in government spending on real goods and services combined with an equal rise in taxation, leaving the budget deficit or surplus unaltered, must increase the national product by exactly the amount spent.

balanced growth
It refers to the growth of all sectors like industry, agriculture, services, etc., and regions of an economy at the same proportional rate. This is unlikely ever to be observed in any actual economy, and it is hard to understand why it should ever have been thought to be desirable. It is true that if growth is so unbalanced that some sectors or regions of an economy actually decline, this may give rise to dissatisfaction among certain sectors and other problems like unequal distribution of income and wealth.

balance of payments
It refers to the following:
1. An overall record of a country's economic transactions with the rest of the world over some period, often a financial year. A table of the balance of payments shows amounts received from the rest of the world and amounts spent abroad. The current account includes exports and imports, i.e., visible trade, and receipts from and spending abroad on services such as tourism.
2. The difference between total receipts and expenditure in any category of payments. Overall payments, including changes in foreign exchange reserves, must balance by definition, but this is not true for any one category of payments. The balance of pay-

ments on current account is the difference between total receipts and expenditures on current account. If receipts exceed spending, there is a current account surplus, and if spending exceeds receipts, there is current account deficit.

balance-of-payments crisis
The term refers to an unsustainable balance of payments. This means that foreign exchange reserves are falling rapidly, or are being maintained only by a level of foreign borrowing, which may lead to difficulties in obtaining further loans. A balance-of-payments crisis may be ended by improving the balance of payments on current account, via a slowdown in domestic activity, or by devaluation.

balancing item
It is an entry in a set of accounts to cover the incongruity between two different figures for the same item. This is used when two methods of measurement produce different results for figures which should by definition be the same, if both methods were completely accurate.

balance of payments surplus
It refers to a number summarising the state of a country's international transactions, usually equal to the balance on current account plus the balance on capital account.

balance of trade
The term denotes the following:
1. It is the excess of visible exports over visible imports. This is a major, but not the only component of the balance of payments on current account.
2. The value of a country's exports minus the value of its imports. Unless specified as the balance of merchandise trade, it normally incorporates trade in services, including earnings, i.e., interest, dividends, etc., on capital.

balance sheet
It is a statement of money values of the assets and the liabilities of an individual, a firm, a company or any other organisation at some moment, particularly the end of a financial year. Assets can include money, securities, land, buildings and other capital equipment, stocks and raw material, and amounts due from debtors. Liabilities include secured and unsecured debts, taxes, insurance dues, etc. The excess of assets over liabilities is the net worth of the firm; for a solvent firm this is positive, and is treated as a liability of the firm to its shareholders. Any firm whose liabilities exceed its assets is insolvent.

banana war
The term refers to a trade dispute between the European Union (EU) and the US over EU preferences for bananas from former colonies. On behalf of US-owned companies exporting bananas from South America and the Caribbean, the US complained to the WTO, which ruled in favour of the US.

bandwagon effect
The term refers to the effect whereby the price of a good falls and demand by some sections or individuals in the community expands. Other individuals or sections follow the reaction and expand their demand too.

bank
It is a financial institution whose main activities are borrowing and lending money. Banks borrow by accepting deposits from the general public or other financial institutions. Bank loans are an important source of finance for firms, companies, institutions, consumers and government. Commercial banks may be all-purpose, or may specialise. Investment banks specialise in loans to firms, merchant banks on financing capital market transactions and international trade. Agriculture Development Banks lend money to buy agricultural inputs. In India, there are Regional Rural Banks (RRBs), which are located in rural and semi-urban areas and cater to the banking services for local people in a region. Sayers defines a bank as "an institution whose debts are widely accepted in settlement of other people's debts to each other." Bank is an institution which individuals entrust with their money when not needed, and an institution that advances money to individuals required by them subject to safety of return. It is a financial intermediary and a dealer in loans and debts. It manufactures credit and facilitates exchanges. The main functions of banks are: mobilisation of savings, supply of finance, creation of money and deposit of credit, development of economy, as agents in purchase and issue of and overwriting shares and securities, collection agents.

Banks may be of following types:

1. *Commercial Banks*: These are the banks that finance trade and commerce with short-term loans. They also give loans to industries for short periods.

2. *Industrial Banks and Investment Banks*: These banks advance loans to industries for longer periods and borrow money for longer duration. They serve as a bridge between capital users and capital savers. They also underwrite and organise the sale of new issue of shares and debentures.

3. *Agricultural Banks*: These are banks that give short-term and long-term loans for agricultural inputs like tractors, pump sets, fertilisers, seeds, etc. The cooperative banks and cooperative credit societies in many countries are agricultural banks. They get financial help from central bank or the government.

4. *Central Bank*: This is the national bank of a country. It has a monopoly to issue currency. It has no direct trade relations with individuals. It is generally government's banker and controls money and credit in the country. There are international banks too, the World Bank, or International Bank for Reconstruction and Development (IBRD) is an investment bank at the international level. The nearest international equivalent to a central bank is the International Monetary Fund (IMF).

bank account

The term refers to an account with a bank, held by an individual, firm, company, or government. Money in an account may be instantly available, as in a current account (as in UK) or a checking account (as in US), or notice of withdrawal may be required, as in a deposit account. An account may be in credit, when the bank owes the customary money, or overdrawn, in which case the customer owes the bank money. Current accounts normally earn little or no interest, and may be liable to handling charges, etc.

banker's draft

It refers to a cheque issued by a bank and sold to a customer. This may be acceptable to a third party who would not accept the customer's cheque for the amount, which may be too large to be covered by any bank card. The bank's credit is better than that of the customer, and a banker's draft is unstoppable.

Bank draft

Bank for International Settlements (BIS)

It refers to an international bank based in Basle, Switzerland to co-ordinate payments of reparations, etc. after the First World War. However, its role as the principal international bank was taken over after 1945 by the International Monetary Fund (IMF). The BIS has acted as trustee for the Organisation for Economic Cooperation and Development (OECD) and the European Monetary Agreement.

banking

It is a broad term referring to the following:

1. According to Banking Companies Act, 1949, banking means "accepting, for the purpose of lending or investment, of deposits of money from the public repayable on demand or otherwise".

2. The provision of payment facilities, credit and capital to individuals, firms and the government. Retail banking is the provision of payments, savings and credit facilities in relatively small quantities to a large number of individuals or small business customers. Investment banking is the provision of credit and capital in large quantities for relatively large businesses. For example, foreign exchange banking is mainly concerned with foreign exchange transactions, issue of letters of credit, etc.

banking system

It is the network of banks and financial institutions responsible for providing banking services. This consists of two parts: (i) there are the actual banks providing services to the general public, which may be universal banks, or specialist institutions dealing with particular types of banking business; (ii) there are higher-level institutions, which are not involved in direct contact with the general public. These are central banks, which act as bankers for other banks and the government, and are responsible for monetary policy and macroeconomic management of the monetary system.

bank loan
The term refers to a loan from a bank to an individual, firm or company. Bank advances for large amounts for business purposes are normally made against security, for example, the title deeds of land and building or stock of goods, other securities like NSCs, life insurance policies, etc.

bank note
It is a paper money, issued by a bank. The issue of notes in most countries is either entirely confined to or subject to strict control by the central bank. A bank note was originally a promise to pay coin on demand.

Bank of Credit and Commerce International
It was a large international bank operating in many countries, whose collapse in 1991 with a shortage of multi-billion pound of funds provoked widespread suspicion of false bookkeeping and money laundering.

bank rate
It is the rate at which the central bank of a country discounts the first class bills. Bank rate, thus, is the rate of discount of the central banks. In contrast, the market rate is the rate of discount that prevails in the money market. In the advanced countries where the money market is well developed and properly regulated, the bank rate is the yardstick for the rate of interest that prevails. When the bank rate is raised, the market rate of interest tends to rise. Borrowing from commercial banks becomes costly. It discourages new loans and puts pressure on debtors to repay existing ones.

bank regulations
They are a form of regulations that subject to banks to certain requirements and guidelines. They are justified by concerns that bank failures may disrupt the rest of the economy in a way that other business failures do not. Commercial banks provide most of the money used in a modern economy, and lend on a large scale. If a bank is run irresponsibly, taking excessive risks and holding too small reserves, this is liable to cause serious problems if its customers suspect it of being illiquid or insolvent.

bankruptcy
It is also called insolvency. It is a legal arrangement to deal with the affairs of individuals unable to pay their debts. Bankruptcy proceedings may be started by the individual, or by unpaid creditors. The assets of a person who has been adjudged bankrupt by a court are taken over by an official and sold. The fund is used to repay creditors as far as possible. Those who have become bankrupt cannot accept credit without warning the lender that they are undischarged bankrupts, and they also face various restrictions on their future activities.

bank statement
It refers to a statement that is prepared by the banker and given to its customers. It gives a detailed account of each debit and credit entry and the balance that stands to the credit at the close. If the customer's bank statement shows a debit account, it means an overdraft which is usually arranged beforehand.

bargaining power
It refers to the ability of a party to get a large share of the possible joint benefits to be derived from an agreement with another party. This depends on the losses which may cause to the parties negotiating. In the absence of agreement, each party has a fallback position. Thus, the less uncomfortable this is, and the longer any party can afford to stay in it, the stronger is their bargaining power.

barriers to entry
The term refers to laws, institutions, or practices that make it difficult or impossible for new firms to enter some markets, or new workers to compete for certain forms of employment. Barriers to entry may take various forms. The law may confer monopoly rights on existing firms, or impose qualifications for licences for new operators which are so obstructively administered as to make new entry difficult.

barter
It is the exchange of one type of good or service for another, without the medium of

money. This was developed to allow society to take advantage of the division of labour and the gains from specialisation. Barter, however, is not much convenient. For example, a person who has goods of one type and wants goods of another type has to find somebody who wishes to make the exchange, either for their own use or as a professional intermediary. Often, the quantity of a good required by one person does not match what is offered by the other in exchange.

base (logarithms)

These are the number whose powers are used as logarithms. The most commonly used bases are 10, where if $b = \log(a)$, $a = 10^b$; and e, the base of natural logarithms, often written ln, so that if $b = \ln(a)$, $a = e^b$. Logarithms to base 10 were originally popular. Before the advent of electronic calculators, they had to be looked up in numerical tables.

baseline

It refers to a projection of how the economy will develop if existing trends and policies continue unchanged. Models of the economy may be based on theory, Econometrics, or a combination of these. It is necessary to construct a baseline projection before it is possible to calculate the effects of changing any aspect of nature, technology, or economic policies.

base period

It refers to the period whose data are identified with 100 (sometimes 1) in constructing an index number. In the UK, for example, in 2001 official data on national income aggregates were using 1995 = 100 as their base.

base rate

It refers to the following:
1. The rate at which the Bank of England lends to discount houses. This corresponds to the minimum lending rate, abolished in 1981. This rate governs interest rates elsewhere in the banking system.
2. The rate of interest used by commercial banks as a basis for charging for loans. Most borrowers pay a premium over the base rate, whose size depends on how risky loans to them are considered to be.

base-weighted index

It refers to a weighted average of prices or quantities, where the weights used are the quantities or the prices of the base period. Where r_{ij} and s_{ij} are the prices and quantities of N goods, i = 1, 2, 3, ... N, in period j, and t labels the latest period and 0 the base period, the base-weighted or Laspeyres price index is given by $P_B = (\Sigma_i r_{it} s_{i0})/(\Sigma_i r_{i0} s_{i0})$ and the base-weighted or Laspeyres quantity index is given by $Q_B = (\Sigma_i r_{i0} s_{it})/(\Sigma_i r_{i0} s_{i0})$

base year

It is called the year in which calculations, usually indexes, commence and with which other years are compared. For example, Consumer Price Index.

basic rate

The term is used for the normal rate of income tax. This was previously called standard rate. In the assessment year 2009-10, it was 10 per cent. This rate applies to all taxable non-saving incomes above a lower limit, above which higher rate is payable.

batch production

Also called the method of production where output emerges in discrete units, it is often used when there is a requirement that a certain quantity of a product, for example, the floor tiles in a building should be of a uniform pattern and quality, but the required characteristics differ between different orders. If there is anything wrong with the product, batch production makes it relatively easy to identify the workers, machines, and materials responsible for any particular part of the output.

Baumol's model of sales revenue maximisation

It is a theory that suggests that firms operating in oligopoly will tend to maximise sales revenue (single period sales) subject to a profit constraint. Total profit is maximised when the firm produces O units of output. Sales maximisation, S refers to maximisation of total revenue (=P'Q) rather than maximisation of P. Total revenue is maximum when MR = 0 and when demand for a company's product is elastic. In the figure, if the firm has to maximise total revenue (without profit constraints), it will choose output Q_1, where TR is maximum (i.e., the slope of TR curve is zero or MR = 0). However, shareholders (owners) demand a level of absolute profit of some amount, which would keep them content. If this minimum acceptable level of profit is π', the firm would produce Q_s and still generate profits greater than π'. Hence, in this situation, it will be worthwhile to produce Q_1. Similarly, if a minimum acceptable profit is π", Q_t will not generate sufficient profits. The firm will have to produce output at reduced Q_s' the optimal output with the profit constraint specified. The first main difference between profit maximises and constrained sales maximises is that the latter can change a lower price to sell the extra output: ($OQ_s - OQ"$). This has to be the case if both have the same demand (AR) curve. The profit maximises produce OQ" and changes a price of OT/OQ" (=total revenue + output). Alternatively, the sales maximiser producers (in the π" constrained cases) Q_s and sells at a price of OR/OQ_s. Baumol argues that it is quite irrational for managers to maximise profits for shareholders when they will get hardly anything themselves. Sales maximisation will on the other hand, expand the size of organisation, enhance the status of managers as well as their promotion prospects, result in increase in wages and compensation (with increase in size), etc.

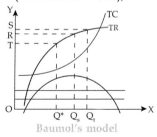
Baumol's model

Bayesian statistics
It refers to a statistical model of how beliefs are updated in the light of experience. It is assumed that beliefs about parameters are regularly revised, using a weighted average of the previous belief, or 'prior', and the most recent observations.

Bayesian techniques
These are the methods of statistical analysis in which prior information has been formally combined with sample data to produce estimates, or test hypotheses.

BBB
It is the Standard and Poor's rating of securities, which are regarded as being of medium riskiness.

bear
It refers to a trader who expects prices to fall. A trader on a stock or commodity market who believes that prices are more likely to fall will sell any shares he/she owns, in the hope of being able to buy them back cheaper when their price has fallen. In extreme cases, bears speculate by selling forward shares or commodities that they do not actually hold, hoping to be able to buy them cheap before delivery is due.

bearer bond
The term is used for a security where the person or organisation holding the certificate of title is entitled to receive any interest and redemption payments. Bearer bonds have no central register of holders, and thus, the owners are at considerable risk of loss by theft or accident. Bearer bonds are attractive to anybody seeking to remain anonymous in order to avoid taxation, controls on capital movements, or legal check. When government or the central public undertaking wants to float public loans, it issues bearer bonds in lieu of the loans so raised from the investing public.

bear market
It is a stock market in which prices are expected to fall in the near future. A widespread belief that prices are more likely to fall than to rise, at least in the immediate future, leads investors to sell shares or defer purchases, and thus the expectation tends to be self-fulfilling.

beggar my neighbour
The term refers to the policies, which were vigorously chased in the foreign trade during the interwar period to weaken a particular country. The futility of 'beggar thy neighbour' policies was ultimately realised because it evoked worse retaliation from the country against which a policy of beggar my neighbour was adopted. To cite an example, a nation took to depreciation of its currency, which raised the prices of the foreign goods and thus it reduced the imports and raised the exports as foreigners could buy more of our goods.

below-the-line
These are the items following but not part of the profit-and-loss accounts of firms or the

income sections of national income accounts. For firms below-the-line, items indicate how profits are used, or how losses are financed. In national income accounts, they are capital account transactions.

benchmarking
It refers to the following:
1. A particular tool for improving performance by learning from best practices by which high performance is achieved.
2. Setting reference points or standards by which behaviours or developments can be measured at a point in time or over time.

benefit principle
It refers to the principle that the cost of public expenditures should be met by those who benefit from them. This is distinct from the ability to pay principle. The benefit principle is extremely difficult to apply. Public support for the disabled or unemployed cannot be paid for by these groups.

benefits in kind
The term refers to the government provision of goods and services for those in need of them. This is different from providing citizens with incomes sufficient to meet their needs by means of the market. Governments wishing to provide for the basic needs of citizens, including subsistence, housing, education, and medical services, have to choose one of these two methods. Providing income is supported by the welfare economics argument that people vary in their individual preferences, tastes and needs, so that an available resources is more efficiently used in providing goods and services, which they choose for themselves.

benefits system
It is the system of provision in cash and in kind of sufficient income and services to maintain minimum standards of welfare among a country's residents. This system has to support those who are unable to provide for themselves because they are too old, too young to work, disabled nor ill.

Bertrand competition
A competition between two or more firms in an industry where each assumes that the others will maintain their prices unchanged. This encourages the use of price-cutting as a form of competition, particularly, if the products are good substitutes.

Bertrand's Duopoly model
The term refers to a model of two firms' market developed by Bertrand in 1883. The model is different from the Cournot Duopoly Model in that in the Bertrand Duopoly model each firm has been assumed to maximise profits on the presumption that the other firm will not change its price. Bertrand's model results in a stable equilibrium for the two firms.

beta coefficient
It is a measure of how variations in the return on a particular share correlate with variations in the return on a market index. The return on a share is the change in price plus any distribution of dividends. If R_t is the proportional return on a share from time t - 1 to time t, and M_t is the proportional return on the market index, β is calculated by finding the best fit to $R_t = \alpha + BM_t + e_t$. $\beta < 0$ means that R_t moves against the market; a zero or low value of β means that the share has mainly idiosyncratic risk.

Beveridge, William Henry
Lord Beveridge was a British economist who took interest in the issue of unemployment and social security. He was the director of the London School of Economics from 1919 to 1937. His report on Social Insurance and Allied Services (1942) had a considerable impact on the extension of the welfare services of the government. His major contribution through the published work to the problem of the unemployment was *Unemployment: A Problem of Industry* (published in 1909).

bias
It is a tendency for estimates of variables to be systematically too high or too low. This may be due to the method of sample selection, the way in which questions are put, or the calculations based on the data collected.

bidrent function
It can be defined as a relationship that indicates the amount of a household or firm will be able to pay for the use of a given quantity of land at varying distances from the centre of an urban area while maintaining a constant level of utility or profit.

big bang
It is a shorthand expression of the view that reforms should be carried out as rapidly as possible. This is distinct from the view that major changes should be made gradually. These views clash in countries undertaking liberalisation or structural transformation.

big push
It is the argument, theory or belief that development can only succeed if various sectors of an economy expand together, since each provides markets for the others. This argument for balanced growth does not take much account of the possible use of external trade to complement a country's own production.

bilateralism
The term refers to trade agreements between two countries. As the trade is between two countries, exporters cannot sell their products in the best market. Therefore, in bilateralism, there is an effort to secure a pre-determined ratio between the exports to each other from each other. It brings a decrease in the volume and profitability of foreign trade. In this system, each country aims to balance exports and imports individually and separately. The external market is broken up into a number of isolated segments.

bilateral monopoly
It refers to a market situation with a single buyer, or monopsonist, facing a single seller, or monopolist. Such a situation could arise where a single supplier firm faces a single government purchaser, for example, the Ministry of Defence, in case of defence equipment or where a single trade union faces a single employer, for example, a nationalised industry.

bilateral trade
It refers to a situation where trade between any two countries has to balance, or any imbalance has to be financed with credits arranged directly between the two countries. This is distinct from multilateral trade, which requires that trade with all other countries should either balance, or be financed by overall credit from other countries. It is believed that bilateral trade has the disadvantages of barter at the national level.

bill
It is a short-dated security, usually maturing in a year. Treasury bills are issued by the UK government; trade bills are issued by firms to obtain short-term finance cheaper than borrowing from the banks; bills of exchange are issued by private firms to finance foreign trade. A bill specifies its maturity date, for example, 91 days from the date of issue, and the currency in which it is to be repaid. Visually, the bills carry no explicit interest. The interest on bills is provided by issuing them at a discount to their redemption value.

bill market
It implies a place where the sellers and purchasers of bills are found. A well-organised bill market is very much indispensable in an economy because of the following factors:
1. The purchaser of the goods is not required to make the payment of goods immediately. He gets some time to arrange funds, etc.
2. The seller also is not at a loss in getting the accepted bill from the purchaser. He can get the sum by discounting the bill from bank or discount house.
3. The bank can also invest its additional funds on a short-term basis.

billion (bn. or b)
It is equal to one thousand million. Its usage is followed by all modern economists. A billion was once used to refer to a million but this meaning can safely be ignored unless dealing with long-dead writers, and in their write-ups and books.

bill of exchange
It refers to the following:
1. A contract entitling an exporter to receive immediate payment in the local currency for goods that would be shipped elsewhere.
2. Any document demanding payment.
3. The term refers to a short-dated security issued to finance foreign trade. The customer pays an exporter not in cash but with a bill payable in usually 3 or 6 months. This can be sold in the discount market to provide immediate cash for the supplier. If the customer is not well known, a bill can be made more marketable by acceptance by a merchant banker, who adds a signature to the bill guaranteeing payment if the issuer should default.

bill of lading
It is a receipt given by a transportation company to an exporter, when the former accepts

goods for transport. It includes the contract specifying transport service being provided and the limits of liability.

bimetallism

It can be defined as a monetary system in which both gold and silver freely circulate as legal tender at a fixed ratio of exchange with each other and are freely minted. This monetary standard has been used since long although it was never seen in practice from the beginning of the twentieth century.

bimodal distribution

It refers to the following:
1. A distribution with two distinct peaks, with a dip between. For example, death rates in human per 1000 are higher in infancy and in old age than the years in between.
2. The distribution giving the expected number of occurrences of a random event as the result of making a number of independent drawings, with a known and constant probability of the event occurring each time. If the probability of the event each time is x, and the probability of non-occurrence is (1 - x), the binomial distribution gives the probability of exactly r occurrences out of n tries, where $0 \leq r \leq n$.

black economy

It can be defined as the economic activities not reported to the tax, social security, and other public authorities. The term is somewhat derogatory, as participation in the black economy usually involves evasion of taxes. It is also liable to involve breach of laws concerning health and safety, employers' liability, job security, etc.

black market

It is the trading, which violates rationing or price control laws, usually both. Black markets can by definition exist only when governments attempt to control prices or ration quantities. It is an illegal market, in which something is bought and sold outside of official government-sanctioned channels. Such markets tend to arise when a government tries to fix a price without providing all of the necessary supply or demand.

black money

It can be defined as the aggregate of incomes, which are taxable but are not reported to tax

authorities. In modern economy, black money is referred to as the sum total of items of receipts deliberately and clandestinely kept out of the books of account by households and businesses in the economy.

blue chip

It refers to the following:
1. The equity shares of large and reputable companies. Such companies normally have high market capitalisation, and a liquid market in their shares.
2. The outstanding equity shares, purchase of which is supposed to be extremely safe and devoid of all risks.

blue collar jobs

These are the manual jobs that are unskilled and involve lots of physical strain on the human muscles.

board of directors

It refers to the governing body of a company, which appoints the company's officers. Most company directors are elected by shareholders at general meetings of the company, but a board may be given powers of co-option. Boards include executive directors, employed by the company for fulltime or for a major portion of their time, and may include non-executive directors.

bond

The term refers to a security with a redemption date over a year later than its date of issue. Bonds may be issued by firms, financial institutions, or governments. They may have a fixed redemption date, an option for the borrower to repay at any date over a period. They may carry fixed interest, or interest variable with notice or linked to some financial index.

bond-rating agency

It is an agency specialising in assessing the creditworthiness of governments, and corporations issuing bonds. Standard and Poor's and Moody's are leading US bond-rating agencies.

bonus

It is a payment to a firm's employees other than their normal pay. Bonuses may be linked to performance, either of the whole firm, a specified section of it, or the individual recipient. Bonuses provide incentives to employees, both to exert themselves and to stay with the firm rather than looking for a better job elsewhere. The calculation of bonus is often based on the basic pay of the employee.

bonus issue
It refers to an issue of additional shares in a company to existing shareholders, in proportion to their holdings. This is different from a rights issue, where existing shareholders are offered first option on new shares, at a preferential price, but only get them if they pay for them.

book value
It is the value that is put on assets in a firm's accounts. This may be the original purchase price, or a revised figure based on a periodic revaluation. It is distingu-ished from trying to value assets at their current market prices. Book value is often used when the assets are non-marketed, so that regular revaluation would be expensive and unreliable.

borrowing
The term refers to incurring debts to finance spending or invested in business. This is done by individuals, companies, firms, and governments. Borrowing can appear desirable when the benefits from using borrowed money are greater than the interest costs. Borrowing may also be because of urgent need for individual spending or sudden falls in income, or favourable investment opportunities for firms. However, injudicious use of credit is liable to cause borrowers severe difficulties when repayments fall due.

bottleneck
It is the effective constraint on the level of an activity. Its use in economics is a physical analogy to the maximum rate at which a liquid can be poured through the neck of a bottle, which slows it down. In production, transport, or administration, the effective constraint is often a shortage of some specific factors like labour, capital, etc. or some particular piece of equipment.

bottom line
In economics, it is the profit or loss on an activity. The expression derives from the custom in drawing up accounts of showing the profit or loss at the foot of the statement.

boulwarism
It is the process of collective bargaining over terms and conditions of employment, which has been normally one of compromise and concession. The two parties involved bargain and approach each other until a point somewhere between their original and present positions that is mutually satisfactory to them is realised.

bound
The term denotes a value, which a given function cannot pass, and may or may not actually reach. A bound may be upper or lower. $f(a)$ is bounded from above, by an upper bond b, if $f(a) \leq b$ for all a. $f(a)$ is bounded from below, by a lower bound y, if $f(y) \geq a$ for all y. A given function may be bounded in both directions.

bounded rationality
It refers to the argument that there is a finite limit to the amount of information the human brain can hold, and the amount of calculations it can understand. Teamwork and computers can vastly increase the amount of information that can be made.

bourgeoisie
It can be defined as the section of industrial society which came into prominence in the course of the industrial revolution as entrepreneurs and professionals. The term is used for describing the property owning middle classes, and ever since Karl Marx's discussion of their exploitative role the term has often carried a pejorative sense.

box diagram
It is an expository device widely used in welfare economics to explain an efficient resource allocation. It is also known as Edgeworth-Bowley box. If an individual, firm, industry, or economy has two types of resources, and uses them for two different purposes, the box shows the amounts of resources available on its axes. Each point in the box represents a possible allocation of resources, measuring the amounts used for one purpose from one corner as the origin, and the amounts used for the other purpose from the other corner.

boycott
It refers to the following:
1. A refusal to trade with a dealer, etc. The

name comes from a nineteenth-century Irish land agent unpopular with his master's tenants. A boycott may involve refusal to buy goods and services from somebody, or to sell to them. It is difficult to make a boycott completely effective, because trade can usually be conducted secretly or indirectly, this involves delay, expense, and inconvenience.

2. Protest by refusing to purchase from some firm, company or otherwise do business with them.

3. In international trade, a boycott most often takes the form of refusal to import a country's goods.

Balance of Payments (BP) curve

It is a curve drawn on the same diagram as the IS and LM curves, showing combinations of Y, GDP, and r, interest rates, at which the overall balance of payments is in equilibrium. In it, the current and capital account balances of payments sum to zero. As higher Y tends to produce a current account deficit, and higher r tends to produce a capital account surplus, the BP curve is upward sloping.

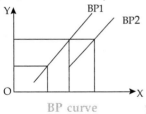

BP curve

brain drain

It is a pejorative description of the tendency of talented people from poor and underdeveloped countries to seek employment in richer and advanced ones. Often, this migration occurs because while similar skills are needed in both poor and rich countries, the rich pay more for them. Brain drain also occurs because the technical and economic backwardness of poorer countries is a major hindrance in the creation of adequate job opportunities.

branch banking

It is the banking system under which banks are allowed to have branches in backward areas. This seems to most economists the only solution to the problem of providing bank services economically to customers in remote areas.

brand

It can be defined as a name used to identify the maker or distributor of a good. A brand was originally a mark burned on the hide of an animal to identify its owner. In some cases, a brand name is that of the original maker, which has been retained by a new owner to draw benefits after the originator ceases to be an independent firm. Brand names help producers and distributors, as they facilitate advertising and building up a reputation for a product or range of products.

branding

It refers to the development of the identity of a product through name selection and related marketing strategies, involving consideration of name creation or brand extension, trademark screening, etc.

brand loyalty

It is the tendency of consumers to prefer familiar names. Consumers frequently buy brands that they have used before, or seen widely advertised on T.V., etc. in preference to unbranded products or unfamiliar names. Brand loyalty is a form of satisfying behaviour, viz. actions that have produced satisfactory results in the past and are repeated unless something goes wrong. This makes it difficult for new suppliers to enter a market, even if their product is in fact just as good or better, and as cheap or cheaper than established branded products.

break-even

The term refers to the ratio of output to capacity just sufficient to allow a business to cover its costs. Demand is always subject to random fluctuations, and equipment sometimes fails, so capacity must exceed the average level of demand to cater to all customers at times of peak demand. Failure to satisfy demand not only loses immediate revenue, but also decreases future demand, as customers may feel they cannot rely on the good or service being available, and seek alternatives.

bridge loan

It is a short period loan advanced by the banker to enable his customer to meet the temporary shortage of funds. For example, a business person may shift to a new line of production, and require funds for installing new type of machinery while his present installed machinery may take some more time to be disposed off.

broad money
It is a relatively broad definition of money. This applies to definitions such as M_2, which includes building society deposits, or M_3, which includes interest-bearing bank deposits. It does not apply to M_0 or M_1.

broker
The term denotes the following:
1. An intermediary between a buyer and a seller. A direct contact between the two is often not possible. So, a person who brings them into contact helps both the buyer in effecting the purchase and the seller in effecting the sale. On the Stock Exchange, brokers are well known for their useful services of buying and selling shares.
2. A person or company who does not trade as a principal, but puts buyers and sellers in touch with one another. Property dealers do this for property, commodity brokers for commodities, insurance brokers for insurance policies, and shipping brokers for charter shipping, etc.

brokerage
It is the commission that is charged by the broker; the intermediary between the buyer and the seller. A stock, for example, charges a given percentage of the value of the shares he buys and sells.

bubble
The term is used for a cumulative movement in the price of an asset whose price is high mainly because the speculators believe it will rise still further. Such speculative behaviour forces the prices to rise for some period on a scale that is eventually realised to be unsustainable. At some point the bubble bursts, but it is hard to predict when this will happen.

bubble economy
It is a term for an economy in which the presence of one or more bubbles in its assets markets is a dominant feature of its performance. Japan was said to be a bubble economy in the late 1980s.

budget
It is a statement of a government's planned receipts and expenditures for some future period, normally a year. This is usually accompanied by a statement of actual receipts and expenditures for the previous period. The word budget originally meant the contents of a package; the budget is so called because it brings government's all the tax and spending plans together. A budget surplus means that total government receipts exceed total spending; a budget deficit means that spending exceeds receipts; and a balanced budget means that income and spending are equal.

budgetary control
It is a device of using budgets to control day-to-day operations to check whether or not performance is being achieved as it was planned. It is the process of comparing the actual results with the corresponding budget data, i.e., with the budgetary plans.

budget constraint
It refers to the limit of expenditure. For any economic agent, whether an individual, a firm, company or a government, expenditure must stay within limits set by the ability to finance it. The finance may come from income, from assets already held, or from loans raised. Loans will be obtainable only if lenders believe that they are sufficiently likely to be repaid.

budget deficit
The term describes the excess of government's total expenditure over its income. This deficit has to be met by borrowing, which increases government debt. Budget deficits can be calculated for any level of government, central or state, in federal countries, or for general government. It is important to distinguish whether the deficit is calculated including the nominal or the real interest as expenditure on government debt. The conventional measures of the budget deficit use nominal interest, but an inflation-adjusted budget deficit would include real interest only.

budget line
A budget line represents those combinations of two goods that a consumer can purchase at specified prices. Thus there are two determinants of the budget line: (i) the prices of goods, and (ii) the consumer's income to be spent on the goods. The budget line will change if either the prices of goods or the in-

come of the consumer changes. Budget line also refers to a graph showing what combinations of quantities of two goods can be afforded by a consumer with a fixed total amount to spend. If each good is available in any quantity at a fixed price per unit, the budget line is a straight line with a slope proportional to the relative price of the two goods. In the figure, AB is the budget line, showing combinations of goods X and Y that can be bought for given total spending. C is a consumer equilibrium, on the highest indifference curve consistent with the budget.

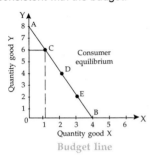

Budget line

budget surplus

It is the excess of a government's total income over its expenditure. This can be used to repay government debt. Budget surpluses can be calculated for any level of government - central, state or local in federal countries such as Germany and the United States, or for general government, which is all these levels combined. It is important to distinguish whether the surplus is calculated including the nominal or the real interest as expenditure on government debt. However, conventional measures of the surplus use nominal interest, but an inflation-adjusted budget surplus would include real interest.

budget year

It is the fiscal year used by the US federal government. This runs from 1 October to 30 September in the following year. UK fiscal year, runs from 6 April to 5 April in the following year.

buffer stock

It refers to the following:
1. A large quantity of a commodity, usually foodgrains held in storage to be used to stabilise the commodity's price. This is done by buying when the price is low and adding to the buffer stock, selling out of the buffer

stock, when the price is high. This is done by the government to reduce the size of price fluctuations. If price is liable to fluctuate, because of variations in supply, demand, or both, a buffer stock operator can limit price rises by selling stocks and can limit price falls by buying stocks. This can be done either at the discretion of the manager, or in accordance with a pre-announced maximum selling price and minimum buying price. The price can only be kept within these limits if the prices set are consistent with long-run market conditions.
2. A stock held by a trade body or government as a means of regulating the supply or price of a commodity. These are stocks built up to moderate fluctuations in supply and price of goods because of changes in demand. It refers to buying and selling out of stock with the purpose of moderating price variations.

built-in stabilisers

In economics, the term is used for devices and features of an economy which more or less automatically counteract the fluctuations in the important sphere of national income, employment and output. In case a slump occurs and reaches higher level of unemployment and lower level of national income, the social security schemes provide the unemployment benefits, on one side and the benefit of a reduced level of taxation, on the other. The disposal income is raised and a fall in the aggregated demand is checked. The policy checks the demand fluctuations during depression and helps in the restoration and revival of the economy. During boom, it helps in checking upward phase, and a sharp rise in the price level and business activity. When the government reduces its public expenditure with full employment, the question of unemployment and other benefits does not arise. Rise in the employment and national income leads to higher taxation yield. Hence, the inflationary and deflationary pressures in the economy are automatically counteracted to a considerable extent by these built-in stabilisers.

bull

As against a bear, bull is that sort of a speculator, who stands to gain with a rise in the price of shares and stocks. He enters into a purchase transaction with a view to selling it in the near future when the price would have risen.

bullion

It refers to gold held in bulk, usually in the form of gold bars. Bullion is largely held by central banks as part of their countries' foreign exchange reserves.

bull market

It is a market wherein prices of shares and bonds are rising. Bulls stand to gain by such a rise in the price. They purchase the shares, bonds of commodities at a time when prices are low and sell the same later when prices have become higher. A widespread belief that prices are more likely to rise than to fall, at least in the immediate future, leads investors to buy shares or defer sales. It is in contrast with bear market.

business

It refers to the following:
1. All forms of industrial and commercial profit-seeking activity. The business cycle refers to fluctuations in the aggregate level of economic activity
2. The ownership/management side of firms, as opposed to their ordinary employees. This group is often referred to as the business community.
3. The firms conducting profitable activities; businessmen are the directors and managers of firms.

business cycle

It denotes the pattern followed by macroeconomic variables, such as GDP and unemployment that rise and fall irregularly over time, relative to trend.

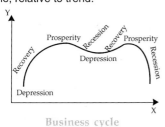

Business cycle

business ethics

It can be defined as the study of what standards a business should observe in its dealings over and above compliance with the provisions of the law. This covers questions such as fair dealing with its labour force, customers, suppliers and competitors, and the impact of their activities on public health, environment, etc.

business finance

The term is used for the necessary arrangement of money for various types of business needs. It may be either short term or long term. Long-term finance is needed for the purchase, manufacture and installation of fixed capital like machinery and plant while short-term business finance is needed for the working and circulating capital. Appropriate financial institutions are needed to cater to the needs of different periods.

buyer's market

It is a market for a commodity, stock, housing, etc. where prices are falling and there are more parties interested in selling than in buying.

buyout

It is a change in control of a company through its previous shareholders being bought out by new owners. These may already be connected with the firm as in a management buyout where the firm is bought by its existing managers. A buyout may alternatively be byoutsiders. Finance may come from the purchasers' own resources, or from loans. In a leveraged buyout, part of the price is raised by fixedinterest loans.

by-product

It defines a good produced incidentally to the production of some other good. Sale of a by-product makes production more profitable than if it had to be thrown away, or were costly to dispose of. The term by-product is used where one good would be produced for its own sake even if the other were useless.

C

C.I.F.
It means the price inclusive of the insurance and freight and all other expenses such as loading and carriage of the goods from a port or airport town to the factory.

calibration
In economics, it refers to assigning numerical values to the parameters of models of the economy so that the quantities predicted for variables such as GDP are realistic. This procedure is used when the available statistics are inadequate to allow econometric fitting of a model and present a true picture of the economy.

callable
1. It refers to a bond issue, all or part of which may be redeemed by the issuing corporation under specified conditions before maturity.
2. The term is also applicable to preferred shares that may get redeemed by the issuing corporation.

call loan
It is a loan that can be concluded or 'called' at any point of time by the creditor or the debtor.

call money
It refers to money lent in the money market, repayable at very short notice. This is a highly liquid asset for the banks and other financial institutions. Because of transaction costs it is only practicable to lend money on these terms in large amounts.

call option
It is a contract giving the holder the right but no obligation to buy a good or security on some future date at a pre-arranged price. A call option will be exercised only if the spot price at the contract date exceeds the option price.

Cambridge Theory of Money
This theory is related to a 'cash balance' form of the quantity theory of money. It has been developed by Cambridge economists like Alfred Marshall and A.C. Pigou (the early Cambridge School) and contained in the equation, $M = kPT$ where M represents the amount of money (bank deposits), k represents the reciprocal of the velocity of circulation, P represents the general price level, and T represents the value of output.

capacity
It can be defined as the maximum output an industrial plant is considered capable of producing, assuming normal working. If single-shift working is normal, output can sometimes be further increased by using two or even three shifts. The capacity of a firm, enterprise or an industry, or even the economy as a whole can only be estimated subject to the problems of aggregation.

capacity utilisation
It is the actual output as a percentage of capacity. Capacity is the maximum output, firms could produce with their existing equipment. Because of the fact that demand fluctuates and equipment is liable to break down, firms normally aim to have more capacity than the average level of demand, and a share less than 100 per cent capacity utilisation.

capital
1. It is a stock of financial assets, which can be used to provide an income. It is the initial stock of money with which a company started trading, plus subsequent retained profits. This capital may be spent on buying capital goods, or it may be in the form of circulating capital, held as money balances or used to give credit to customers. The capital market is the system through which firms are provided with capital.
2. Man-made means of production. Capital goods are goods designed to be used in production, for example, machinery. Capital consumption is an estimate of the investment needed to keep the capital stock constant.
3. Human capital refers to skills and experience, which enhance a worker's productivity. Human capital differs from material capital in the sense that it cannot be bought or sold and thus cannot be used as collateral for loans.
4. Human capital is the social class of those who derive most of their income from owning property. Capitalists are individual members of this class.

capital account
It describes transactions which do not involve

income or expenditure, but change the form in which assets are held. Receipt of a loan, for example, is not income, but just an exchange of cash now for a promise to repay, usually with interest, in the future. In a country's balance of payments, the capital account is a record of international exchanges of assets and liabilities.

capital accumulation
It refers to an increase in man-made equipment like machinery, tools, building and other structures, and stocks of goods, used for or capable of being used for the production of goods and services. It is one of the main sources of economic growth in the short and medium run. Whether capital accumulation can raise longrun growth is a matter of controversy. Solow-style growth models hold that in the long run, growth rate is set by population growth and the rate of technical progress.

capital adequacy
It is defined as the possession by a firm or bank of sufficient capital for the business, it is doing. This matters to the firm/bank itself. If it is undercapitalised, a small adverse shift in circumstances can impair its solvency. Capital adequacy, therefore, matters to a firm's creditors/bank's account-holders. In the case of banks and other financial institutions, it also matters to the regulatory authorities.

capital allowances
They are deductions from a firm's taxable profits in respect of investment expenditure. This encourages investment, since for any given level of gross profits, the more investment a firm does, the less tax it has to pay.

capital appreciation
It describes an increase in the prices of the assets owned by an enterprise. When increases in the value of land, buildings, equipment, or stocks are only proportional to general inflation in the economy, it is believed that they do not increase the real value of a business.

capital consumption
It refers to a value of loss of capital equipment due to use, ageing, or obsolescence because of change in technology. Part of the value of the capital stock owned by a firm or by an enterprise is lost in any period through wear and tear in use. The passage of time also reduces its expected remaining useful life.

capital controversy
It denotes a debate between the Cambridge School represented by Cambridge University, England and the Neoclassical School, of the Massachusetts Institute of Technology, Cambridge, about the validity or otherwise of the neoclassical approach to economics. Debate has centred around the correct concept of capital to use and its place, if any, in an aggregate production function. The possibility of a reswitching of techniques argued forcefully by the Cambridge School has been sufficient to render many of the assumptions of neoclassical economic theory invalid. Some experts do not accept that neoclassical theory should be abandoned in totality.

capital deepening
It refers to the following:
1. A process of accumulating capital at a faster rate than the growth of the labour force bringing rise in the capital labour ratio. The term also refers to an increase in capital intensity, normally in a macro-economic context, where it is measured by something analogous to the capital stock available per labour hour spent. It could also mean the amount of capital available for a worker to use, but this use is rare.
2. A macroeconomic concept of a faster growing magnitude of capital in production than in labour.

capital expenditure
It defines expenditure by a company, which cannot be treated as a cost in calculating its profits. Such expenditure has to be paid for either out of post-tax income, or by raising external finance. Capital expenditure may be on actually creating new capital goods, but is more usually on buying them from outside suppliers.

capital flight
It refers to a large-scale and sudden movement of capital from a country by residents or foreigners. The causes of capital flight include fear of economic problems, political uncertainty, public disorder or persecution leading to personal danger to its owners, fear of confiscation, drastically increased taxation, and fear of rapid inflation leading to a loss of its value by the country's currency.

capital formation
The term denotes the following:
1. The amount, which a community adds to its capital during a period. It implies increase in real capital of a country.
2. The amount invested during a year in the fixed assets, e.g., land, buildings, plants, machinery, etc.; raw materials and stock; finished goods and goods under process of production.
3. Also the process of adding to the stock of real productive equipment of an enterprise, either by actually constructing it, or more usually by buying it from outside suppliers.

capital gain/gains
The term refers to the following:
1. An increase in the value of assets. This is the difference between their present value and the price at which they were purchased. If the general price level is stable, real and nominal capital gains are equal. If there is general inflation of prices, capital assets show real gains only if their prices increase proportionally faster than the general price level.
2. All increases in the value of all property except merchandising profits on goods as a business activity. Capital gain occurs when land, buildings, capital equipment, stocks and shares are sold at prices higher than the ones originally paid for them.

capital goods
It refers to goods intended for use in production rather than by consumers. Some goods such as power generating stations and oil-drilling equipment can clearly only be capital goods. Many goods are in fact capable of being used either for production or for consumption. Capital goods are goods, which help in further production of goods, like machinery, equipment, tools, etc. The capital goods will, therefore, be demanded only when there is demand for such goods, which capital goods help in producing. So, the demand for capital goods is a derived demand.

capital issues
The term refers to the main way in which new shares come into existence. Money to fund newly floated companies, or to finance the expansion of existing ones, can be obtained by selling newly issued shares to the public through IPOs, i.e., initial public offers. New issues are regulated by the stock exchange.

capital loss
It is a fall in the price of an asset. A capital loss is incurred when the price of an asset falls below its purchase price and is realised when an asset is sold for less than its cost. Sale at a lower price means a nominal capital loss. A real capital loss is incurred if an asset rises in price less than in proportion to general inflation since it was acquired, and is realised if it is sold for less than its purchase price adjusted for inflation.

capital market
It refers to the following:
1. A market that deals in long-term loans. It supplies industry with fixed and working capital and finances medium-term and long-term borrowings of the central as well as state governments. The capital market deals in ordinary stocks, shares and debentures of corporations, and bonds and securities of governments.
2. The stock exchanges and other institutions where securities are bought and sold. The securities concerned include both shares in companies and various forms of private and public debt. The capital market allows firms, governments, and countries to finance spending in excess of their current incomes. It also enables individuals, firms, and countries to lend to others' savings that they cannot employ as profitably themselves.

capital mobility
The term can be defined as the extent to which capital can be shifted between different uses, and in particular between different countries. This is restricted in various ways. Capital in use may be entirely sunk, or it may be possible to withdraw it from its present use only gradually, as existing equipment wears out. Capital mobility is hindered if the investors do not have sufficient information, or enough confidence that the information provided to them is reliable, about opportunities in different industries or foreign countries.

capital reserves
It is a part of the net assets of a company in excess of the share capital originally contributed by shareholders. Capital reserves may arise from the sale of new shares at a price above their par value, from retention of profits, from the revaluation of assets, or from capital gains made by a company. Capital re-

serves are not normally distributable as dividends. This is in contrast to revenue reserves, which are available to maintain dividends in years of low current profits.

capital stock adjustment

It is a model using the capital output ratio to explain investment. It assumes that firms have a target capital-output ratio. If at any time actual capital stock is less than that is implied by this ratio, the firm invests in order as to close part of the gap during the next period. Partial adjustment is assumed, in view of both uncertainty and costs of adjustment.

capital-intensive economy

It refers to an economy in which the majority of production techniques deployed are capital-intensive. Most advanced countries are capital-intensive.

capital movements

These refer to international flows of funds, which may be undertaken by either private individuals, institutions or governments. It is an important element in the balance of payments.

capital saving innovation

In the present times of fast economic activity, the proportion of capital to labour is raised by the introduction of costly and latest plants that economise the use of labour. When a move is made in the opposite direction, when a reduction in the use of capital per worker takes place, it is termed capital saving innovation. Many countries are faced with the problem of rising numbers of labour and badly need such an innovation.

capital turnover criterion

It refers to an investment criterion, which was suggested for use in some developing countries. It suggests that projects should be selected in accordance with their incremental capital output ratio and that priority be given to those with the lowest ratio. The rationale was that in capital scarce countries a high rate of capital turnover would give rise to an efficient allocation of resources. This criterion would also bring about a utilisation of labour-intensive production techniques, which would be appropriate in developing countries.

capital stock

It is defined as the total stock value of the physical capital of an enterprise, including inventories as well as fixed equipment. This can be measured in following ways: (i) historical cost is what the equipment originally cost to buy; (ii) written-down value is historical cost of equipment minus deductions for ageing and wear and tear in use; while; and (iii) replacement cost is what it would cost to replace existing equipment with equivalent new items.

capital structure

It is used for a firm which is broadly made up of its amounts of equity and debt.

capital tax

It is a tax on the value of the capital assets held by a person. It may be imposed on the annual yield of the capital asset or on the annual value of the capital asset. Such a tax requires capital to be valued, and would be difficult to collect if it could not be paid out of income received from the capital over some short period. Capital taxes are of different types: (i) an annual capital tax or annual tax on net wealth, (ii) a capital levy, i.e., a once-for-all charges, (iii) death duty, i.e., a tax paid on inherited property.

capital transfer

It is the transfer of assets between individuals, by gift or inheritance, where the recipient regards the receipt as an addition to their capital rather than part of their income. There are no objectives with transfers of this nature.

capital transfer tax (CTT)

It is a tax on capital transfers from one person to another by gift or bequest. Governments have two motives for using such a tax rather than a wealth tax if they want to tax capital: (i) a CTT is less discouraging to saving than a wealth tax. A CTT is less likely than a wealth tax to be resented, and thus avoided or evaded by taxpayers; and (ii) a wealth tax involves the regular identification and valuation of assets, which is not always possible.

capital widening

It is investment to increase capacity using unchanged techniques. This allows increased production, using more labour, fuel, and materials through employing more capital. Capital widening is in contrast with capital deepening, where investment makes possible an unchanged level of output at lower cost, through saving of other inputs.

capitalism
It is the economic system based on private property and private enterprise. Under this system, at least a major proportion of economic activity is carried on by private individuals or organisations with a profit motive. Land and other material means of production are largely privately owned. Capitalism does not imply complete *laissez-faire*, i.e., no government intervention. It is compatible with having parts of the economy in public ownership, and with varying degrees of regulation of the private sectors on grounds of security, safety, etc.

capitalist
It refers to a person or a group whose income comes from the ownership of capital. In a capitalist economy with a well-developed occupational pension system and where the majority of homes are owner-occupied, most workers are to some extent also capitalists. The term is, however, normally used only for people who derive a significant proportion of their income from property.

capital-intensive techniques
These are production techniques having a higher proportion of capital than any other factor of production, particularly labour. It is in contrast with labour intensive.

capital-output ratio
It is the ratio of the capital used in a process, firm, company, enterprise or industry to output over some period, usually a year. This ratio for any process depends on the relative cost of different inputs. Where technology makes alternative techniques feasible, firms normally choose the one which is the cheapest. Capital-output ratios tend to be high when capital is cheap relative to other inputs. For a firm, company, enterprise or industry, the capital-output ratio will depend on the mix of different outputs produced and different processes used. This ratio can be measured as an average ratio, comparing total capital stock with total output, or as a marginal ratio, comparing increases in capital used with increases in output.

capitation
It refers to the system of payment for each customer served, rather than by the service performed.

carbon tax
It refers to a proposed tax in some countries on the use of fossil fuels, designed to reduce world output of carbon dioxide (CO_2). The proposal has been prompted by fears that excess accumulation of CO_2 in the atmosphere will have serious effects on world climate.

cardinal utility
It is the concept of personal welfare as being measurable. Statements about both the level of welfare and the size of a change in welfare are, therefore, quite meaningful. Cardinal utility is distinct from ordinal utility, in which the level of welfare is not measurable, so that only statements about the direction of changes in welfare are meaningful. Some experts believe that distinction raises severe problems.

cardinal utility theory, assumption
It is a theory based on the following assumptions:
1. The utility that the consumer makes is measurable. This assumption was, however, severely criticised later. The consumer is rational. He tries to spend the money at his disposal in such a manner as to maximise his satisfaction from the purchases made with the amount of money at his disposal.
2. The utility is measurable in terms of money.
3. The marginal utility that is derived from the successive units of a commodity consumed at a particular time keeps on falling. This assumption is quite valid, the law of diminishing marginal utility is based on this assumption.

carry forward losses
It is the right to deduct past losses from present profits in calculating tax liability. Most tax systems collect taxes from companies and unincorporated businesses, which make profits, but do not make payments to firms making losses, because it is widely believed that the fraudulent production of apparent losses would be too easy. This asymmetry in the treatment of profits and losses perhaps tends to discourage investment.

cartel
It is a formal or informal agreement between a number of firms in an industry to avoid or at least restrict competition. Cartel agree-

ments may provide for setting minimum prices, setting limits on output or capacity, abolishing non-price competition, dividing markets between firms either geographically or in terms of type of product, or taking other measures to restrict entry to the industry.

cash

Literally, it means notes and coins, but cash is mostly used in economics as a synonym for money in general. Cash in hand is currency, etc., kept by firm, etc., for making immediate or short-term transactions. The cash flow of a firm is the pattern over time of its receipts and payments in money, as distinct from the pattern of sales and purchases, which may well be on credit. Cash down means payment in money, and not in credit. A cash discount means that the net price charged for goods is lower if payment is made immediately by means of currency, cheque, credit card or electronic transfer.

Cash

cash discount

It is a discount for prompt payment. Where goods are commonly sold on credit, it is often possible to obtain a reduction in price for prompt payment, in cash, by credit card, or by electronic transfer. Sellers are willing to offer cash discounts because immediate payment saves delay in receiving their money, and possible administrative costs.

cash flow

It is the pattern over time of a firm's actual receipts and payments in money, as opposed to credit. A major responsibility of the finance director of any business is to forecast its cash flow, on both current and capital account, and to ensure that the timing of receipts and payments is such that money is always available to meet any payments that have to be made. Sometimes, such business as appears profitable on the basis of present discounted value may prove disastrous if the

receipts come in too late relative to the payments due.

cash ratio

It refers to minimum ratio of cash holdings to total liabilities of banks or other financial institutions. Cash ratios are said to guard against the collapse of such institutions because of lack of public confidence in their ability to repay deposits. It is hard to see how they provide protection to depositors if an institution's other assets are inadequate so that it is insolvent.

catch-up

It is learning by copying. A country's real economic growth may gain from the possibility of copying techniques from other countries with higher levels of productivity. Catch-up is believed to be most effective for countries that are relatively open to trade and capital movements.

causation

It is the relationship that results when a change in one variable is not only correlated with but also causes the change in another one.

caveat emptor

It is Latin word for 'let the buyer be beware', which means that the consumer is supposed to know about the uses, harmful effects as well as qualities of a product. Considered as a legal principle, this is, however, inconsistent with much modern legislation and many regulations designed to promote public health and safety by protecting buyers, who cannot reasonably be expected to be experts on all the products they purchase, and that they should not suffer from the consequences of their own ignorance and the greed or incompetence of sellers.

ceiling

In economics, it is the maximum level or aggregate real output the economy can attain. The effective constraint may be shortage of labour or capital, or limits on the money supply. Due to growing population, increasing investment, and technical progress, the ceiling rises over time, but only at a limited rate. If the economy rows faster than this, and output reaches the ceiling, the rate of growth of actual output will fall.

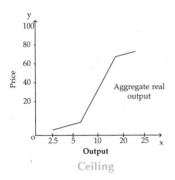

y
100
80
60
Price
40
20

Aggregate real
output

0   2.5   5   10   20   25   x
Output
Ceiling

ceiling price
It is the highest permitted price of a good or service. If a government or other regulatory body wishes to prevent the price of a good from exceeding a ceiling price, this can be done through legal regulation or market intervention. The second option is considered where the stabilisation authority holds a buffer stock of the good and stands prepared to sell it in unlimited quantities at the ceiling price.

census
It is an official enquiry concerning the number and characteristics of the population of a given area. Censuses are normally carried out by official bodies, by means of questionnaires, reply to which is compulsory. In most countries census is conducted every ten years. Census has a unique importance in the day-to-day functioning of our economies, and in the formulation of the sound and appropriate policies.

census of production
It refers to a systematic survey of productive enterprises, carried out by an official body having powers to compel firms to reply to questionnaires. Information is typically collected from enterprises on topics such as the nature of their products, the quantity and types of inputs used, the number and types of employees, and value added.

central bank
The term refers to the apex institution and head of the banking system of a country. It has power of supervision and control over all other banks, and manages and controls the monetary system. The Bank of England and Federal Reserve Bank are central banks in UK and USA respectively. The central bank

of a country controls the volume of currency as it has the sole authority to issue notes as legal tender money. It controls the volume of credit by influencing the lending policies of commercial banks.

central government
It is the highest level of government in a country. It is contrasted with local government, and with state governments in federal countries such as the United States.

central bank independence
Independence of the central bank from immediate short-run control of its aims and operations by the government. This can be promoted by removing the government's right to sack the central bank's directors or to dictate its policies. An independent central bank desired by those who believe stable money is good for the economy. This may sometimes conflict with government aims, whether these are increased employment or the protection of various vested interests in the economy.

central limit, the theory of
It is a theory that states that the sum of a set of random variables will follow a normal distribution if the sample has been sufficiently large, regardless of the distribution from which the individual variables come. The theory is used to justify the assumption of normality of the error term in econometric work, which allows for the use of the usual t-statistics for hypothesis testing, since this error term is supposedly composed of the sum of a set of random omitted factors.

central planning
It is the operation of a command economy through centralised decision-making. In a centrally planned economy, decisions are taken at the centre and orders are issued to enterprises in various sectors like industry, agriculture, services, etc., concerning their production and investment plans. The advantages claimed for this system of a command economy are that all resources in an economy are used in the public interest, and wasteful duplication of effort is avoided. Critics of central planning argue that the amount of information required to achieve efficiency in a centrally planned economy is too great, and the incentives to supply the centre with reliable information are too small, for such a

system to be able to perform as well as a de-centralised system based on competition between independent decision-makers.

certainty equivalent
It refers to the certain outcome, which would give the same utility as an actual distribution of expected outcomes. For an investor with a linear utility function, the certainty equivalent of a distribution of uncertain outcomes is equal to the mean expected value of the uncertain outcomes, and thus makes such an investor risk-neutral.

Certificate of Deposit (CD)
It is an accounting term in which money is deposited for a pre-set length of time that must yield a slightly higher return to compensate for the reduced liquidity.

certificate of incorporation
It is a certificate issued by the Registrar of Companies to a public limited company when it has submitted certain documents and completed the requisite formalities. The promoters of the public limited company (whose minimum number is 07) are required to file two basic documents with the Registrar of Joint Stock Companies.

certificate of origin
It is a document certifying that a good was produced in a given country or region. Such certificates are necessary in free-trade areas, where the members do not have uniform external tariffs. Such certificates of origin are needed to confine duty-free entry to goods produced in member countries, to avoid goods from non-members being imported to the free-trade area through members with low external tariffs and re-exported to members with higher external tariffs. A certificate of origin is also a confirmation to the importer that goods are from the specified country/area as desired by him.

ceteris paribus
It is Latin for 'other things being equal'. This means that other things that could change are for the moment being assumed to remain the same. All statements in economics include such a clause, either explicitly or implicitly. Such things include price, demand, supply, consumer behaviour, among other things.

chairman
He is the member of a committee or board of directors elected or appointed in a company, bank or other such body to preside over its meetings. The chairman frequently has a casting vote. The holder of this office can also be female. In this case, some authors prefer to refer to her as a chairperson.

chancellor of the exchequer
He is the UK's chief finance minister. The chancellor is a member of the cabinet, and is in charge of HM - Her Majesty's Treasury - the UK ministry of finance. The chancellor is responsible for overall supervision of monetary and fiscal policies.

chartalism
Also called as 'state theory of money', it is a 19th century monetary theory, based more on the idea that legal restrictions or customs can or should maintain the value of money, not the intrinsic content of valuable metal.

chartist
The term is used for a person who believes that there are recurring patterns in the behaviour of market variables over periods of time, so that study of past variations assists in predicting the future. The name comes from the use of charts or graphs to show the past behaviour of variables such as share or commodity prices.

cheap money
It refers to the maintenance of low interest rates during a period of recession or slow-down to encourage investment. This policy was followed in the UK during the 1930s and 1940s; in America, Europe and Asia during global recession in 2008-09. It was not very successful in stimulating investment in every sector of economy in the 1930s, except in housing, but proved effective in 2008-09 and 2009-10. Cheap money is a necessary condition for recovery.

checking account
It is an account with a US commercial bank, which can be drawn on without notice, in cash or by writing a cheque. Until recently, such accounts paid no interest.

cheque
It is a written order by a customer to a bank

to pay cash, or to transfer money on deposit to another account. It is convenient but not legally compulsory to use a form provided by the bank for this purpose. Cheques are widely accepted but they are not legal tender, and there is no compulsion to accept them. Most businesses require cheques to be supported by a bank backing/card, unless the customer is well known to them. Cheques not supported by a bank card can be stopped, that is, the bank can be instructed not to honour them.

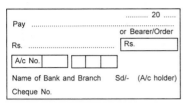

Cheque

Chicago school
The term refers to a group of economists who, inter alia, believe that changes in the money supply have been a major determinant of short-run changes in the level of economic activities.

Chinese walls
In economics, the term refers to the requirement that financial firms prevent transfers of information between staff members who are dealing with different clients, which could lead to conflicts of interest or even to insider dealing.

choice of techniques
It is the choice of method of production where more than one method is possible. A technique refers to a set of inputs capable of producing a given output or set of outputs. If more than one set of inputs can produce the outputs, a choice of techniques has to be made. A firm, which aims at profit-maximisation prefers the technique for which the total cost of inputs is lowest. If some costs are sunk, e.g., in buying long-lasting machines, choice of technique has to take account of expected input prices over the whole useful life of the machines. A firm that aims at maintaining/improving quality, prefers to adopt latest technology.

circular flow of incomes
It is a simple model of a static economy, based on the assumption of a one-period lag between income and expenditure. If there were neither injections of new purchasing power into this flow nor leakages out of it, total income in each period would be equal to the spending arising from incomes in the previous period, and total income would remain constant over a given period of time. Injections of new purchasing power not derived from last period's income can be made by means of investment, fresh borrowing government spending, or return from exports.

circulating capital
It refers to the flows of value within a production organisation. It includes stocks of raw material, work in process, finished goods inventories and cash in hand, needed to make payment to workers and suppliers of inputs before the products are sold.

claimant
It refers to a person applying for any benefit from the state. Benefits, for example, jobless, sickness, or disability benefit, need to be claimed for two possible reasons: (i) in some cases, the person has a clear legal right to the benefit, but the civil servants administering the benefits system need to be informed of the facts; and (ii) in other cases, payment of the benefit is discretionary wherein the claimant has both to establish the facts and convince the administrator that he or she has a good case for receiving the benefit.

classical dichotomy
It is the view that real variables in the economy are determined purely by real rather than by monetary factors, and nominal variables are determined purely by monetary factors and not by real ones. Keynesian economics is strongly opposed to this view.

classical economics
It is the economics that deals with the economic thought of the period from the mid-18th to the mid-19th century, of which great bulk emerged from the U.K. The major practitioners were Adam Smith, David Ricardo, J.S. Malthus, J.B. Say and T.R. Mill. Classical economists are economists prevalent before the Great Depression, who believed that the basic competitive model provided a good description of the economy and that if short periods of unemployment did occur, market forces would quickly restore the economy to full employment.

classical model

It is a model of the economy in which it is assumed that prices, wages and interest rates are flexible. In such an economy, factors are fully employed, and the growth of output depends on the growth of available factor supplies. The Solow growth model is an example of a classical model. Classical models are at variance with models in which either nominal or real price rigidities prevent markets from clearing, and unemployment can occur in equilibrium. It is obvious that classical models are not 100 per cent realistic; it is a matter of controversy how much light they shed on long-term trends in real world economics.

classical unemployment

It can be defined as unemployment caused by wages being too high relative to productivity, so that the firms in an economy cannot profitably employ all the labour on offer at these real wages. This type of unemployment can be reduced by a fall in wage costs relative to producer prices.

Clayton Act

It is a US Act of 1914, which extended the federal antitrust law. It forbade price discrimination, trying arrangements and exclusive dealing, and the acquisition of another corporation's stock where this led to monopoly or decreased competition.

clearing bank

It is the system for settling payments due from one bank to another. There are numerous commercial banks, and in most transactions settled by a transfer of bank balances from buyer to seller, the two parties hold accounts with different banks. The bank clearing is an arrangement to reduce the amount of funds, which needs to be transferred to settle all these payments. All the cheques are sent to a clearing-house usually through the bank's centralised clearing department, where the amounts payable to and from the customers of each bank are added up.

clearinghouse

It is an institution where claims by various banks against each other are offset. This greatly reduces the need for transfers of funds between banks, as each bank need only remit the net excess of its gross payments out over gross payments in, or receive the net excess of payments in over payments out.

cliometrics

It is known as the study of economic history.

close company

It is a company with very few members.

closed economy

It is an economy without contacts with the rest of the world. No economy is entirely closed, but the various possible forms of contact with the outside are restricted in several ways, e.g., China and Russia. Trade in goods and services may be limited by poor transport facilities, or by human agency. Some of this, such as tariffs and quotas on trade, is deliberate; other restrictions are by-products of conditions making a country unattractive to foreign firms, including poor infrastructure, disorder, lack of a satisfactory legal system, and corruption.

closing price

It refers to the price in a stock or commodity exchange at the end of a day's trading.

cluster

It denotes a concept associated with Michael Porter's work. He defines a cluster as "a geographically proximate group or geographic concentration of 'interconnected companies', specialised suppliers and service providers, firms in related industries and associated institutions linked by commonalities and complementarities".

clustering

It is the theory that firms in certain industries flourish best in areas where there are other firms of a similar type. This enables them to use the services of related industries providing inputs of goods and services, and probably to gain from the training provided by other firms in a cluster by restricting their skilled labour force. This is held to explain the tendency of industries to concentrate in particular areas, for example, software hubs in Bangaluru, and Silicon Valley in California, with a high density of electronics and computer-based industries.

cobweb

It is a simple model used to denote the danger that time lags may introduce fluctuations into the economy. Suppose that the demand for a good is a decreasing function of its current price, but, because of the time taken to plant and harvest crops, its supply is an increasing function of last year's price. The equilibrium price is where the supply and demand curves cross, but if price is not at this level in year 1, it will be above equilibrium level in year 2 if it was below in year 1, and vice versa. The price will thus oscillate, with increasing oscillations if the absolute slope of the demand curve is greater than that of the supply curve.

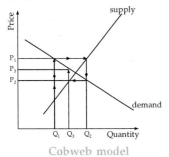

Cobweb model

as the sovereign's portrait to certify that their weight and fineness are guaranteed. Sovereigns discovered that they could make profits by debasing the coinage, so that the material was of less value than the face value of the coin. This eventually led to the rise of token money, which does not claim to have intrinsic value. Since the rise of paper money, coinage has been largely used as small change. Now coins form only a small part of the total money supply.

Coins

Cobweb theorem
It refers to the simplest form of a dynamic model in which the supply of a good has been a function of the goods price in year t-1 and where, in any period, price is adjusted so as to clear the market.

coefficient
It is the number of algebraic expressions giving the structure of an expression or equation. For example, in $y = ax^2 + bx + c$, a is the coefficient of x^2, b is the coefficient of x and c is the constant term.

coefficient of variation
It is a measure of the importance of variability relative to average size. Size is measured by the mean, and variability is measured by the standard deviation, which is the square root of the mean square of deviations from the mean. Thus, if there are N observations, x_i for $i = 1, 2, ..., N$, the mean is: $\mu = [\Sigma^N_1 x_i]/N$, the standard deviation and the coefficient of variation is $c = \sigma/\mu$.

coins
They represent money consisting of solid tokens, usually of metal. Coins were originally made of precious metals, normally gold or silver, and were imprinted with patterns such

co-insurance
It is an insurance covering only a proportion of total losses. This is often desirable since cover for the entire loss would create too much moral hazard. For example, the insured would take too few precautions to avoid the risk, of fire or accidents, etc.

co-integration
It is the property of a set of timeseries, that a linear combination thereof exists which is of a lower order of integration than the highest-order series in the set. For example, two series are co-integrated if one can be expressed as a linear function of the other(s) plus a stationary disturbance term.

collateral
It is a valuable article or property pledged as the security for a loan. In mortgages, land or buildings are used as collateral; share certificates, National Saving Certificates (NSC), life insurance policies with a surrender value are used as collateral for bank loans; in pawnbroking the collateral pledged can be any portable valuable like car. If payments of interest and repayments of the principal are not made on time, in the last resort the lender can sell the collateral asset.

collectivism

It can be defined as a doctrine or belief that is reverse of individualism. Individualists advocate and uphold the interest of the individual, with a firm belief that his/ her interest also maximises the interest and welfare of the society. Collectivism, on the contrary, upholds the belief that it is the collective wellbeing of the society that is far more important and if need be, the individual can be sacrificed for the society's advancement.

collusion

It refers to an action without any formal agreement. For example, firms may refrain from undercutting each others' prices, or from selling in each other's market areas. Collusion is common when anti-monopoly legislation makes explicit agreements illegal or unenforceable.

collusive tendering

It refers to restrictive practices in which firms tendering for a particular job agree to submit a common price, or to allow one of their numbers to submit a lower tender, thus allocating orders between themselves.

column

It is a list of variables arranged vertically. This may be part of a table, or a vector. A column vector is sometimes enclosed in brackets. The elements in either case may be numbers or algebraic expressions. A column is contrasted with a row, which is a list of variables arranged horizontally.

command economy

The term is used for an economic system, which is dominated by central planning. It is distinguished from a free enterprise economy with a minimum of state interference. The features of command economy are not restricted to socialist economies. The system, which encourages free enterprise, maintains a powerful apparatus of central control and influence though much in it may be of an indirect character with the use of monetary and fiscal policies.

commercial bank

It is a bank dealing with the general public, accepting deposits from and making loans to a large number of households and small firms. These banks also provide various services for depositors, including provision of cash and credit cards, storage facilities for valuables and documents, foreign exchange, stock-broking, mortgage finance, and executor services. Commercial banks conduct a general rather than a specialised type of business. They accept deposits on varying terms, but including demand deposits; and their lending to private sector business for non-fixed capital purposes, generally accounts for the greater part of their assets.

commercial bill

It is a bill that is drawn to finance trade or other commercial or production activities. It is distinct from a Treasury Bill and Local Government Bill, which have been instruments of public financial operations.

commercial paper

It is said to be another term for commoditised short-term corporate debt.

commercial policy

It defines the policies followed by governments affecting foreign trade. This covers the use of tariffs, trade subsidies, quotas, voluntary export restraint agreements (VERs), and other non-tariff barriers to trade, restrictions on rights of establishment for foreign businesses, and the regulation of international trade in services such as insurance, transfer of funds, etc.

commission

It is a kind of payment for the services of an agent or intermediary in a transaction. This payment is usually an increasing function of the value of the transaction. Commission may be payable by the buyer, the seller, or both. Working on a commission basis includes sales staff, estate agents, stockbrokers and auctioneers, etc. They are examples of agents.

commitment

It is a promise by governments or central bankers about future policies. Commitment, sometimes pre-commitment, promises that monetary or fiscal policies will not be changed, or that if policy changes are needed, they will take specified forms.

commodities market

It is a place or institution through which commodities are traded. Markets were originally places or buildings, where traders could come together, which facilitated comparisons of price and quality. Non-standardised commodities such as fish, fruit, flowers and fresh vegetables, which need to be physically inspected, are often still traded in such markets. Commodity markets include both 'spot' markets, where goods are traded for immediate delivery, and forward and futures markets, where prices are agreed in advance for trading at various dates in the future. Such trading is facilitated by market conventions on the specification and quality of the goods traded.

commodity
It refers to a good, that is generally a primary good, which is used in manufacturing timber, cotton, wool, and copper.

common external tariff
It is the tariff charged on trade with non-members by all countries in a customs union or common market. When used with capitals, it normally refers to the external tariff of the European Union (EU).

common market
It is a fully integrated market area. This covers not only complete freedom of internal trade, as in a customs union, but also free mobility of labour and capital. Full mobility of labour involves the right to reside and accept employment in all member countries, and mutual recognition of professional and technical skills, subject to satisfying local language requirements. Full capital mobility requires lack of exchange controls, and full rights of establishment for firms in all countries.

commons
The term refers to the resources which are not owned, either privately or by the state, but are left open for free use by all comers. Examples include the air, fishery and forest resources as well as public highways. As there is no price on using them, every user has an incentive to use them until the private marginal return falls to zero. If the resources are in unlimited supply, this is efficient. But if each user in fact reduces the supply available for others, it may be termed as inefficient use.

common stock
It is the equity capital of a US corporation. Holders of common stock are entitled to attend and vote at general meetings, to receive declared dividends, and to receive their share of the residual assets, if any, if the corporation is wound up or goes into liquidation.

communism
It can be defined as a stage of economic development which is said to take place when all classes in society have been absorbed into the proletariat. In this ideal society, the state would have withered away and each person would contribute according to his/her ability and receive according to his/her needs. This utopia was envisaged by Karl Marx and has been seen as the stage of economic development which follows on from capitalism and socialism. Nowadays the term is, however, generally used to denote the planned economic system operated in the communist countries.

community indifference curve
It is a type of curve used in international trade theory, similar in shape to an individual's indifference curve, but purporting to describe the tastes of a country. The community indifference curve through any collection of goods shows the amounts of goods needed to bring every member of the community up to their utility level in the original situation.

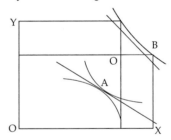

Community indifference curve

company
It is a form of organised business, with a legal personality distinct from the individuals taking part in it. This has been found essential in organising large and complex businesses. The formation of companies is controlled by the state. At various times in the UK, companies have been formed by Act of Parliament, or registration with the Registrar of Companies. A company is empowered to own assets, incur debts, and enter into contracts, and may be sued and taxed. It may or may not have limited liability for its shareholders. In case of without limited liability, shareholders are in the last resort responsible for meeting the company's debts. In case of limited liability, com-

panies are liable only to the extent of any unpaid part of the book value of their shares.

company law
It is the law relating to the formation and operation of companies. Laws are necessary for the existence of companies, which are often described as artificial persons whose rights and obligations exist only in a legal framework provided by the state. Company law lays down the rights and duties of directors and shareholders, and determines the extent of limited liability for a company's debts.

company reserves
The term refers to the business enterprises registered under the Companies Act, which instead of distributing the entire net profit amongst the shareholders, set a part of its profit in the shape of reserves for specific or general purposes. It is known as company's reserves.

company taxation
It is the system for taxing company profits. Two systems are possible: (i) in the 'classical' system the company is taxed as such; any dividends have to be paid out of post-tax company income, and are taxed again as the income of shareholders; (ii) in the 'imputation' system, company dividends are not then taxed again.

comparative advantage
According to this concept given by David Ricardo, a country has a comparative advantage in producing a good, relative to another country or the rest of the world, if the relative cost of producing the good, that is, its opportunity cost in terms of other goods foregone, is lower than it is abroad. The comparative advantage encourages a country to export goods to other countries.

comparative cost, the theory of
It explains as to how and why different nations trade with one another. In other words, it explains the basis of international trade. The basis is the differences in cost. Different nations produce a given article at different cost ratios. Such differences can be difference in costs, viz.: (i) absolute difference in cost; (ii) it is equal differences cost under which no trade is possible; (iii) comparative difference in cost. The greatest bulk of international trade takes place due to the comparative differences in cost. It encourages a country to export goods to other countries.

comparative dynamics
The term refers to a method employed in dynamic economics with a special feature that the rates of change in the equilibrium values of the variables have been constant.

comparative statics
It is the analysis of how the equilibrium position in an economic model would change if the assumptions of the model were altered. Such changes can affect exogenously given quantities, e.g., a country's population, or parameters describing behaviour, such as the propensity to save. 'Comparative' indicates that two or more equilibrium states of the economy are being compared.

compensated demand curve
It can be explained as below:
1. A curve in which the income effect of a price change has been netted out so that, along the demand curve real income has been held constant. The demand curve then exhibits the shape it does because of the substitution effect only. The demand curve given by Alfred Marshall includes both income and substitution effects.
2. It is the demand curve for a good as it would be if consumers were compensated for the effect of changes in its price. As this removes the income effects of price changes, the compensated demand curve for a normal good is less elastic than the market demand curve, which includes income effects.

compensating variation
It is the amount of additional money needed to restore an individual's original level of utility if the price of any good consumed rises, or it ceases to be available. This is based on the assumption that the prices and availability of all other goods are unchanged. The compensating variation is contrasted with the equivalent variation, which can be described as the amount of additional money needed to give the level of utility that an individual could have reached if the price of a commodity fell.

compensating wage differential
It is a differential in wages intended to compensate workers for special non-pecuniary

aspects of a job. Examples would be extra pay for work which is not palatable or involves staggering hours.

compensation for externalities
It is the principle that those causing adverse externalities should compensate the victims. There are two different points involved here. The economic benefit of 'making the polluter pay' is that it creates an incentive to avoid causing pollution, unless avoiding it is too expensive to be worthwhile. This internalises the externality concerned, and makes for economic efficiency, whether or not the charge the polluter pay, goes to the victims of pollution.

competition
It is the situation when anybody who wants to buy or sell something has a choice of possible suppliers or customers. In a market with perfect competition, there are so many suppliers and customers, with such good contact between them, that all traders ignore the effects of their own supplies or purchases on the market, and act as price-takers, able to buy or sell any quantity at a price which they cannot influence. However, such intense competition is rather unusual in real life. The usual condition is monopolistic or imperfect competition, with a limited number of buyers or sellers. In this case, buyers and sellers realise that the amount they can trade is affected by the price they offer. With monopoly, there is only one seller, but this is also unusual. Monopolistic competitors have some monopoly power, but this is limited in the long run by potential competition from possible entrants to a market as well as actual competition from other rivals who have only recently entered the market. Most economists welcome competition as a stimulus to cost reduction and quality improvement, many businessmen and trade unionists protest that competition is liable to lead to shoddy goods as prices are cut, and to depressed incomes for producers who may reduce wages.

competitive devaluation
It is an attempt by two or more countries to improve their competitive position relative to the others by devaluing their currencies. For each country, devaluation gives at least a temporary cost advantage, which improves the competitiveness of domestic firms. They can either maintain their prices in domestic currency and cut their foreign currency prices, or raise their prices in domestic currency and use the revenue so gained to improve the quality of their products.

competitiveness
It is the ability to compete in markets for goods or services and is based on a combination of price and quality. With equal quality and an established reputation, suppliers are competitive only if their prices are as low as those of rivals. A new supplier without an established reputation may need a lower price than rivals to compete.

complementarity
It is a relation between two goods or services in which a rise in the price of one decreases demand for the other. Complements are contrasted with substitutes, when a rise in the relative price of either good increases demand for the other. Examples of pairs of goods which are complements are butter and eggs, or car tyres and petrol or cups and saucers.

compliance costs
They are the costs to a firm of complying with laws and regulations affecting the markets it trades in. This may include extra record-keeping, using extra staff to maintain 'Chinese walls' between departments, and employing compliance officers to monitor the behaviour of other members of staff.

composite demand
It is the total demand of a commodity or service, which has more than one use. For example, electricity is used for light and industry power or for running trains. Thus, demand of a commodity having many uses is called composite demand.

composite quasi-rent
It is the excess above the return necessary to maintain a resource's current service flow, which can be the means to recover sunk costs. Composite quasi-rent can also be defined as that portion of the quasi-rent of resources that depends on continued association with some other specific, currently associated resources.

composite supply
A supply of different commodities satisfying the same want is called composite supply.

These different commodities are substitutes for each other. For example, tea and coffee or supply of colas and other aerated waters.

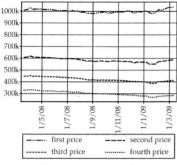

Composite supply

compound interest
It is a loan where the interest due each period is added to the amount outstanding. The interest of earlier periods, thus itself earns interest in later periods. At an interest rate of 100r per cent per period, after 1 period, an original loan of A amounts to $A(1 + r)$; after two periods to $A(1+r)^2$; and after N periods to $A(1 + r)^N$, where r is the rate of interest.

computerised trading
It is use of a computer programme to track various pieces of market information, such as share or commodity prices, and to execute specified trades if certain conditions are observed. For example, the computer could be programmed to track the share prices of companies A and B, and to sell A and buy B if the excess of B's price over A's falls below 15 per cent.

concentration ratio, n-firm
The proportion of a market taken up by the n largest firms. This is normally expressed as a percentage of the market as a whole. Size may be measured in various ways, including output, employment, and market capitalisation of various firms. The n-firm concentration ratio takes no account of the distribution of firm sizes either between the largest n-firms, or within the tail of smaller firms.

conceptual framework for economic geography
The term refers to the structure that serves to hold the conceptual parts concepts toge-

ther and within which the ideas, facts, principles, insights and circumstances of economic geography exist and are related to each other.

conditional distribution
It is the distribution of some characteristic for fixed values of some other characteristic(s). For example, if c stands for number of dependent children and a for the age of the head of family, then $f(c)(a_i)$ is frequency distribution of the number of dependent children in families with heads aged a_i.

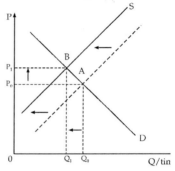

Conditional distribution

conditionality
The practice by which the International Monetary Fund (IMF) makes its loans conditional on the borrowing country adopting an approved adjustment programme or policy package. Some critics argue that the actual conditions are sometimes based more on economic dogmas than on understanding of the borrowing countries' real problems, and in particular that they tend to be too deflationary.

confidence interval
It is the interval that contains the true value of a parameter of the population sampled with a given probability, for example, 95 per cent, as inferred from a sample. The width of the confidence interval is an increasing function of the probability required.

conglomerate
It is a business conducting activities in different industries with very little in common.

conglomerate merger
It is a merger between firms, which operate in different sectors of the economy. Such a merger offers no economies of scale ex-

cept possibly in raising finance, but it is believed to reduce riskiness.

conglomerates
It is a firm operating in several industries.

connected lending
It means loans to companies or persons connected with the institution lending the funds.

conservative central banker
It refers to a central banker appointed in some countries with a higher valuation of price stability relative to activity levels than the average for a country's population. It is argued that since a conservative central banker can acquire a reputation for antiinflationary policies, appointing such a central banker may allow a country a more favourable trade-off between employment levels and price stability.

consignee
The term denotes the person in whose favour the consignment is despatched. Thus, the consignment is sent by the consigner to the consignee. A consignment note is prepared. It contains the description of the goods being despatched along with the name and address of the consigner and the consignee.

consolidated account
They are accounts of an undertaking which has several subsidiaries and are prepared in such a manner so as to show the overall accounts and correct picture of each of the subsidiaries as well. Such an exercise is known as consolidated account.

consortium
It is a group of companies or banks combining to run a project. This method is used for projects too large or risky to appeal to any one firm or enterprise on its own. Many power generation projects in the world have been set up by a consortium. When one particular firm in spite of its size and resources and technology finds it beyond its capacity to cope with the execution of the projects that it may be entrusted with, it may combine with a few more independent firms and shoulder collectively its risk and operations.

consortium bank
It is a bank which is formed by groupings of existing banks usually drawn from different countries. These banks appeared in the 1960s and have now established in several financial centres. They are mainly involved in medium-term lending, frequently extending loans to multinational companies.

conspicuous consumption
It is the theory that some consumption expenditure is undertaken not to maximise independent individual utility functions, but to impress other people. Consumers who spend to display their wealth will not necessarily prefer cheaper goods to dearer ones, provided a high price is well publicised. Some examples are buying expensive paintings, antiques, big cars, etc.

Constant Absolute Risk Aversion (CARA)
Also known as exponential utility, it is a class of utility functions. It has the form for positive constant 'a': $u(c) = -(1/a)e^{ax}$ Under this specification, the elasticity of marginal utility is equal to '-ac' and the instantaneous elasticity is equal to '1/ac'. The coefficient of absolute risk aversion is 'a', thus the abbreviation CARA for Constant Absolute Risk Aversion.

constant of integration
It is an arbitrary number which can be added to any indefinite integral. Consider a function f(a). Its first derivative is $df(a)/dx = g(a)$. f(a) is thus the indefinite integral of g(a). But the first derivative of any function $h(x) = f(a) + k$, where k is any constant, is also g(a), since $dk/da = 0$. Thus, h(a) is also an indefinite integral of g(a).

constant returns to scale
It is a constant ratio between inputs and outputs. With constant returns to scale a uniform percentage increase in all inputs in a productive process results in an equal percentage increase in output.

constrained maximum
It is the maximum possible value for a function, consistent with satisfying one or more inequalities. For example, a consumer seeks to maximise utility subject to a budget constraint, that is, a limit on the amount he or she can spend. In this case, if wants are assumed insatiable, the budget constraint is always effective, but in other problems constraints may not be effective.

constrained minimum

It refers to the minimum possible value for a function, consistent with satisfying one or more inequalities. For example, if a firm seeks to minimise the costs of producing a given output, the constraint is always effective, but in other problems constraints may not be effective. There may be any number of constraints, each of which may or may not be effective. For example, consider the problem of minimising $C = f(a, b)$ subject to $g(a, b) \geq 0$, where a and b are inputs. If it is known that the constraint is not effective, it can be disregarded. If it is known that it is effective, that is, $g(a, b) = 0$, then it may be possible to use the constraint to express a in terms of b, turning C into a function of b only.

constraint

It can be defined as a condition which has to be satisfied for any economic activity to be feasible. Constraints may arise from facts of nature, e.g., a country has only a certain amount of land available. Constraints may arise from human actions in the past, e.g., a country's capital stock is predetermined by its past investment, and its working population by its past immigration policies. Such constraints can be changed by human action, but only slowly, over a period of time. Constraints may also arise from the limits on available technology which again can be improved on by research and development, but only gradually and subject to uncertainty.

consultant

The term refers to an outside specialist hired by an enterprise to advise on some particular technical, commercial, or legal aspects of its activities. A person or firm employed as a consultant normally has a reputation for technical expertise and experience.

consumer

The term can be defined as a purchaser of goods and services for the personal satisfaction as distinct from use to generate further income. Consumer credit is credit given for the purchase of consumption goods.

consumer behaviour

It can be defined as the way in which consumers choose how to spend their incomes. One theory of consumer behaviour views consumers as having utility functions depicting the levels of satisfaction, they will derive from every possible set of goods and services. They choose their expenditures to maximise their utility subject to the constraints imposed by their incomes. This view is based on the assumption that tastes are given, independent, and are fully known, and that information is free, complete, and reliable. Those who oppose this view point out that the set of available goods and services is continually changing.

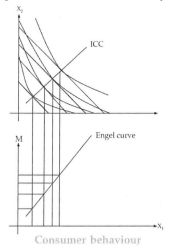

Consumer behaviour

consumer confidence

It is the willingness of consumers to spend their incomes. This is invariably higher if their expectations concerning future incomes are optimistic, and lower if they are worried about job security. Long-term and short-term income expectations have an impact on consumer confidence through people's ideas of their permanent income; short-term income expectations also affect people's spending through tightening or relaxing liquidity constraints for those subjected to them.

consumer consumption

The term refers to the individuals and corporations that buy products and services. In economics, consumption refers only to consuming that involves a monetary transaction.

consumer debt

It is the amount owed by consumers at any time as the result of past acceptance of consumer credit. The amount of consumer debt increases each month through new purchases on credit, and the addition of interest payable on existing debt, and it falls each month through repayment.

consumer demand, the theory of
It refers to that area of economics that defines testable theories of how the consumers behave in response to change in variables like price of the good, a consumer wants to buy and the price of other goods which act as substitute income changes and so on.

consumer durables
They are long-lived goods bought for final consumption. Their services are expected to be enjoyed over a period longer than that (normally a year) used in national income accounting. They include cars, buses, trucks, furniture, televisions, video recorders, refrigerators, washing machines, air conditioners, microwave ovens, and so on. Footwear and clothing are not normally treated as consumer durables, although they are frequently made to last for several years.

consumer expenditure
It is the spending on private consumption. This can be divided into spending on non-durable goods, (such as food, drink, or fruits), spending on consumer durables, (such as cars and furniture), and spending on services, (such as travel and entertainment, among other things).

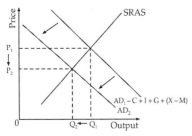

Consumer expenditure

consumer goods
The term refers to the goods designed for use by final consumers. These are mostly bought by consumers, but some, such as business cars, are bought by enterprises, while many are exported.

consumerism
It is the view that economic life should be organised for the benefit of consumers, rather than producers. It is based on the fact that consumers are individuals while producers are mostly organised in firms, companies, etc., and the consumers spread their purchases over a much wider variety of goods and services than those, which are produced by the most firms, consumers are mostly less well informed and less organised than producers.

consumer non-durable
It is non-durable goods, such as food, drink, vegetables, fruits, etc., designed for the final consumers. Some of these are in fact used by businesses. Some nondurables such as wine actually has quite long shelf lives, but they are nondurable in the sense that they can be used only once when they are finally consumed.

consumer preference, the theory of
It is the theory based on the replies of consumers who have been asked if they prefer set of goods or they are indifferent to it.

consumer price index
It is a price index covering the prices of consumer goods. It is distinct from a more general price index, such as the GDP deflator, which also includes the investment goods and the goods purchased by the government.

consumer protection
It refers to the laws that protect consumers. These laws concern minimum health and safety standards, information and labelling requirements, provision of advice as to the use, etc., and regulation of consumer credit.

consumer rationality
The term denotes the assumption that consumers, at least sane and sober adults, are the best judges of their own interests. This assumption is the basis for leaving consumption patterns to be decided by the market. The consumers thus pay fixed prices of goods and services, which reflect the costs of production.

consumer sovereignty
It refers to the proposition that it is the tastes of consumers rather than the preferences of producers, which determine what goods are to be provided and in how much quantity. This is in contrast to the theory of producer dominance wherein the industry decides what and how much to produce, and how

much advertising is successful in brainwashing consumers into buying it. Neither view is completely justified. In a market, consumers cannot be compelled to buy any particular goods, and many new products and new brands of existing products fail to secure a market share.

consumer surplus

It is the excess of the benefit a consumer gains from purchases of goods over the amount paid for them. An ndividual demand curve shows the valuation put by a consumer on successive units of a good. Goods whose value to the consumer is higher than the price at which they are bought continue to attract customers. Purchasing stops when their marginal utility is equal to the marginal utility of money. If the marginal utility of money is treated as constant, consumer surplus can be measured by the area below the demand curve but above the price. The marginal utility of money is not in fact believed to be exactly constant, but if the good absorbs only a small proportion of income the error involved is quite small and can be ignored. The consumer surplus can be determined by the following figure, which shows market demand curve for a commodity. The figure shows that the market price is $5, and the equilibrium quantity to be demanded is 5 units. It is obvious from the market demand curve that consumers may pay $9 for the first unit, $8 for the second unit, $7 for the third unit, and $6 for the fourth unit. Nonetheless, they can purchase 5 units just for $5 per unit. The surpluses from the first unit obtained by the consumers are:

Surplus from the first unit: $9 - $5 = $4
Surplus from the second unit: $8 - $5 = $3
Surplus from the third unit: $7 - $5 = $2
Surplus from the fourth unit: $6 - $5 = $1
Total surplus: $(4 + 3 + 2 + 1) = $10

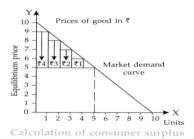

Calculation of consumer surplus

The sum total of these surpluses is called consumer surplus.

consumer's preference

It refers to the preference of the consumer for a particular commodity as compared with some other commodities. We have innumerable wants and spend the money in a manner that gives us the maximum satisfaction. If article A has greater utility as compared with article B, it means the consumer has preference for A to B.

consumption

It is defined as an act of using goods and services to satisfy current wants. Withal, different groups of economists define consumption differently. Mainstream economists consider it as only the final purchase of goods and services. Others define it as the aggregate of all economic activities.

consumption function

The term refers to a function showing how the consumption of an individual or a country as a whole is determined. Individual consumption is an increasing function of income, for those individuals whose income is exogenously determined. For individuals who can choose how much to work, consumption and income are jointly determined, but they tend to rise or fall together. Consumption is also affected by a number of other factors, including size of dependent family, total assets, and factors affecting 'permanent income', such as job security, pension prospects, liabilities towards loans availed, etc.

contagion

It is the tendency of investors to doubt the solvency of some firms or countries when others are in trouble. Default by one bank or financial institutions, for example, may trigger a doubt about the credibility of other banks, or default on its debts by one LDC government may make it harder for others to borrow, even when there is no concrete evidence to justify this. Fears of contagion may force central banks to support institutions in financial difficulties. The contagion was visible during the recession of 2008-09, particularly in America.

contestable market

It is a market that can be entered without

sunk costs and left without loss. In such a market, the potential as well as actual competition is a constraint on what the actual producers can charge. It is difficult to produce examples of fully contestable markets as most activities involve some sunk costs for entrants.

contingency reserve
It is witnessed in the preparation of the budget and allocation of resources, when different heads of expenditure are allotted different accounts. Contingency reserve has great importance, for it is from such a reserve that expenses which arise out of suddenness or out of a peculiar unexpected development are proposed to be met.

contingency theory
It is the design of an effective organisation, as necessarily having to be adapted to cope with the 'contingencies', which arise from the circumstances of technology, scale, resources, work, task and some other factors.'

contingent fee
It is a fee payable only if an activity is successful. For example, an estate agent receives commission only if a sale is achieved. The lawyers, however, do not work on a contingent fees basis, and get paid whether or not they win their client's case.

contingent liability
It is a liability that will only arise in certain specific circumstances. For example, a guarantee of somebody else's debts will only have to be honoured if they fail to pay up. Insurance companies incur contingent liabilities when they issue fire or accident insurance policies, i.e., they will only have to pay out if policy-holders have fires or accidents.

contingent market
It is a market in which contracts will only be carried out in certain states of the world. Some contingent markets do exist, e.g., options market, where the holder of a put option will only choose to exercise it if the market price is below the option price, and the holder of a call option will only choose to exercise it if the market price is above the option price.

contingent protection
The term denotes instruments of import restriction, which are not actually used unless they are thought to be needed, but are available in case a domestic industry is threatened by a surge of imports. This includes measures such as anti-dumping duties.

continuity
It is the absence of sudden jumps in a function. A function $b = f(a)$ is continuous if as a changes by arbitrarily small amounts there are no sudden changes in b. Some functions are continuous for all values of a, for example, $y = a^2$.

continuous variable
It is a variable, which can take any value, and is not confined to particular values, such as integers. The techniques of calculus apply only to continuous variables. Many economic variables, including prices and incomes, are measured in money terms. But since money comes in discrete units, it is not a continuous variable.

contra cyclical policy
It is a deliberate policy adopted by the government to counteract the taking place of trade cycle. During boom periods, when the economy registers an upward phase, the government imposes higher direct and indirect duties, while in the sphere of public expenditure, the government spends the absolute minimum as private investment in itself is very high.

contract
It is a legal agreement between two or more parties, specifying the actions to be taken and payments to be made by each of the parties to the contract. A contract may also specify how any dispute over its interpretation will be resolved, through arbitration or a court of law. A contract of employment is a contract between an employer and an employee specifying the work to be performed by the employee and the payments and working conditions to be provided by the employer.

contract curve
It refers to the line in a box diagram running between the two origins, showing where indifference curves or isoquants for the two outputs are tangential. Only points on this curve represent Pareto optimal allocations of resources, while points off it are not Pareto

optimal. If the indifference curves or isoquants through any point in the box are not tangential, then a shift in resource allocation to some point on the contract curve may allow more or either of the two types of output to be obtained without giving up any of the other.

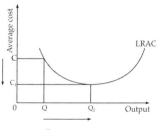

Contract curve

contractual savings
They are savings made on a regular basis in conformity with a contract. This could be through life insurance policies, pension plan, investment in a Mutual Fund or a repayment mortgage. Individuals may adopt these forms of savings as a method of self-discipline. They have the disadvantage that violation of the contract generally involves financial penalties. Liabilities under contractual savings may cause problems if income falls, for example, through unemployment, or if special needs arise.

contributory pension scheme
It is a pension scheme in which scheme members are required to contribute to the scheme's funds, usually by deduction of a percentage of their pay. This may be distinguished from a noncontributory pension scheme, where the entire cost is borne by the employer. In a contributory pension scheme, the employer normally also bears part of the cost.

controllable costs
These costs are subject to control or check by executive vigilance, while noncontrollable costs are those that cannot be subjected to administrative control or supervision. But a cost which is non-controllable at one level of the executive may be regarded as controllable at some other level.

convergence
It is a tendency for two or more economies to become more similar. This may be, in respect of per capita incomes, GDP growth rates, in-flation rates, interest rates, methods of economic organisation, fiscal position, plans for socioeconomic development, etc.

convertibility
Convertible securities are the ones, holders of which have an option to them by the company to get them converted into shares. Convertibility in context of foreign exchange means the change of the currency of one country into the currency of another country like the rupee being converted into dollar or vice versa. A fully convertible currency is convertible by any holder, for any purpose. A currency may be convertible for nonresident but not for resident holders.

convertible currency
It is a currency, which the holder has the right to change into any other currency. A fully convertible currency can be exchanged into any other currency by any holder. However, some limited forms of convertibility are possible: currencies may be convertible only by non-residents, or only for current account but not for capital account purposes. If a currency is convertible only by non-residents, the government must control payments from residents' into non-residents' bank accounts.

convexity
It is a property of sets whereby if any two points are members of a set, any convex linear combination of them is also a member. If points with coordinates shown by $(x_1, x_2, x_3, ..., x_N)$ and $(y_1, y_2, y_3, ..., y_N)$ are members of a convex set, any linear combination $(z_1, z_2, z_3, ..., z_N)$, where $z_i = \lambda x_i + (1 - \lambda)y_i$ for all i, $0 < \lambda < 1$, is also a member of the set.

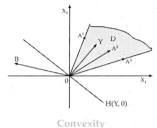

Convexity

cooperative banks
These are the small local institutions, which are generally organised by a group of individuals with a common purpose. They are designed to give members easier and cheaper access to credit.

coordinates
The term refers to the method of specifying position on a diagram. The most common form in economics is Cartesian co-ordinate, i.e., a grid with the axes at right angles.

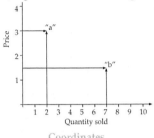

Coordinates

co-ordination failure
It is a situation where activities, which could have benefited two or more parties does not take place because they fail to concert their plans. For example, in a least developed country (LDC), one might find mineral resources, which are not mined because there is no transport to export them, and a railway, which is not built because there is no freight for it to carry.

copyright
It is the exclusive right to reproduce literary, artistic, dramatic, or musical work, or to authorise its reproduction by others. Copyright persists for a finite period after the author's death, usually 60 years. Copyright can be sold or inherited. It also extends to films and TV, theatre and is one of the main forms of intellectual property.

core
It is a central region in an economy, with good communications, transportation and high population density, which conduce to its prosperity. The core is distinct from the periphery or outlying regions with poor communications, transportation and sparse population. Some economists argue that the differences between core and periphery tend to increase as migrants and investment are attracted to the core. Large populations give core regions considerable voting power, which means that government policies tend to be more responsive to core than to peripheral needs.

core inflation
It is a measure of inflation of consumer prices excluding the prices of certain items. This may apply to food, whose prices are subject to seasonal fluctuations, fuel, whose prices are subject to large variations, for example, because of actions of OPEC, and other oil cartels.

corner solution
It is a solution to a system of equations where some variables are zero. For example, firms characteristically do not produce many goods, and individuals do not consume all available goods. Corner solution is different from an interior solution, in which all variables are non-zero.

corporate equity
It refers to the net assets of a company after paying all creditors, including debenture and preference shareholders. This is the net amount available for ordinary shareholders.

corporate income tax
It is a tax on the profits of firms, as distinct from taxation of the incomes of their owners. There are strong arguments for having separate income tax schemes for firms and individuals because the system of allowances and progressive tax rates appropriate for a tax on individual incomes is always different from a system for taxing firms.

corporate sector
It refers to that part of the economy, which is conducted by companies working for private profit. This is contrasted with the parts of the economy run by the government, nationalised industries, individuals, or voluntary bodie such as NGOs charities, which are considered a part of the personal sector.

corporation
It can be defined as a collective body carrying on economic activities, able to sue and liable to be sued, and to pay taxes, as an entity distinct from the individuals running or employed by it. A private corporation is a synonym for a company. Corporate tax (UK) and Corporation Income Tax (US) are taxes on the profits of companies. Corporation also refers to a contemporary form of business organisation in the United States of America and elsewhere, having two distinct character-

istics: (i) it is a legal entity separated from its owners, viz. the stockholders; and (ii) it is usually on a scale much too large for the sole proprietor or partnership to manage or fund.

corporatism

It is the system of reaching economic decisions through negotiation between centralised corporate bodies representing economic groupings, particularly employers and workers. It is distinct from a reliance on decentralised bargaining between individuals or limited groups. The supporters of corporatism always hope that it could improve the trade-off between inflation and unemployment, by inducing all parties to adopt a consensus view on prices, incomes and other factors like demand and supply.

correlation

It is the extent to which two variables vary together. Linear correlation between two variables a and b depends on the sign and size of $\sum_i (a_i - \mu_a)(b_i - \mu_b)$, where μ_a and μ_b are the means of a and b. The two variables are positively correlated if this sum of products is positive, and negatively correlated if the sum of products is negative. The strength of correlation is measured by the correlation coefficient: $r = [\sum_i (a_i - \mu_a)(b_i - \mu_b)]/[n\sigma_a\sigma_b]$.

correlation of returns

It is the extent to which the returns on one project are good or bad at the same time as the returns on another. Suppose that a and b are the returns on two risky projects, with expected means μ_x and μ_y. The returns are positively correlated if the expected value $E[(a - \mu_x)(b - \mu_y)]$ is positive, they are negatively correlated if this expected crossproduct is negative, and they are independent if the expected crossproduct is zero.

corruption

Simply speaking, it is the use of bribery to influence politicians, civil servants and other officials. Bribes may be in cash or in kind; almost any official action or inaction can be influenced by corruption. Officials may have to be bribed to do things they are legally supposed to do anyway, and to do them promptly. They may be bribed to neglect their duties, to the advantage, for example, of speculative builders putting up flats without planning permission and in disregard of construction regulations.

corset

Introduction of corset by the central bank is designed to place a limit over the interest bearing eligible liabilities which is a primary category of bank deposit with the commercial banks. It is believed that sound monetary policy cannot be effective so far as it does not exercise a strict control over the aggregate money supply of a country.

cost

The term refers to the following:

1. It is the price one pays in exchange for something. In economics, cost is usually defined as how much money one pays for something. However, there are costs beyond monetary price and many prices do not reflect the true cost of items. For example, the price of petrol does not reflect the environmental costs associated with driving a car.

2. It is the value that must be given up to acquire a good or service.

3. It is the value of the inputs needed to produce any good or service. This has to be measured in some units of money.

4. The term cost is also used in various other contexts : (i) opportunity cost is cost measured in terms of alternative output forgone in order to produce a good. (ii) total cost includes fixed or overhead costs, and variable costs. (iii) fixed costs must be incurred if any output is produced, for example, paying for buildings and a manager. (iv) sunk costs are fixed costs, which cannot be recovered even if an enterprise is closed down completely, for example, the cost of sinking a mine shaft or digging a canal. (v) social cost is cost including the external costs of an enterprise, such as the value of smoke, damage, noise, and river pollution, as well as the direct costs to its proprietors. (vi) cost-plus pricing is a system of setting prices in contracts by measuring costs and adding an agreed percentage mark-up. (vii) normal cost pricing is the system applied not to actual costs but to what costs would have been at a normal level of output. (viii) the cost-of-living index measures the cost of buying a fixed bundle of consumer goods, selected to resemble the purchases of a typical household. (ix) factor cost is the prices of products facing producers, subtracting from market prices any indirect taxes and adding any subsidies.

cost accounting

It is the branch of accounting concerned with the costs of economic activities including measuring the costs of activities already carried out, so that their profitability can be assessed, and estimating the expected costs of future activities, to assist management in planning and in tendering for contracts. It is concerned only with private costs.

cost-benefit analysis

It denotes the following:
1. An attempt to compare the total social costs and benefits of an activity, usually expressed in money terms. The costs and benefits concerned include not only direct pecuniary costs and benefits, but also externalities, i.e., external effects not traded in markets. These include external benefits such as reductions in travelling time or a more comfortable journey.
2. A systematic comparison between the cost of carrying out a service or activity and the value of that service or activity, quantifying, as far as possible, all costs and benefits whether direct or indirect, financial or social.

cost-benefit ratio

This ratio is calculated as gross benefit/ gross cost. The gross cost and benefits have been discounted over the life of the project by a selected annual rate of interest. The difference between the two amounts has been the present value of net benefits. The ratio of the two amounts is termed as the gross cost-benefit ratio.

cost-effectiveness

It refers to the achievement of results in the most economical way. It assesses efficiency by checking whether resources are being used to produce any given results at the lowest possible cost. It is believed that cost-effectiveness is most relevant as a concept of efficiency in cases such as the provision of education, defence, health care, administration, or environmental protection, where a monetary evaluation of the results achieved is not easy and is often controversial.

cost centre

It is a section of a firm whose costs and revenues are distinct from those of other sections. In most cases, costs and revenues can be reliably attributed to a particular cost centre, so that the profitability of each cost centre can be measured.

cost control or cost reduction

It is an extremely important and highly useful concept for both private and public sectors. In some countries, however, it is the private sector that has turned its full attention to this concept of cost reduction. Maximisation of the profit is the golden rule of the private sector. Its attainment is possible only when all possible waste in terms of labour and material is avoided.

cost curve

It is a curve relating cost to the quantity of a good produced. The total cost curve shows total cost at each level of output. The average cost curve shows total cost divided by quantity produced, while the marginal cost curve shows the addition to the total cost caused by any increase in output.

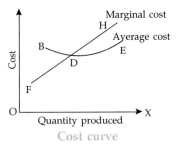

Cost curve

The cost curve is U-shaped because at low levels of output, fixed costs must be spread over few units, while at output levels which are high relative to plant capacity, marginal costs tend to be high. Long-run average cost curves may not be U-shaped. In the given diagram, BDE is the average cost curve. FDH is the marginal cost curve. D is the minimum point of the average cost curve.
Left of D, FDH<BDE, so BDE falls.
Right of D, FDH > BDE, so BDE rises.
At D, FDH = BDE and $d(BDE)/dQ = 0$.

cost function

It refers to a function of input prices and output quantity. Its value is the cost of making that output given those input prices. Cost function may be utilised in forecasting the expenses associated with the production. It would obviously help in determining the price strategies that must be used to achieve hoped profit margins.

cost inflation

The term can be defined as inflation due to increases in particular prices or wage rates being passed round the economy. Increases in costs cause producers to raise prices; increases in prices cause workers to demand higher wages; and increases in wages in one occupation lead to demands for increases in others to restore differential. The cumulative effect of all these processes leads to a cost-inflationary spiral, which is extremely difficult to stop. It is also sometimes called cost push inflation, in which powerful unions have been blamed for making large wage demands in the absence of excess demand in the labour market.

cost minimisation

The term refers to the following:
1. For any given level of output, it implies that choice of input combination provides the smallest possible total cost. The choice of a cost minimising firm is between fixed input prices and using the two factors input. Capital and labour can be illustrated using isocost lines and isoquants. The cost minimising choice for output level X_2 has been represented by the input combination A, where the isoquant labelled X_2 has been tangent to the lowest possible isocost line I_2.
2. It is the assumption that any enterprise will try to produce its output at the lowest possible cost. This is clearly desirable for a profit-maximising firm. It appeals to public bodies because a saving of cost in any one project will either allow lower taxes, or free resources for other desirable uses. Cost minimisation, however, has to be taken with following facts:

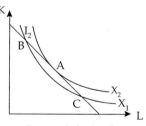

Cost minimisation

(i) it refers to the cost of providing goods or services of a specified quality, which does not mean achieving lower costs by cutting standards.
(ii) it does not imply operating at the lowest point of a U-shaped cost curve, unless the market will accept the level of output which this entails.
(iii) actual firms have to anticipate that demand will fluctuate over some range, i.e., cost minimisation means achieving low average costs over a range of outputs.

cost of capital

It refers to the rate of return that an enterprise or a firm has to offer to induce investors to provide it with capital. The cost of loan capital is the rate of interest that has to be paid. The cost of equity capital is the expected yield needed to induce investors to buy shares. When a firm or an enterprise uses both methods of raising capital, its cost of capital is the average of the costs of capital raised by the two methods, weighted by the proportion of funds raised in each way.

cost of living index

It refers to an index of the cost of maintaining a given standard of living. This is obtained by measuring the total cost of some given basket of goods and services. The composition of the basket has to be changed periodically, to take account of changes in the proportions of income spent on different goods as relative prices change. It is a synonym for the retail price of living index. When on the preparation of an index, member articles are shown on the retail prices. It is called cost of living index. It comes in contrast with the wholesale price index in which the products are shown as they rule in the wholesale market.

cost of protection

To an economy it is the total cost of adopting protectionist trade policies. To consumers it is the cost of having to buy more expensive domestic products rather than cheaper or better quality imports. This normally exceeds the private gains to domestic producers. Those who favour protection hold that if the labour employed in protected production would otherwise have been unemployed, there may be a net gain to the country.

cost, insurance, & freight (cif)

Cif value is the value of goods when they reach the port of entry to their country of destination. It includes their purchase price in the country of origin, and the freight and insurance costs of shipping them to a foreign port. However, it does not include import duty or costs of transport within the country of destination.

cost-plus pricing

It is a contract providing that price will equal measured costs plus an agreed percentage mark-up for profit. This procedure is sometimes criticised because it gives the producer no incentive to keep down costs. Instead, the incentive is to increase costs needlessly, thereby increasing the profit margin also. However, cost-plus pricing is often used in projects.

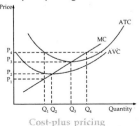

Cost-plus pricing

cost-push inflation

It is the inflation primarily caused due to the rise in the production cost.

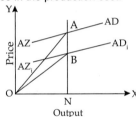

Cost-push inflation

counter-cyclical policy

It refers to an appropriate fiscal and monetary policy of the government specifically designed to avoid the occurrences of trade cycles. In boom time, the government restricts its public outlays increases interest rates to control money circulation, and raises the taxation limits.

counter party

The term refers to the other party in any transaction. For an exporter, the counter party is the foreign customer; for a lender, the counter party is the borrower. In any transaction, counter-party risk is the risk that the other parties may fail to fulfil their side of any contract. In some markets, these market makers can reduce counter-party risks for both sides by substituting themselves as the counter party for both outside buyers and sellers.

counter-trade

It refers to international trade conducted by barter. In general, barter is inefficient compared with the use of money, just as bilateral trade is inefficient compared with multilateral trade. Countertrade is thus clearly a second-best policy. It has been practised in the past by many countries, including former planned economies.

counter trading

The term describes the bilateral international trading relationships between companies.

countervailing duty

It is the imposition of customs duty by the importing nation on the import of the products on which the exporting nation has given subsidy. Grant of subsidy enables the producer of the home country to export the product at comparatively cheaper rate. The import duty is imposed with a view to raising the price to its original point, if they had not been given. Countervailing duty imposed to offset the effects of some foreign policy such as an export subsidy, which domestic producers claim gives an unfair advantage to foreign competitors.

countervailing power

It is the tendency of market (monopoly) power to be reduced by the emergence of countervailing groups and forces. The idea/thesis was given by British economist J.K. Galbraith. It also refers to the use of organisations to protect their members against monopolistic exploitation by others. The formation of co-operatives to protect onsumers from suppliers and the formation of trade unions to protect workers against monopsonistic employers are some examples of countervailing power. The alternative is control of the monopolists by public regulatory authorities.

coupon bond

It refers to the following:
1. A bond in which interest coupons attached to the oupons have been clipped as they become due and have been presented by the owner for the payment of interest.
2. The bond that pays the holder of the bond a specified amount of money at given dates until maturity. Then, the face value of the bond is paid at maturity. The total value of the coupons in a year over the face value of the bond is called the coupon rate.

coupons

The term refers to the following:
1. The tokens, usually paper, used as evidence of entitlement under rationing schemes.
2. The dividends due on a security. With a bearer security, the holder claims payments due by using a physical coupon attached to the documents of title.
3. These are the bearer bonds which are payable at the presentation of the bond at the counter at the expiry of the stipulated period. The bearer bonds may have attached to it a coupon book with the format of scheduled interval of three, six or twelve months. The detachable coupon is presented for collection of the interest on the bond.

Cournot duopoly

It refers to a market situation with only two sellers, each of whom fixes their own output on the assumption that the other will hold quantity sold unchanged.

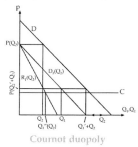

Cournot duopoly

Cournot's duopoly model

It is a model based upon the behavioural assumption that each of the two firms in a duopoly will maximise profits assuming that its competitor's output remains constant.

crawling peg

It refers to a compromise arrangement between a fixed exchange rate and a floating exchange rate, where the exchange value of a currency has been allowed to alter over a period of time but only by some previously agreed percentage each year.

crawling peg exchange rates

The term denotes the proposal that official intervention in foreign exchange markets should take the form of limiting the rate of change of exchange rates, as against setting any particular level. A 'crawling peg' could take several forms. The authorities could preannounce a trend rate of movement at par exchange rates by small regular changes in the same direction, for example 0.25 or 0.50 per cent a month.

creative accounting

It refers to devising new financial methods, or new way of presenting old ones, in order to evade controls on one's activities. Examples are the creation of special accounts to which the transactions can be relegated so as to appear as off-balance sheet items; and selling assets and leasing them back, thus exchanging present receipts from the sale for future liabilities in the rentals payable.

creative destruction

The term applies to the effect of technical progress in one part of the economy in lowering the value of existing capital in other parts. If a new item displaces demand for an old one, the capital used in making the old item may become worthless, or of much less value. If a new method of production has lower costs even including any necessary capital costs than the variable costs of producing on old equipment, the price of the product is likely to fall to such extent that operating the old machines becomes uneconomic.

credentialism

The term implies that there is problem of hiring standards that have been too severe for the limited skill requirements of the lower grade jobs.

credibility

In economics, it refers to the extent to which policy announcements are believed. Policy announcements by monetary or fiscal authorities are credible only if people are convinced that the authorities will in fact stick to their announced policies. Credibility is thus relatively easy to achieve if the announced policies are compatible with what people would predict on the basis of the authorities' past conduct and the general condition of the economy.

credit

1. It is the system by which goods or services are provided in return for deferred rather than immediate payment. Credit may be provided by the seller, or by a bank or a finance company.
2. A positive item, that is, a receipt or asset in a balance sheet.

3. Also the reputation for financial soundness, which allows individuals or companies to obtain goods and services without cash payment.

credit card

It is a card made of plastic etc., which allows the holder to obtain goods and services up to some limit without immediate payment. The supplier is paid by the bank or other financial institution issuing the card. The card-holder pays off the debt in arrears, often by instalments.

credit control

It refers to the following:
1. The policy of controlling aggregate demand by means of restriction on access to credit. This may simply be through monetary policy instruments, i.e., the quantity of money and the interest rates. It may also involve regulation of particular types of lending.
2. The systems by which commercial organisations seek to ensure that they get paid in due time for goods and services supplied on credit.
3. The system of monetary control by Central Banks whereby banks are required to maintain minimum reserve ratios.

credit creation

It is defined as the process by which the banks collectively can make loans in excess of extra base money they receive. If base money increases, through a balance-of-payments surplus or open market operations by the central bank, this will mostly be paid into somebody's account with a commercial bank. The bank concerned can then lend most of the extra money to borrowers, which in turn raises deposits at other banks.

credit cycle

It refers to the theory that trade cycles are caused by fluctuations in credit. Booms occur because banks and other financial institutions become over-optimistic in granting credit. At some stage, their mistakes lead to defaults and a loss of confidence, leading to a slump. During this time, lenders are overcautious, and bad debts are provided for and gradually written off.

credit instruments

They are documents containing terms of a credit transactions and obligations of the concerned parties. Some of the main credit instruments are mentioned below:

1. *promissory note*: it is a written promise to pay a certain amount of money on demand or on a certain date. Promissory notes drawn by the central bank or the government and payable on demand are regarded as legal tender and circulate as money.
2. *bill of exchange*: it is an order by a seller on the buyer to pay a certain sum of money to a specified party or to his order, at sight or after a specified period of time. The amount of bill is fixed including interest. Bills may be drawn for settling a debt or for advancing loan. Such bills are known as finance bills or accommodation bills.
3. *cheque*: a cheque is a bill of exchange payable by a bank. Cheques are called money substitutes because they are readily acceptable in place of cash.
4. *hundi*: a hundi is a negotiable instrument written in vernacular. Some hundies are exactly like bills of exchange, some are like cheques or promissory notes.

creditor nation

A nation is called a creditor nation when it has an excess of exports over the imports and has to realise the balance amount from the importer nation for the excess exports so made. If this is the result of the normal disequilibrium in the balance of payment position, there is no cause for concern, but when an economy due to the impact of war or growth needs gets into a structural disequilibrium balance of payment position, it places heavy responsibility on the creditor nation to help the debtor nation.

creditors

The term refers to the balance-sheet item showing debts owing to others. This is divided between payments due in under a year, i.e., short term, and other debts, i.e., long term.

credit rating

It is an assessment of the probability that an individual, firm, enterprise or country will be able and willing to pay its debts. Such an assessment is based on all available information about the subject's total assets and liabilities, exposure to risk, and debt service ratio past record in making prompt payment of interest and principal when due. An individual, firm, or government with a good credit rating (i.e., A+ or AAA) can borrow or obtain goods on credit more easily and cheaply than one whose credit rating is poor.

credit rating agency
The term is used for a firm, which collects information affecting the credit-worthiness of individuals or companies, and sells the resulting credit rating for a fee to interested parties. These include firms considering lending to the individual or company, or providing them with goods or services on credit. CRISIL Credit Suise, Goldman Sachs, etc. are some major credit rating agencies.

credit rationing
The term describes restriction of loans. This occurs when lenders do not make loans to all applicants willing to pay the interest rate demanded, even though they satisfy all collateral requirements and other tests of credit-worthiness. The absence of credit rationing does not mean that lenders raise the interest rate and grant loans at it to all comers. In other words, it is a situation where no lender is willing to give loan to a borrower or the amount lenders are willing to lend to borrowers is limited, even if the borrower is willing to pay more than other borrowers of comparable risk who are being granted loans.

credit squeeze
It is a policy package intended to restrain the level of demand by restricting credit. This may include restricting the money supply, raising interest rates, restricting the level of lending by particular banks or other credit intermediaries, or restricting certain sectors for which credit is available.

creditworthiness
The term refers to the opinion of potential borrower. This sometimes is a matter of judgement. Apart from governments, the people to whom it would be perfectly safe to lend come under high creditworthiness. Certain external factors also influence creditworthiness. The profits of firms are liable to variation through bad luck, bad management, or fraud; the incomes of individuals are liable to variation through unemployment, poor health, or folly.

creeping inflation
It refers to inflation at moderate rates but persisting over long periods. This is the normal state of affairs in many countries. If inflation is rapid, it causes serious losses and builds up strong political support for measures to control it. Once inflation falls to low levels, other problems such as maintaining full employment come under the focus of the authorities, and measure to reduce inflation further command little political support.

cross elasticity of demand
Under demand function, it is mentioned that demand for a commodity is not only a function of its own price but also a function of the prices of related goods. Hence, the concept of elasticity of demand can be applied in a situation where two commodities are related to each other. The elasticity in this case is called cross elasticity of demand. The concept of cross elasticity of demand is useful in handling inter-commodity demand relations. The sign of the measure of cross elasticity depends upon the nature of interrelationship between the two goods. If the two goods are substitutes, the value of cross elasticity will be positive. Cross elasticity of demand is the ratio between the proportional change in demand for a good and the proportional change in the price of a different good. This is calculated assuming that the price of the good itself is constant. Thus if q_x is the quantity of good x, and p_y is the price of good y, the cross elasticity of demand is given by

$$\varepsilon_{xy} = (dq_x/q_x)/(dp_y/p_y) = (p_y/q_x)(\partial q_x/\partial p_y).$$

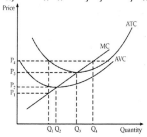

Cross elasticity of demand

cross holding
It is the position when each of two companies holds shares in the other. If such holdings were of large size, this would make it difficult for either company's shareholders to displace the existing management.

cross subsidy

Cross subsidy refers to when a given producer produces two or more products of different type or trade marks. It may, for various constraints, undergo a loss in the sale of one product; a loss which the producer makes up by the profit made in the sale of another product. Cross-subsidisation is the provision of a good or service at a loss, which is met by the supplier from profits made on other goods and services. Where the goods and services concerned have joint costs, or are complementary in demand, the extent of any cross-subsidy is not easy to determine. Some economists believe that lack of transparency leads to inefficient decisions as to which goods and services should be subsidised.

cross-validation

It is a way of choosing the window width for a kernel estimation. The method is to select, from a set of possible window widths', the one that minimises the sum of errors made in predicting each data point, by using a kernel regression on the others.

crowding

It may occur when an extremely large sized buyer (e.g., a government or a big business house) enters the market making it very difficult for the other buyers who are relatively very small in effecting their purchases.

crowding hypothesis

It refers to the theory that entry barriers and informational imperfections will be able to converge certain groups, chiefly women and blacks, into a limited range of occupations and in the process lower the relative wage of these occupations.

crowding out

It is the possibility that an increase in one form of spending may cause another form to fall. This may happen in various ways. In case the government spending on public works rises, it might use scarce resources, such as skilled engineers, diverting them from alternative investment projects which are thus delayed. Alternatively, if increased demand causes inflation, it may lead to tighter monetary policy, thus cutting other forms of spending.

cryptography

In trade, it is a secret language used to encode information to conceal secret messages from unauthorised parties. It has traditionally been used for military and national security purposes. Cryptography makes use of algorithms to transform data, which then cannot be retrieved, unless one has access to the cryptographic key.

cum dividend

The term refers to the sale of shares including the right for the purchaser to receive a dividend already announced or approved but not yet paid. This is in contrast with ex dividend, which is the sale of shares where the vendor retains the right to a dividend already announced but not yet paid.

cum drawing

It means with benefit of the current drawing. If there is no benefit, it means with the liability for loss of drawing.

cumulative frequency distribution

It is also known as the proportion of a frequency distribution below any given value. If F(a) is the frequency distribution, where a is continuously distributed between a minimum value x and a maximum value of y, the cumulative frequency distribution is written $F(x) = 0$; for $x < c < y$, $0 < F(z) < 1$; and $F(y) = 1$.

cumulative preference share

It is a share where dividends to the holder must be paid, including any arrears due from previous years, before any dividends can be paid to ordinary shareholders.

currency

It is another name for money. A country's own currency, i.e., local currency is that used for internal transactions. Foreign currency is the money of other countries. For example, rupee is India's local currency while dollar, pound, euro, yen, etc. are foreign currencies for India.

currency account

The term refers to transactions where the payments are income for the recipient. A country's balance of payments on current account include trade in goods, i.e., visibles; trade in services, i.e., invisibles; payments of factor incomes, which include dividends, interest and migrants' remittances from earnings abroad; and international transfers, etc.

currency reform

It is the replacement of a currency by a new one. This has frequently been done simply for convenience because inflation has made the value of units of the old currency so small that it becomes inconvenient to transact in it. It may sometimes have been hoped that a new name for the currency would assist in making a promise of less inflationary monetary policy more credible.

currency risk

It refers to the risk that changes in exchange rates will affect the profitability of an activity between the time when one is committed to it and the time when it is actually carried out. This adversely affects foreign trade, foreign lending, and foreign direct investment. Commitment may arise from a contract such as in export sales or foreign currency loans, or from incurring sunk costs such as in foreign direct investment.

current account

It refers to a bank account bearing no interest and requiring no notice for withdrawals. This is contrasted with a fixed deposit account, where interest is paid and notice of withdrawal is required. A current account is used for business purposes, while savings and fixed deposit accounts are meant for saving, etc. The distinction has become blurred with the introduction of bank account under various proprietary names, which are withdrawable on demand but yield some interest, generally at a very low rate.

current account deficit

It is an excess of expenditure over receipts on current account in a country's balance of payments.

current account surplus

It is an excess of receipts over expenditure on current account in a country's balance of payments.

current assets

They are the assets turned over frequently in the course of business. These include cash in hand, debtors (other than bad debts), and stocks of finished goods. Current assets are contrasted with fixed assets, which last some years and are depreciated, e.g., plant and machinery.

current liabilities

These are the debts due to creditors, which are due for payment within the next 12 months. These include short term debts, interest payable, insurance and taxes due within the current year. These have to be shown separately in balance-sheets from longer-term liabilities.

current prices

The term refers to the measurement of economic magnitudes using the prices actually prevailing at any given time, for example, 2010-11 GDP at 2010 prices. This may mean the prices in force at some particular date, for example, 1 April, or the average of prices observed over the year, in years of high inflation these could differ significantly.

current-weighted index

Also known as Paasche index, it is a weighted average of prices or quantities, where the weights used are proportional to the quantities or prices of the most recent period. In this index where p_{ij} and q_{ij} are the prices and quantities of goods i = 1, 2, ... N in period j, 0 labels the base period and t the latest period, the current-weighted or Paasche price index is given by $P_c = [\Sigma p_{it}q_{it}]/[\Sigma_i P_{i0}q_{it}]$.

customs and excise

It refers to the tax authority responsible for collecting indirect taxes, including customs duties, revenue duties on alcoholic drinks and tobacco, and value-added tax (VAT), etc.

cuts in expenditure

It refers to reduction in government spending. These may refer to changes in actual government spending, which have already been announced in the budget or plan, or, more usually, to announcements of planned reductions. Cuts in actual spending may be due to the application of unchanged spending rules in changing circumstances as in case of a reduction in unemployment benefits when employment is rising during a boom.

cyclic adjustment

It is the adjustment of figures such as GDP, government spending, or the budget deficit to show how much the amount would be if total activity was at its normal level. This can only be done by the use of a model showing how these aggregates are related to the level of activity.

cyclical unemployment

It refers to unemployment during the recession phase of business cycles, which can be expected to disappear during the next boom. Because of continual changes in techniques and tastes, it is difficult to tell during any recession how much of the increase in unemployment is cyclical on Keynesian lines, by a recovery in the industries where people were formerly employed, and only by the rise of new forms of activity.

cyclically adjusted budget deficit

The term can be defined as to a calculation of what the government's budget deficit would be if the economy was at a normal level of activity. This is normally based on the assumption that the rules and rates concerning spending and taxes are unchanged. As taxes are an increasing and government spending is a decreasing function of national income, during a recessionary phase, the cyclically adjusted budget deficit will be smaller than the actual, and an actual deficit may correspond to a cyclically adjusted budget surplus.

D

damage cost

It is the monetary cost of damage done by pollution. In economics, pollution is generally considered to be an instance of an externality. Placing money values on externalities is a complicated and often dubious procedure similar as with valuing injuries, death, loss of recreational land, loss of forest cover, wildlife, etc.

damping

It means bringing a reducing effect. For example, at low levels of market demand, some people might be able to withdraw from the labour market, thus damping the rise in unemployment figures.

data mining

It is the production of spurious relationships in econometrics by running too many regressions. Standard tests of significance answer the question. Given the variance of the data, what chance is there that an apparent relation could have arisen by chance? A coefficient is significant at the 10 per cent level, for example, if a result thus far removed from zero would only have arisen by chance in 10 per cent of cases.

DDD

It refers to a Standard and Poor's credit rating indicating that servicing of a security is in default or in arrears.

de minimis

The term denotes a legal term for an amount that is small enough to be ignored, too small to be taken seriously. It is used to restrict legal provisions, including laws regarding international trade, to amounts of activity or trade that are not extremely small.

deadweight burden of taxes

It is defined as the excess of the total harm done by a tax over the actual revenue raised. An indirect tax raises the price of the taxed good to the consumer. The quantity sold falls, as consumers only buy units of the good for which their benefits exceed the price inclusive of tax. There are thus some units where the benefit to the consumer would be higher than the cost of production, but lower than the taxinclusive price.

deadweight debt

It is the debt incurred without leading to the creation of any specific asset from which the cost of debt service can be met. Personal debts incurred to finance consumption, business debts incurred to finance operating losses, and government debt incurred to finance wars or unemployment benefit are some examples of deadweight debt.

dear money

The term implies higher interest rates, which make it expensive to borrow. How high rates need be to constitute dear money depends on the rate of inflation because only interest rates greater than the rate of inflation make borrowing expensive in real terms. If the central bank (e.g., RBI) is using monetary policy to reduce aggregate demand, dear money and tight money, or difficulty in gaining credit, tend to go together.

death duties

These are the taxes levied on a person's estate after their death. These may be levied to discourage inherited wealth, or simply as a convenient source of government revenue.

debasement

It refers to a deliberate attempt by the government to reduce the intrinsic value of the coins. These days, the governments have been forced to debase the coins due to the limited availability of the metals, on one hand, and the huge expansion of currency brought by the increase in the production and trade, on the other.

debenture

It refers to a secured loan raised by a company, with a fixed rate of interest and sometimes with a fixed redemption rate. Debenture holders have no control over the company so long as their interest is paid and all conditions of the loan are complied with, but if the interest is not paid or the conditions are broken they can claim control of the company. They rank before other shareholders in the event of liquidation.

debit

It is recorded as negative (-) in the balance of payments. Any transaction that gives rise to a payment out of the country, such as an import, the purchase of an asset (including official reserves) or lending to foreigners. In banking, the rule applied is debit what comes in, credit what goes out.

debt

It is the money owed by one person, a firm or an organisation to another. A debt contract states the terms of borrowing, viz. what interest and redemption payments the borrower must make, and what collateral must be provided. Debt contracts stipulate the currency in which payment is due. For example, foreign currency debt is debt where the interest and redemption payments due are paid in some currency other than the debtor's own. Debt may have an interest or redemption payments linked to a price index.

debt burden

The term refers to the cost of servicing debt. To an individual or business, this is what they have to pay in interest and redemption payments. In the case of a government debt, it would appear that what is paid from one set of citizens goes to another, the aggregate debt burden should be zero. This is subject to the objection: that where the debt is held externally, payments to non-residents are a real burden on residents.

debt crisis

It is a situation in which a country, usually a Least Developed Country (LDC), finds itself unable to service its debts.

debt deflation

It refers to a situation when spending is depressed because individuals and firms have too much debt. This causes them to be cautious about both spending and further borrowing, preferring to reduce their debts. As one person's debts are another person's assets, debt can only reduce aggregate spending if debtors have higher spending propensities than their creditors have of investing.

debt finance

It refers to the use of loans by companies to finance their operations, especially capital expenditure through long-term loans. The overall cost of capital may get reduced by the use of debt. Governments also borrow to finance their operations as also to help regulate the volume of aggregate activity in the economy.

debt for equity

It is a system by which firms, companies or countries with excessive debt exchange a part of their debt obligations for equity, held initially by the former creditors. This may be beneficial for both debtors and creditors. The debtors gain from a reduction in gearing, i.e., when the profits of firms or export receipts of countries are low, less of them as to be spent on debt service.

debt management

The term applies to the management of the debt of a company, enterprise or government to keep down its expected cost and ensure that funds are always available when needed. This includes forecasting when net borrowing may be needed, choosing the type of securities to be issued or redeemed, and timing the maturity dates of outstanding debt to prevent excessive concentration of redemption payments on particular dates, which might create difficulties in funding them.

debtors

This is the part of the assets shown in a balance sheet consisting of debts due to a firm, company or enterprise. Debts due to be paid in the next accounting period have to be distinguished from those due to be paid later.

decentralisation of an industry

It is the reverse of centralisation or concentration of industry. While the latter means establishing all the units of an industry at one particular place, territory or region the former means to establish various units of the same industry at different places or regions.

decentralisation

It refers to the following:
1. The dispersal of the power and duty to take decisions away from the centre and towards other bodies. Within the public sector this means leaving decisions to local or regional rather than central government.
2. It may also be pursued by transferring decisions from the state to private bodies such as housing associations, or by breaking up monopolistic companies.
3. Sharing the authority of decision-making with lower levels of management. Everything which goes to increase the importance of subordinates' role is decentralisation. When lower levels of management are allowed to

make decisions regarding activities to be undertaken in an enterprise it is called decentralisation.

debt overhang
The term refers to a situation in which the external debt of a country is larger than the sum that the country will be able to repay, often due to having borrowed in foreign currency and then having its own currency depreciated.

debt relief
It is an agreement among the creditors including banks and governments of an indebted firm, enterprise or country to accept reduced or postponed interest and redemption payments from the debtors. This may be in the interest of creditors if they believe they can expect more from debtors making real efforts to pay reduced bills than from hopelessly pursuing insolvent debtors who may simply default. Debt relief may be given by the government to help certain sectors like small farmers' who may have suffered crop failure/damage due to floods/droughts.

debt service
1. It refers to the payments due under debt contracts. This includes payment of interest as it becomes due, and redemption payments. Where debt is long-dated, a large proportion of debt service is comprised of interest payments. Where debt is short-dated, most debt services consist of redemption payments.
2. The term also refers to the actual payments made by a borrower on their debt, usually including both interest payments and partial repayment of principal.

decile
In economics, it is the boundary of a tenth part of a distribution. If all incomes, for example, are arranged in descending order, the first decile is the income such that 10 per cent of the income lie above it, and 90 per cent lie below.

decouple
It is the provision of support to an enterprise, usually a farm, in a manner that does not provide an incentive to increase production. Farm subsidies that are decoupled are included in the green box and are, therefore, permitted by the WTO. In international eco-

nomics, decoupling means not to be too much affected by the events happening in other parts of the world.

decreasing balance depreciation
It refers to the system of accounting for the depreciation of assets by assuming that they lose a fixed percentage of their remaining value year after year (usually 10 to 20%) until they are finally scrapped, when their remaining value is written off.

decreasing function
It is a function whose value falls as its argument rises. If y = f(x), y is a decreasing function of x if and only if dy/dx ≤ 0 for all x. If dy/dx < 0 for all x then y is a strictly decreasing function of x.

decreasing returns to scale
1. It is a ratio of output to inputs that falls as inputs rise. A uniform proportional increase in all inputs results in a less than proportional increase in output.
2. A property of a production function such that changing all the inputs by the same proportion changes the output less than in proportion. It is also called simply decreasing returns.

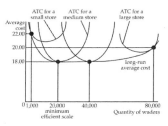

Decreasing returns to scale

deductibility
It is a tax concession available in many countries by which certain contributions to charities can be deducted from gross income to arrive at taxable income. The argument for these concessions is that through them the state can encourage donations to worthy causes.

deductibles
The term refers to the part of any insured loss which has to be borne by the insured party. The UK term for this is an excess. The point of making the insured bear the first part of any loss is partly to reduce moral hazard.

deduction

It is also known as deductive reasoning-process of inference, which leads from general principles or universal premises through logical reasoning to expectations or conclusions about particular cases.

deepening of capital

It is a creation of capital assets of new kinds and not just duplication of existing varieties of capital. This happens when growth of capital, i.e., accumulation of capital is faster than labour growth.

default

It is a failure to make payments such as the interest or redemption payments or debt on the due date. Default may be partial or total, ranging from a slight delay in payment and promises that payment will soon be forthcoming, to total and defiant repudiation. Default is frequently avoided by creditors agreeing to reschedule debt, which they may prefer as it avoids showing bad debts in their balance sheets.

defence spending

It is the military spending by governments. It is not in fact possible to determine whether military expenditure is for national defence, for offensive operations of threats, to develop a credible deterrence or for internal repression. The classification of military and civil spending is often arbitrary.

deficiency payment

It refers to subsidies paid to farmers in some countries when the prices at which certain products can be sold are below a target set by government policy.

deficit financing

It refers to creating new money to meet a budget deficit. The term refers to the policy of arranging finances needed to cover the budget deficit. When the government cannot raise enough capital resources through taxation, i.e., increase its revenue, it finances its development expenditure by running down its own cash balances with the central bank or by borrowing from it.

deficit units

These are economic units which cannot meet their expenses in a given period from their incomes during that period - from the sale of their labour - or their assets, such that they have been dependent on borrowing money or obtaining credit.

deflation

It refers to the following:
1. A progressive reduction in the price level. This would make real interest rates exceed nominal interest rates, which might make it impossible to lower nominal interest rates during a slump adequately enough to make real investments appear profitable.
2. A reduction in activity due to lack of effective demand. This could be brought about deliberately by the monetary authorities in order to reduce inflationary pressure, or could occur due to an erosion in confidence, which the authorities have been unable to avert.
3. It is the opposite of inflation. When the inflation rate is negative, the economy is in a deflationary period.

deflationary gap

1. It is an aggregate expenditure that runs short of what is needed to produce a level of national income which would ensure full employment. In the income expenditure model, it is shown by an aggregate expenditure function, which cuts the 45° line, where E = Y, at less than the full employment level of national income.
2. It is an estimate of the difference between the level of effective demand required for a normal level of economic activity at any time, and the actual level during a recession. The deflationary gap provides an estimate of the amount by which effective demand needs to rise to restore a normal level of activity.

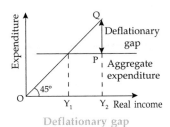

Deflationary gap

3. Also the excess of the full employment demand or aggregate supply or output at full employment level over the aggregate demand. As supply is more than demand, prices tend to fall.

deindustrialisation

The term refers to the tendency for the industrial sector to account for a decreasing proportion of GDP and employment. In advanced countries like America, England, France, etc., large improvement in industrial productivity in the twentieth century increased real incomes. Consumers and governments have chosen to spend these largely on services, including education, medical care, transportation, communication, banking and insurance and entertainment and tourism.

delta

In economics, the term is used with respect to options. The rate of change of a financial derivative's price with respect to changes in the price of the underlying asset. Formally, this is a partial derivative. A derivative is perfectly delta-hedged if it is in a portfolio with a delta of zero. Financial firms also make some effort to construct delta-hedged portfolios.

demand

It refers to the quantity of good or service that people want to buy or consume. The demand function relates demand to the factors determining it: these including customers' incomes, the good's own price and the prices of competing goods, i.e., substitutes and of other goods in general; as well as factors affecting the demand of individuals. The demand curve relates the demand for a good to its own price, holding all other factors constant. There are various types of demand: (i) Price elasticity of demand is the proportional increase in quantity demand divided by the proportional reduction in price; (ii) Income elasticity of demand is the proportional increase in quantity demanded at a given price divided by the proportional rise in income; (iii) Aggregate demand is what is actually demanded, as contrasted with notional demand, which is what people would demand if all markets were in equilibrium.

demand curve

The term refers to a graph relating demand for a good or service to its price. The price of the good is usually shown on the vertical axis and the quantity demanded at each level of its own price on the horizontal axis. Other factors affecting demand are assumed constant, including incomes, the prices of other goods, and other factors such as fashion and the weather. Demand curve is assumed to be constant. A demand curve may represent the demand of an individual consumer, or of the market as a whole.

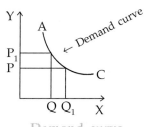

Demand curve

demand deposit

1. A bank deposit that can be withdrawn on demand. The term usually refers only to checking accounts, even though depositors in many other kinds of accounts may be able to draw cheques and regard their deposits as readily available.
2. The money stored in the form of savings account at banks.

demand-determined output

It refers to the situation when effective demand is the only constraint on output. This is generally the case only during a deep slump. At most times there are shortages of particular skills or types of equipment which restrict output in some parts of the economy, even when output in other parts is determined mainly by demand.

demand draft

It is drawn by a bank on its other branch. It is issued in favour of a person, company, firm or institution at the request of the purchases for value received.

demand function

It is a function showing how the demand for any good or service is determined. Both at the individual and aggregate level, demand depends on income, and on the price of the good concerned. The demand curve plots demand against the goods, own price, assuming other factors constant. Demand also depends on other factors, including the prices of other goods, particularly those of close substitutes and complements; and on factors such as the weather or changes in fashion.

demand inflation

It is price rise due to excess demand. As resources are not perfectly mobile between different regions and sectors of the economy, demand inflation can occur even if the level of effective demand in the economy as a whole is below the level needed for normal levels of employment. The higher the aggregate level of activity, the larger the proportion of areas and industries which experience excess demand for goods and labour of various types, hence the demand-inflationary pressure is more powerful.

demand management

It is the use of monetary and fiscal policy to influence the level of aggregate real effective demand in the economy. Policymakers may aim at various targets, for example, a high and stable level of activity and employment; a somewhat lower level, designed to cure inflation; or the balance of payments. Whatever be the aim, the monetary and fiscal authorities can only influence the level of effective demand, and cannot decide it, and this may be done by a large number of decentralised consumers, investors and export customers.

demarcation

It is the reservation of particular tasks to workers with specialised skills. Some degree of demarcation is essential to health and safety, for example, insisting that gas-pipe installations are fitted by qualified engineers. Members of professions or craft-based unions face the temptation to insist on high levels of demarcation to exploit their monopoly power.

demographic transition

It refers to the following:
1. Model of population change based on European experiences. The model explains the effects of changes in fertility and mortality, associated with industrialisation, urbanisation and health care improvements.
2. It refers to a fundamental change in the characteristic trends of a population, viz. a transition from high birth rates and high death rates to low birth rates and low death rates.
3. Also the process by which countries pass from a situation of high birth and death rates to one of the low rates. Least developed countries (LDCs) typically have high birth and death rates. But, as development starts, death rates tend to fall earlier than birth rates, resulting in rapid population increase of up to 3 per cent per year.

demographic transition theory

It is a theory that relates to the population growth statistics, the study of the birth rate and the death rate. These statistics have a great relevance and bearing on the economic growth of a nation. The theory is subdivided under following parts: (i) Initially, when a nation is underdeveloped its birth rate and death rate are both high. (ii) With better public hygiene, sanitation and medical health, the death rate tends to decline; but the birth rate continues to be at the same high level. This raises up the survival rate. (iii) Final stage of demographic transition is a steady decline in the birth rate due to better and higher education, higher awareness and enlightenment amongst the people as a result of higher standard of living and higher education, particularly amongst the females.

demographic unemployment

The term refers to the type of unemployment immediate cause of which is changes in the labour force. Demographic unemployment can arise if the number of new workers entering the labour force through natural increase or inward migration exceeds the number leaving the workforce through retirement or emigration.

demography

It is the study of size, growth and age and geographical distribution of human populations and births, deaths, marriages, sex ratio and migrations, etc.

demurrage charges

The term refers to levy per day charged by the Transport Authority, Railways, or the Shipping Company or the Airway when the cargo is not taken delivery of by the consignee at the place or port of arrival. The purpose behind the imposition of demurrage is to ensure that there is a prompt collection of the goods by the consignees for the storage accommodation is very precious and limited.

dependency theory

It is a theory that states that the developing countries are poor because they allow themselves to be exploited by the developed countries throughout international trade and investment.

deposit

It refers to an account with a bank or other financial institution, such as a building society. Deposits may be on current account, or cheque account or sight deposits which bear no interest and can be withdrawn on demand, or deposit accounts, savings accounts or time deposits which bear interest but require notice of withdrawal. In recent years, new types of account have blurred this distinction somewhat.

deposit account

It is a deposit with a bank which requires notice for withdrawal, and where interest is paid. It is in contrast with a current account which is repayable on demand and does not bear interest.

deposit insurance

It refers to the insurance of the depositors with banks or other financial intermediaries against default by the bank. This is normally either paid for through premiums charged to all banks, or funded by a central bank or government. The advantage of deposit insurance is that it safeguards individuals who have deposit accounts with a bank, as well as keeps the credibility and confidence of depositors intact.

depreciation

The term applies to the loss of value of capital goods like fixed assets due to wear and tear, ageing, or obsolescence. The value of such assets is assumed for accounting purposes to decrease each year. The amount by which to 'write down' an asset in a balance-sheet can be estimated in two ways: (i) Straight line depreciation assumes that the asset loses an equal amount of its value each year over its expected lifetime, the number of years allowed for write-down depending on the type of asset; (ii) Percentage method adopts a fixed percentage of precaution of (10 to 20%) of an asset each year over the previous year's value.

depreciation, currency

It denotes a fall in the price of a currency in terms of other currencies. This makes a country's imports dearer relative to home-produced goods, which tend to decrease imports, and it makes exports cheaper abroad, which tends to increase exports.

deregulation

1. It refers to the removal or relaxation of government regulation of economic activities. Advocates of deregulation argue that excessive regulation increases costs and restricts entry to markets in industry, finance and transport. According to them, consumers are better protected by competition. The finance, communication, housing and transport sectors have been extensively deregulated in recent decades in many countries.
2. The term also denotes the lessening or complete removal of government regulations on an industry, especially concerning the price that firms are allowed to charge and leaving the price to be determined by the market forces.

derivative

It refers to the following:
1. The rate at which the value of a function increases as its argument increases at some point, if this is defined. In a graph, the first derivative of a function is its slope. If $y = f(x)$, its first derivative at a point p0 is the limit, which tends to become indefinitely small.
[$f(p_0 + a) - f(p_0)$]/a
2. The second derivative is defined as the first derivative of the first derivative, and so on. If a function has several arguments, its partial derivatives are its derivatives with respect to one factor, holding the other factor constant.
3. A tradeable security whose value is derived from the actual or expected price of some underlying asset, which may be a commodity, a security or a currency. Derivatives include future contracts, futures on stock market indices, options as well as commodities.

derived demand

It denotes the following:
1. The demand for an input to a productive process. This depends on the output of the good or service being produced. Derived demand also depends on the price of the input and the prices of other inputs, which are either substitutes for or complements to it. If other inputs are good substitutes, the elasticity or derived demand is high, but if other inputs are poor substitutes, the elasticity of derived demand may be very low.
2. It can be defined as the demand that arises or is defined indirectly from some other demand or underlying behaviour.

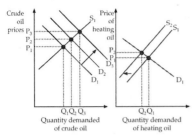

Quantity demanded of crude oil

Quantity demanded of heating oil

Derived demand

derogation

The term is used in the trade literature, implying a departure from the established rules, as when a country's policies are said to constitute a derogation from the WTO.

destabilising speculation

It is the speculation, which increases the movements of the price in the market where the speculation occurs. Movement may be defined by amplitude, frequency or some other measure.

determination of the market period price

Market period is the period where no adjustment in the supply is possible. It refers to the period of a day or so. Supply in such a case brings the adjustment in the price and the final equilibrium between the forces of demand and supply.

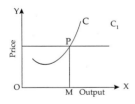

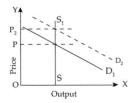

Determination of the market period price

If there is a rise in demand due to some festival like Christmas, Diwali, the price would keep on rising so far as the fall in demand does not become equal to the fixed supply. Market period price determination is shown when supply curve S, is shown vertically. It is fixed irrespective of the price in the market period. When D_2 is the demand curve, price is OP. When the demand curve rises to OD_2, the demand curve, price is OP to OP_2.

detrending

It is a process by which a time trend is removed from data, often by prior estimation of a time trend, and the calculation of residuals.

Deutschmark (DM)

It was the currency of West Germany, and since 1990, of the whole of Germany. The DM has now been replaced by the Euro in 2002.

devaluation

It denotes the following:
1. A fall in the value of a currency that has been pegged, either because of an announced reduction in the par value of the currency with the peg continuing or because the pegged rate is abandoned and the floating rate declines.
2. A fall in the value of a currency in terms of gold or silver. But this is meaningful only under some form of gold or silver standard.
3. A fall in the price of a currency in terms of other currencies. Less foreign currency can be bought with a unit of the currency that has been devalued. If the price of the pound in dollars falls from $2.00 to $1.50, the pound is devalued by 25 per cent.
Devaluation and depreciation are similar. Devaluation is generally used for a discrete change in the exchange rate brought about as a policy matter whereas depreciation occurs gradually throughout the working of the foreign exchange markets.

developing country

The term refers to a country whose per capita income is low by the world standards. Such a country is marked by low literacy, low employment rate, lack of capital, inadequate infrastructure, underutilisation of resources, etc.

differential

It refers to the rate of change of a variable

over a period of time, where time is treated as a continuous variable. The rate of change of y, dy/dt, is frequently denoted by a dot over the y, or d^2y/dt^2 is represented by two dots over y, and so on.

differential effect
In shift and share analysis, that part of the total regional shift, which is due to the fact that local industries may develop differently from their counterparts, in the larger (usually the national) benchmark region. Thus, these effects on shift arise from the fact that some industries in some regions are expanding or contracting more rapidly than the same industries in other regions.

differential equation
It is an equation that relates the value of a variable to its own derivatives with respect to time, treating time as a continuous variable. This is distinct from difference equations in which time is treated as a discrete variable. A first-order linear differential equation, for example, can be written as $y(t) = x + z(dy/dt)$ or $y = x + zy$.

differentiated product
1. It is a firm's product that is not identical to the products of other firms in the same industry.
2. The term is also applied to products produced by a country, even though there are many firms within the country whose products are the same, if buyers distinguish products on the basis of the country of origin. This is also called the Armington assumption.

diffusion theory of taxation
It is a theory given by Lord Mansfield that states that taxes that are imposed by the government get automatically diffused over the various sections of the community. So, no separate study of the incidence of taxation need to be made. But this theory is not acceptable to some economists who hold that this is not to deny that some taxes do get diffused but that does not imply that all the taxes likewise shift in some automatic and equitable manner. If it were so, then there would be such a hue and cry that we witness in case of some taxes in particular.

diminishing marginal product
It is the tendency for successive extra units of any input to a productive process to yield smaller increases in output. If one input to a productive process rises, while the other inputs are held constant, total output may increase in which case the input has a positive marginal product. However, as successive extra units of an input are applied, after a certain point output is likely to rise at a diminishing rate.

diminishing marginal utility
The term refers to the phenomenon whereby it is assumed that the marginal utility attached to an extra unit of any good diminishes as more and more of that good has been purchased. In the cardinal utility approach to demand theory, the existence of diminishing marginal utility explains the downward slope of the demand curve, assuming other things to be equal. The principle has been also widely used to explain the convexity of indifference curves since more and more of one good will be required to compensate for the surrender of extra units of any other good.

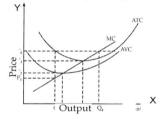

Diminishing marginal utility

diminishing returns
It denotes the fall in the marginal product of a factor or factors that eventually occurs as the input of that factor rises, holding the input of at least one other factor fixed.

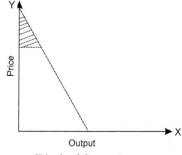

Diminishing returns

director factor content
It is a measure of factor content that includes only the factors used in the last stage of production, ignoring factors used in producing intermediate inputs.

direct labour
The term refers to the use by an authority of its own employees for work such as refuse collection or aintenance of its housing stock. This is at variance with the system of having such work contracted out to independent firms. Supporters of the direct labour system argue that it gives the authorities full control over the quality of work done.

direct tax
It refers to a tax on income or capital, for example, income tax is called direct tax. Direct tax is so called because it is normally assumed that the real burden of payment falls directly on the person or firm immediately responsible for it and cannot be passed on to anybody else.

disappreciation
It means a movement of prices which, while downward in direction, was just a correction of a previously excessive rise.

discount
Simply speaking, a reduction in prices is called discount. A cash discount or a discount for prompt payment is a reduction in price allowed to customers who pay cash, or pay promptly. A security like share or bond stands at a discount if its present market price is below the price at which it is due to be redeemed.

discount factor
In a multi-period model, agents may have different utility functions for consumption, etc. in different time periods. In such models, they usually value future experiences to a lesser degree than present ones. The factor by which they discount next period's utility may be a constant between zero and one and is called a discount factor.

discount house
It refers to a business institution which will buy acceptances from their owners for less than their face value and hold them to maturity. The difference between the price paid and the face value, expressed as a percentage per annum, is termed the row. Discount houses borrow at call from banks and other financial institutions. Such funds may be called in by the banks and other financial institutions.

discount rate
1. It is the interest rate at which future receipts or payments are discounted to find their present value. If the discount rate is 100r per cent per annum, the present discounted value of a payment of A due in n years time may be denoted as:
$V = A/(1 + r)^n$.
2. It is the interest rate that the central bank charges when the commercial banks want to borrow money. It is known as bank rate or minimum lending rate (M.L.R.).

discrete distribution
It refers to the distribution of a variable that can take only discrete values, such as integers. If $f(a_i)$ is the frequency of occurrences of ai where i = 1, 2, 3, ... N, in a discrete distribution.

discrete time
It implies to the treatment of time in dynamic economic models as a discrete variable. Processes in discrete time are described by difference equations.

discrete variable
It is a variable, which can only take certain particular values, e.g., integers. This is in contrast with a continuous variable, which can take any value over some interval. Calculus is only applicable to continuous variables.

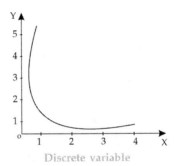

Discrete variable

discretionary policy
It refers to a policy where the choice of policy

measures, their extent and their timing, is entrusted to the judgement of policymakers. This is distinct from rules-based policy, where policymakers either follow pre-announced rules or always follow well-defined procedures.

discretionary spending
It implies a spending, which a government body is empowered but not legally required to undertake. This may include both spending on real goods and services, such as public works, and grants to individuals, organisations or sectors.

discriminating monopoly
It is a situation where a single firm sells in more than one market, and needs not change the same price in each. For maximum profits a monopolist sets prices in such a way that at the amounts sold, marginal revenue in each market equals marginal cost. Simply speaking, it is the ability of a monopolist to charge different prices from different customers and it is called discriminating monopoly.

discrimination, trade
It refers to a treatment of imports on a different basis according to their country of origin. In it, in a free-trade area, customs union, or common market, imports from non-members are subject to tariffs, while imports from other members are admitted tax free. Even treating free-trade areas and common markets as single trading units, it is possible to discriminate between different non-members in some ways. There may be preferences in tariffs for goods from particular countries, or special quota arrangements applying to particular sources of imports.

discriminatory tariff
It is a higher tariff against one source of imports than against another. Except in special circumstances, such as anti-dumping duties, this is a violation of Most Favoured Nation (MFN) status and is prohibited by the WTO against the other members.

diseconomies of scale
It is the reverse of economies of scale. Normally, with the increase in the scale of production, number of economies rise, which raise the profit of the producer by lowering its cost. But when the long run average cost increases with the raising of the output, it is

termed as the diseconomies of scale. These may be subdivided into internal and external. Diseco- nomies may be affected either due to the rise in the administrative cost or due to the rise in the cost of transport in the carriage of raw materials from distant places.

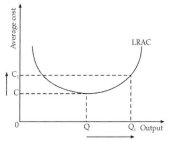

Diseconomies of scale

disembodied technical progress
The term refers to an improvement in technical knowledge that allows more output to be obtained from given inputs without the need to invest in new equipment. Disembodied technical progress is distinct from embodied technical progress, where improved techniques can be exploited only by investing in new technology.

disequilibrium
It describes the following:
1. Inequality of supply and demand.
2. An untenable state of an economic system, from which it may be expected to change.
3. It is a situation in which plans cannot be carried out. Ex ante plans for spending and selling, or for producing and consuming, cannot be carried out if they are inconsistent with each other, or with objective facts. Disequilibrium can arise in specific markets, in the level of activity as a whole, or in the external relations between countries.

disguised unemployment
It refers to unused labour, which does not appear as open unemployment. Firms hoard labour for which they have no use, because sacking workers may be illegal or politically risky, or because they are subsidised to do so. In some countries, more people are engaged in farming than are necessary. The excess or extra workers may be termed as disguised employment.

dishoarding

It is the reverse of hoarding. When an individual or a group of individuals decide to utilise the hoarded money for investment, it is termed as dishoarding.

disincentives

These are the economic arrangements, which weaken the inducements to work or save, or make it actually pay not to. High marginal tax rates provide disincentives to the effort, and means-tested benefits may lead to the poverty trap, which means that it may not benefit individuals to accept work, which does not fetch good wages.

disintermediation

It refers to the following:
1. The prevention of banks from flowing money from savers to borrowers as an effect of regulations.
2. Circumventing middle-men, intermediaries and even agents from transactions between businesses or between businesses and consumers, now often involving direct digital transactions through 'e-commerce' on the Internet.

disinvestment

It is the process of reducing the capital stock. So far as fixed capital is concerned, disinvestment may come by scrapping, or by non-replacement of capital goods as they wear out. Stocks and work in progress can also be reduced. It takes place in two ways: (i) The producer of a product may dispose of some of the surplus or old technique plant, and convert the same into cash; (ii) He may set aside more amount into the depreciation than the actual wear and tear that may be taking place.

displacement effect

It denotes an observed tendency for public expenditure to rise during a war or other national crisis but not to fall to the original level after the crisis. In this way, such crises lead to a permanent increase in government expenditure. This phenomenon has formed part of the explanation of public expenditure growth given by A.T. Peacock and J. Wiseman.

disposable income

It refers to personal income, which is available for spending. This is total or gross income minus direct tax, insurance due, EMIs to be paid or other bills like water, electricity, phone which have to be paid. Disposable income may either be spent on consumption or can be saved.

dissaving

It refers to a decreasing net assets by spending beyond one's income. This may be done by spending money taken from bank balances, i.e., past saving or the proceeds of selling assets, or by incurring debts. People with positive net assets can dissave relatively easily.

distance elasticity of demand

It is called the relative response of effective demand to a change in the distance (or transport costs) that a consumer has to overcome in order to purchase a good or service at a given price.

distortions

These are economic situations in which the incentives facing firms and individuals fail to reflect true social opportunity costs. Distortions can be created by externalities, taxes, or monopoly. The effects of some externalities could be corrected by levying taxes and duties.

distribution

It denotes the following:
1. The process of moving goods and services from producers to final consumers, by means of a network of wholesalers and retail shops.
2. The share of income received by different sections of the community. The functional distribution of income refers to the shares of income derived from using the factors like labour, land and capital.
3. Also a function showing the probability of various possible outcomes of a stochastic process.

disutility

It is the psychological cost of work or other unpleasant experience. There is no separate disutility function. An individual's utility is assumed to be a function of both consumption and work performed, with utility an increasing function of consumption and a decreasing function to work.

diversification

The term denotes the following:

1. A policy designed to reduce the dependence of a regional economy on specialised types of activities or markets. This may be done by shifting to a broader range of activities or markets.

2. The concept that considers the advantages and shortcomings of different regional economic structures, including specialised and diversified structures.

3. A spread of the activities of a firm or a country between different types of products or different markets. Many firms are diversified to varying degrees. The truly single-product firm may be an exception, and even it may supply various markets. Even very small shops usually sell a range of products.

divestment

The term refers to the disposal of part of its activities by a firm. Sometimes it reflects the commercial judgement that the activity concerned would be more profitable if operated independently or run by another firm. In other cases, divestment is required by anti-monopoly regulators to reduce a firm's monopoly power.

dividend

The term refers to the part of the net profit, which the joint stock company decides to distribute amongst the shareholders. Dividend is usually declared as a percentage of the value of the share capital, but it may also be as an absolute amount per share. Rate of dividend is decided in the annual general meeting of the shareholders.

dividend control

It refers to the restrictions on the distribution of dividends by firms. These may be imposed as a part of prices and incomes policy. These controls usually take the form of preventing or limiting increases in dividends. If wages are controlled, political considerations may require a balancing restriction on profits.

division of labour

It is the system by which different members of any society do different types of work. This has two advantages: (i) it allows individuals to specialise on types of work at which they have a comparative advantage over others and (ii) it allows them to acquire specialised skills, both through training and by learning from experience on the job how to work effi-

ciently. The division of labour in modern industrial societies has become so extreme that no individual could create unaided more than a small part of the goods and services he or she uses.

doctrine of *laissez-faire*

It refers to the belief of most of the 19th century economists that the government should confine its activities to the maintenance of internal peace and the prevention of outside aggression, i.e., law and order, and defence, respectively. In all other matters including economic matters, the government should remain neutral and all such matters should be left to the initiative and enterprise of individuals and private sector. In other words, the government should not intervene in economic activities. The state is not concerned with economic matters and therefore it should not have any economic policy. However, complete non-intervention by the state is not possible.

documents against acceptance (D/A)

These are inland or foreign bills sent along with the trade documents, e.g., invoice, bill, etc.; documents, sent to the banker with the instruction that he may hand over the possession of the documents in getting the unqualified acceptance of the bill of exchange by the buyer.

documents against payment (D/P)

Today credit has assumed shape of the varying orders. Depending upon the circumstances and the understanding between the seller and the buyer, documents that are to entitle the buyer to take the delivery such as the Railway Receipt or Bill of Lading, the Marine Insurance Policy, etc. may be sent to the banker with the instruction that the banker would hand over the documents when the payment for the goods is made by the buyer of goods on whom the bill of exchange is drawn.

Doha ministerial round

It refers to the WTO ministerial meeting held in Doha, Qatar, in November 2001, in which it was agreed to begin a new round of multilateral trade negotiations, which later came to be known the Doha Round. This meeting holds great importance as it framed important conditions of trade among the WTO members.

Doha round
The term refers to the round of multilateral trade negotiations that began in January 2002 as a result of agreement at the Doha Ministerial Round.

dollar ($)
It is a unit of currency adopted by several countries, notably the United States. Other countries using dollars include Australia, Canada, Fiji, Hong Kong, Jamaica, Singapore and New Zealand. Any mention of a dollar without qualification normally refers to the US dollar, unless it occurs in a context which implies that it means the local currency.

dollar standard
It refers to a system of exchange rate management in which other countries peg the exchange rates of their currencies with the US dollar, and hold their foreign exchange reserves mainly in the form of US dollars. It was argued that the Bretton Woods exchange rate system operating in the 1950s and 1960s will hold effectively a dollar standard.

Domar aggregation
The term refers to the principle that the growth rate of an aggregate is the weighted average of the growth rates of its components and is weighted by the share of the aggregate it makes up. The idea was given by Domar and comes up in the context of national accounts and national statistics.

domestic
It means from or in one's own country. A domestic producer is one that produces the home country. A domestic price is the price inside the home country. It is opposite of foreign or world.

domestic credit expansion
It is the part of any increase in the money supply, which is not due to a balance-of-payments surplus, on either current or capital account.

domestic distortions
The term refers to factors causing departures of a country's internal economy from Pareto-optimality. Such factors include the existence of externalities, monopoly, and discriminatory taxes.

domestic product
The term refers to the value of the total product of enterprises operating in a country, irrespective of their ownership. This is in contrast with national product, which is the product of enterprises owned by residents, no matter of where they may be operating.

domino effect
It is the tendency of one country's accession to an organisation, or adoption of a policy, to induce other countries to follow suit. In the case of joining trade blocs, this could be because the bloc benefits members at the expense of outsiders.

dotcom company
It is a name for companies devoted to providing Internet access and various activities including sales over the Net. Many dotcom companies have come up recently. A bubble in dotcom shares developed, and burst in 2001.

double counting
It is the attempt to find the total product of an economy by adding up the gross sales of each enterprise, without subtracting purchases of inputs from other enterprises. As firms buy large amounts of fuel, materials, and services from one another, simply adding gross outputs results in double counting of output.

double entry
It is the system of keeping accounts in which, as a check on accuracy and consistency, every payment appears twice, in different accounts, once as a credit and once as a debit. In this system, a sale appears as a credit for the department making it, and a debit for the buyer; a purchase appears as a debit for the department making it and a credit for the supplier.

double taxation
It refers to the collection of taxes on the same income by two countries. This is liable to happen when an economic asset earns income in one country but is owned in another. If countries tax both the profits of firms operating in their territories, and the incomes of their residents, double taxation will take place

unless there is an agreement or arrangement between the two countries to prevent it.

Dow Jones Industrial Average
It refers to a leading index of US stock market prices. This is an index of the thirty most widely traded US industrial shares. Dow Jones also publishes indexes of transportation and utilities stocks, and a composite index which is an average of all three.

down payment
It is the part of the price of goods sold on hire purchase or instalment credit that has to be paid immediately. When hire-purchase controls became part of some countries' monetary policy, variations in the required minimum down payment was used to influence demand for the goods concerned.

downside risk
It refers to the risk that the outcome of a new project will be below the expected mean return. From the point of view of a lender financing a project, the downside risk is that a project may not yield enough returns to enable the borrower to repay a loan.

downward-sloping demand curve
It refers to a demand curve showing that the quantity demanded decreases as price increases. Demand curves are normally assumed to slope downwards, which is consistent with the outcome of empirical demand studies.

drachma
It was the currency of modern Greece (Athens, in ancient times) replaced by the Euro in 2002.

drawing rights
The term refers to the right for members of the International Monetary Fund (IMF) to acquire foreign currency from the fund in exchange for their own, to an extent proportional to the size of their quota. Drawing rights were extended after 1970 with the creation of Special Drawing Rights (SDRs).

dual economy
It refers to an economy in which modern industries, mines or plantation, agriculture exist side-by-side with backward sectors such as primitive farming, village and cottage industries, with little interaction between them. This situation may occur in Least Developed Countries (LDCs) with foreign investment in extractive industries using expatriates for their more skilled work.

duality
It refers to the fact that economic problems stated in terms of one set of variables can also be considered in terms of an alternative set. For example, in linear programming, the problem may be to maximise the value of output despite resource constraints. The dual problem corresponding to this involves choosing shadow prices to minimise the value put on resources, consistent with firms, breaking even point.

dual labour market
It is a segmented labour market in which one part is usually and in broad terms, characterised by high skills and wages, job security, career development conditions, while the other part has low wages, inferior benefits, a temporary or unstable nature, little chance of advancement, poorer working conditions, etc.

dumping
1. It refers to export price that is 'unfairly low'. It is also defined as either below the home market price hence, price discrimination or below cost. With the rare exception of successful predatory dumping, dumping is economically beneficial to the importing country as a whole though harmful to competing producers. It often represents a normal business practice.
2. It is a form of price discrimination exercised by the monopolist and is considered an unfair practice. While goods outside the country are sold at a lower price. The same quality goods are sold at a higher price inside the country.
3. Selling goods in a foreign country at a price which local producers regard as unfairly low. This may mean selling at less than the long-run average costs of production plus transport costs, charging a lower price in export markets than it is charged for comparable goods in home markets.

duopoly
It refers to a market situation with only two sellers - each of whom must take account of the other's expected reactions. A Cournot duopolist assumes that the rival will hold the

constant his quantity produced, while a Bertrand duopolist believes that the rival will hold the constant the price charged.

duopsony
It is a market situation with only two buyers. This is the parallel on the demand side to duopoly, which is a market situation with only two sellers.

Dutch disease
It denotes the following:
1. The adverse effect on a country's other industries that occurs when one industry substantially expands its exports, causing a real appreciation of the country's currency.
2. The effect of an increase in one form of net exports in driving up a country's exchange rate, which handicaps the sale of other exports and impairs the ability of domestic products to compete with imports. The name comes from the supposed effects of natural gas discoveries on the Netherlands economy.

duties
They refer to anti-dumping duty, countervailing duty, customs duty, death duties, estate duty, excise duty, and stamp duty.

duty drawback
The term is used for the payment of customs duty refunded by the government. In case of the goods that are imported into a country and exported to some other country, the customs duty that was charged earlier on these goods is refunded.

duty-free
The term refers to 'without tariff', and is usually applied to imports on which normally a tariff would be charged, but that for some reasons are exempted. Travellers, for example, may be permitted to import a certain amount of articles duty-free.

dynamics
It is the study of how economies change over time. Change may occur as a result of exogenously determined factors, and endogenously as individuals, firms, and governments react to observed disequilibria. Dynamics is distinct from comparative statics, which is concerned with how changes in exogenous factors or behavioural assumptions will alter equilibria.

E

earmarking
In economics, it is a linkage between a particular tax and a particular type of state expenditure. Such linkages are not very popular with treasuries because of their rigidity.

earned income
It refers to income received in return for work. This is distinguished from unearned income, which comes from property, such as rent, dividends, interest, etc.

earnings
These are the salary/pay of the employed labour force. These include payment for overtime and bonuses, as well as basic pay. Earnings should be distinguished from wage rates, which refer to normal time working only and exclude bonuses.

earnings per share (EPS)
It denotes the amount of company earnings available per ordinary share issued. These earnings may be distributed in dividends, used to pay taxes, or retained and used to expand the business. Earnings per share of a company are a major determinant of its share prices.

East Asian tigers
The term is used for four East Asian economies, namely Hong Kong, Singapore, South Korea and Taiwan, whose incomes and trade have grown extremely rapidly in the period since the 1990s.

easy fiscal policy
It is a policy of cutting taxes, increasing government spending, and not worrying about the resulting budget deficits and increases in government debt. Such a policy is generally advocated when the economy is depressed. While this policy is tempting when the investment and the employment are below normal, it may prove counterproductive in the long run.

easy monetary policy
It refers to a policy of having low interest rates and easy access to credit to stimulate real economic activity. Such a policy is adopted in times of depression when investment and employment are both below normal. Easy monetary policy was adopted by America, Europe and Asia during the global economics crisis of 2008-09.

EBRD
It stands for the European Bank for Reconstruction and Development.

e-commerce
It is the practice of advertising and selling goods and services over the Internet. This is growing as a substitute for the traditional use of mail-order catalogues by people who prefer or are obliged to shop from home. Business to business (B2B) use of the Net is also growing.

econometric models
These are mathematical models given by Klein which are designed to assist in forecasting the needs and demands of the national economy some years ahead. Such models are constructed for static or dynamic economic situations, and the interaction of forces can be isolated and analysed.

econometrics
It refers to the application of statistical methods to economics. In econometrics, a model of some aspect of the economy is established and stated in mathematical terms. This model is compared with the available statistical facts about the economy. The model and the facts will invariably fail to match precisely. Econometrics uses statistical tests to tackle various questions.

economic base multiplier
The term is used for a form of regional multiplier which is able to estimate the effect of changes in an area's economic base on the economy of the region as a whole.

economic cost
It is the cost calculated in terms of the best alternative foregone in the making of a thing.

economic friction
The term is used for influences - natural or deliberate - which tend to impede the full or rapid operation of economic laws.

economic growth stages
The term refers to the stages that a nation has to pass on the road to economic growth.

W.W. Rostow in his famous book, *Stages of Economic Growth* has listed five stages:
1. The traditional society.
2. The preconditions of the take-off.
3. The take-off.
4. Drive to maturity.
5. Era of high mass consumption.
The most crucial stage that a developing nation has to get through is the take-off stage. These five stages can be abridged to three, viz. underdeveloped, developing and developed. The first two stages make a nation underdeveloped while the last two stages make her a developed one.

economic imperialism
It is the domination of the economies of colonies by their rulers, or of politically independent countries by foreign or multinational companies. Some economists argue that true independence is impossible for poor and backward countries which are faced with domination of their trade, and possibly their extractive industries, by large, sophisticated and monopolistic firms based in the advanced countries.

economic integration
When two or more nations seek to co-ordinate and link up their economies, it is termed as economic integration. It can be in various forms. It may develop itself into a free trade area or it may convert itself into a full economic union. Member nations thus formulate common monetary and fiscal policies. European Economic Community (EEC) is one of the instances of economic integration. Member nations have decided to impose no customs duties on the products of one another and also agreed to impose a uniform customs duty on the products that come from the other nations outside their zone or association.

economic liberalism
It refers to the doctrine which advocates the greatest possible use of markets and the forces of competition to co-ordinate economic activity. It allows to the state only those activities which the market cannot carry out, e.g. the provision of public goods.

economic planning
It refers to the broad economic plans of a country. It can be classified as: (i) imperative and (ii) indicative. Imperative planning is applicable to a centralised macroeconomic plan in an economy which has been dominated by the public sector; while indicative planning is more directional.

economic problems
These refer to the underlying factors behind the economic problems of the paucity of resources and unlimited wants. Scarcity is the phenomenon that holds good for all the nations. With scarce resources in terms of skilled workers, wealth and material, each nation has to make certain fundamental decisions to solve the three major problems: (i) how to produce, (ii) what to produce and (iii) for whom to produce. Each nation tries to allocate its productive resources in such a manner as to raise its productivity to the maximum.

economic rent
It refers to the following:
1. The differential gain that accrues to the owner of the super marginal land on account of its superiority over the marginal land. The superiority may be due to either higher fertility or better situation or both. The concept was given by Marshall.
2. A payment for the services of an economic resource which is not necessary as an incentive for its production. Unimproved land, which is valuable purely on account of its location, commands a rent based on its value to the user. Since nobody had to be paid to make it, so rent paid to a landlord is economic rent. In the case of land, which has been improved, however, for example, by the irrigation, part of the rent is a necessary incentive for the improvements.

economics
It can be defined as a social science which is concerned with how people, either individually or in groups, try to accommodate scarce resources to their wants through the process of production, substitution and exchange. As per Adam Smith, economics is an enquiry into the nature and causes of wealth of nations. Alfred Marshall in 1890 in his masterpiece book *Principles of Economics* defined it as "a study of man in the ordinary business of life". It enquires into how he gets his income and how he uses it. Thus, it is on the one side a study of wealth and on the other hand it is the study of man. Marshall, thus established the fact that man was of greater importance than wealth. A.C. Pigou likewise

emphasised man and his welfare. According to him, "Economics is the study of economic welfare which can be brought, directly or indirectly, into relationship with the measuring rod of money." At a time when the issue of the definition of economics was settling down, Prof. Lionel Robbins in 1932 in his book *Nature and Significance of Economic Science*, defined economics as, "The study of human behaviours as relationship between ends and scarce means that have alternative uses." There are various branches or types of economics:

(i) Macroeconomics considers how aggregates such as output, employment, and the general price level are determined.

(ii) Positive economics is concerned with what actually happens, or what would happen under various conditions.

(iii) Normative economics considers what would be the best methods of economic organisation, from the point of view of both equity and efficiency.

(iv) Welfare economics is concerned with socio-economic welfare of people.

economic sanctions

When a nation adopts some measures in the functioning of its economy with a view to adversely affecting some other country, these are called economic sanctions. It can be compared to a political sanction. Economic sanctions can take different forms. The usual method is that of the restrictions placed on the normal flow of goods.

economic theory

It is a generic term for theory concerned with the formulations of economic generalisations and laws concerning man in relation to his economic pursuit. Study of economic theory occupies a primary place in the science of economics.

economies of scale

The term refers to the factors which make it possible for larger organisations or countries to produce goods or services more cheaply than smaller ones. Economies of scale which are internal to firms are due to indivisibilities and the division of labour. Specialised equipment usually comes in units of some minimum size, so that a larger total output makes it economic to use more specialised equipment. The division of labour denotes that it is possible with a larger workforce to restrict the range of tasks performed by each individual worker. In a larger firm, the breakdown of any particular piece of equipment, or the absence of any individual worker, causes less disruption to production.

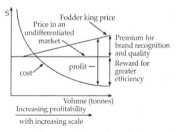

Economies of scale

economies of scope

They are the benefits arising from carrying on related activities. These are similar to economies of scale, but the major difference is that whereas with economies of scale cost savings arise from carrying on more of the same activity, with economies of scope cost savings arise from carrying on related activities.

effective demand

It refers to the following:

1. Demand which is measured by spending on consumption, goods and services more or less used up immediately; on investment, e.g. plant, buildings, equipment, stocks; and on the difference between exports; which adds to demand for output at home and imports which tends to satisfy home demand without adding to home output.

2. Ex ante spending, that is plans to purchase, by people with the means to pay. It is distinct from notional demand, the demand that would exist if all markets were in equilibrium. Effective demand thus excludes the extra goods that unemployed workers would buy if they could get jobs.

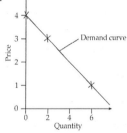

Effective demand

efficiency

It implies getting any given results with the smallest possible inputs, or getting the maximum possible output from given resources. Efficiency in consumption denotes allocating goods between consumers so that it would not be possible by any reallocation to make some people better off without making anybody else worse off. Efficiency in production means allocating the available resources between industries so that it would not be possible to produce more of some goods without producing less of any others.

efficiency audit

It is a process of checking whether an organisation is working as efficiently as it can. This may be done either internally as management tries to improve profitability, or externally by bodies, for example, those responsible for supervising privatised utilities.

elasticity

It is defined as the ratio between proportional change in two variables. Economists find this concept useful because comparisons of proportional changes are pure ratios, independent of the units in which the variables, such as price or quantity, are measured. There are various forms of elasticity: (i) Price elasticity, sometimes called own-price elasticity, compares proportional change in quantity of a good supplied or demanded with proportional change in price. (ii) Elasticity of supply is the ratio of proportional increase in quantity supplied to proportional increase in own price. (iii) Elasticity of demand is the ratio of proportional rise in quantity demanded to proportional fall in price. This is usually defined as $(p/q)\,(dq/dp)$, where p is price and q is quantity; the negative sign makes the elasticity of demand positive.

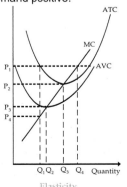

Elasticity

elasticity of demand

It is the ratio between proportional change in quantity demanded of a good and proportional change in its price. This is based on the assumption that income and other prices remain unchanged. When q is quantity and p is price, elasticity of demand is given by $\varepsilon = -(p/q)(dq/dp)$.

elasticity of expectations

It refers to the ratio of the proportional change in the expected value of a variable to a proportional change in its current value.

elasticity of supply

It is the ratio of the proportional rise in the quantity of a good supplied to a proportional rise in its price. The concept is only appropriate to an industry in which the firms are price-takers, i.e., the market sets the price and firms adapt their outputs to it. For any one firm, elasticity of supply will be larger in the long run than in the short run.

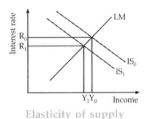

Elasticity of supply

electronic trading

It refers to trading stocks and shares or commodities with a computer network. The network provides information on offers to trade by market makers and others, and data of trades conducted. It can also be made to do the actual trades, though this part is often done by telephone.

embargo

The term refers to the following:
1. A prohibition on releasing or quoting published material before a given deadline. This is generally intended to avoid diplomatic embarrassment or opportunities for insider trading.
2. A prohibition on trading with a country, or in some particular goods. A general embargo is intended as an expression of disapproval, for example, of practices such as against the policy of apartheid practised in South Africa in the 1970s.

emerging markets

These are the stock exchanges in those countries where investors are not used to trading. These are mainly newly industrialised countries (NICs), such as China, India, South Africa or Brazil, or newly liberalised economies, such as Hungary or Poland.

emigration

It is the reverse of immigration. When people come to our country from some other country, it is called immigration. But when our residents leave to settle permanently in some other country, it is called emigration.

employee

An employee is a person working for somebody else, for wages or salary, rather than working on their own account and selling their product or services. In the official economy, the distinction between them is: an employee has a contract of employment, and employers are liable for damage caused either by or to employees in the course of their duties.

employee stock ownership plan (ESOP)

The term refers to an arrangement for a company to provide shares for its employees through a trust fund. Company contributions to ESOPs are exempt from income tax. Employee share ownership is believed to make employees better motivated, better informed about their employer's business, and more loyal to the company.

employer

An employer is an individual, company or government body that pays somebody wages to work for them. This is distinguished from hiring a self-employed person to do the work. Often, the employers have legal liabilities for the health and safety of employees. They are required to be insured for employer's liability, who are responsible for deducting income tax from their employees' pay, etc.

employment

It refers to the following:
1. The state of being paid to work for somebody else.
2. The state of being gainfully occupied. It includes self-employment as well as working for somebody else. Full employment is a state in which everybody wishing to be so is gainfully employed.

emoluments

They can be defined as that portion of management's salary and non-pecuniary benefits which are not part of the entrepreneurial supply price.

endogenous

The term arises from the working of a system. This is opposite to exogenous, which means imposed on a system from outside. Monopoly in an industry, for example, could be endogenous, where economies of scale allow larger firms to drive out smaller ones, or it could be exogenous, where it is imposed by the state giving one firm a legal monopoly.

endogenous growth

The term refers to the economic growth where the long-run growth rate is determined by the working of the system. This is in contrast with exogenous growth, where the long-run growth rate is determined from outside the system such as by population increase and an exogenously given rate of technical progress.

Engel Curve

It refers to a line which plots the relationship between an individual's income and his consumption of a specified good. An Engel Curve is illustrated in the following diagram.

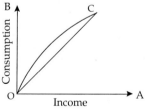

Engel curve

The slope of the curve at any point will give the individual's marginal propensity to consume the good and the ratio of change in consumption to change in income. The ratio of total consumption of the good to total income will give the average propensity to consume the good, which is equal to the slope of a line such as OA. The ratio of the marginal propensity to consume the good to the average propensity to consume has been the income elasticity of demand for the good.

Engel's law
It refers to a generalisation which states that the proportion of income spent on food tends to decline as income grows, with given tastes, or preferences. This law or tendency was postulated by Ernst Engel (1821-96) in a paper published by him in 1857.

enterprise
It implies the following:
1. A business venture, which can be either private or public.
2. The combination of initiative, foresight, and willingness to take risks required to make a success of running a business.

entrepreneur
1. He/she is a person with overall responsibility for decision taking in a business, who receives any profits and bears any losses. Entrepreneurs need not necessarily contribute either labour, which can be hired, or capital, which can be borrowed. But they must contribute either one of these or a credible guarantee, that their responsibility for possible losses is genuine.
2. A manager whose status changes from company employee to proprietor of an independent firm. This change is encouraged and possibly financed by the former employer.

envelope curve
It refers to a curve showing the maximum possible output obtainable by using a combination of two or more independent processes to pursue any objective. If all processes have constant or increasing returns to scale, it is always possible to produce any amount efficiently using only one of the processes. It pays to combine processes only when each has decreasing returns. It applies to the use of different plans by a firm, or the use of internal production and external trade for a country.

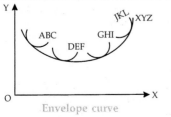

Envelope curve

environment
In socio-economics, it refers to the conditions under which people, creatures, and plants have to live. The natural environment concerns matters such as the purity of air to breathe, water to drink and soil to cultivate, and several further aspects of living. The built environment concerns the effects on quality of life of human constructs such as buildings, roads, dams, or power lines.

equality
The term refers to the property of having the same value. This is symbolised by = and applies to numbers or algebraic expressions. If a and b are real numbers, a = b means that a and b are the same.

equation
It is a requirement that a mathematical expression takes some particular value. A quadratic equation, for example, takes the form $ay^2 + by + c = 0$. A solution is any value of y for which this is true. An equation may have more than one argument. For example, $ax^2 + bxz + cz^2 = 0$. A solution to this is any set (x, z) for which this equality is satisfied. With simultaneous equations, two or more equations must be satisfied by the same set of their arguments.

equilibrium
It is a situation in which nobody has any immediate reason to change their actions, so that the status quo will continue, at least temporarily. This concept is applied in economics in a number of related ways, particularly in microeconomics, macroeconomics, and game theory, as explained below:
1. In macroeconomics, equilibrium refers to situations where activity and price levels are such that the plans of various groups like savers and investors are consistent, so that they can all be implemented. For example, there is no reason, why the ex ante savings and investment of any individual or firm should be equal.
2. In microeconomics, the simplest form of equilibrium analysis looks at a single market. Due to the reason that repercussions in the rest of the economy are ignored, this is called partial equilibrium analysis. Equilibrium price is that at which quantity supplied and quantity demanded are equal. Equilibrium quantity is that at which the marginal valuation put on

the good by purchasers equals the marginal supply price, which for competitive producers is their marginal cost. Under normal assumptions, the demand curve in a competitive market slopes downwards, and the supply curve slopes upwards.

3. In game theory, a strategy is a rule adopted by an individual agent whose own actions are made conditional on those they observe in others. An equilibrium in strategies exists if, given the strategies that all other agents are using, no individual agent finds any change of strategy.

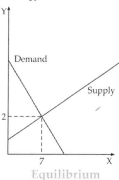

Equilibrium

equilibrium price
It refers to a price at which the quantity of a good supplied is equal to the quantity demanded. If the supply curve is upward sloping and the demand curve is downward sloping, this price is unique.

equilibrium quantity
It is the quantity of a good supplied and demanded when the price is such that these quantities are equal, so that the market is in equilibrium. With normally sloped supply and demand curves, if the price is above the equilibrium price, the quantity supplied is above the equilibrium quantity.

equimarginal returns
At times, production is carried out in a manner that the cheaper and the more efficient factor of production replaces the more expensive and the less efficient factor of production. It maximises their profits and equalises the returns at the margin from the different factors of production. It is known as equimarginal returns.

equities
These are the ordinary shares or common stock of companies. The owners of these shares are entitled to the residual profits of companies after all claims of creditors, debenture holders, and preference shareholders have been satisfied.

equity
In economics, it refers to fairness and the concept of distributive justice which is used in welfare economics. Equity as fairness has several possible meanings. Sometimes it means equality; sometimes that difference in efforts should be followed by differences in rewards; and sometimes that expectations should always be met.

equity leasing
It refers to lease under which the lessor contributes the entire capital cost. It is distinct from leveraged leasing where the lessor contributes only a minor portion of the capital.

equity-linked insurance
It refers to a system of life insurance where the benefits to be received are linked to the level of an index of equity share prices. The benefits may have some guaranteed minimum, but above this, they reflect the behaviour of equity prices up to the time when the policy matures.

ergonomics
It can be defined as the creation of such conditions that the output in a factory is maximised. It tries to raise and maximise the output of each worker by the introduction of proper design of machines and an ideal layout for factories.

escalator clause
In economics, it is a clause in a contract linking the price or wage to be paid to some other price, or to the cost of living. This linkage may apply to all increases in costs, or only to those beyond some threshold level. If escalator clauses are widely used in contracts or wage bargains, they contribute to cost inflation and make inflation extremely hard to contain.

estate duty
It is a tax formerly levied on the estate of a dead person. It was based on the total value of the estate, with exemption for small estates.

estate economy

It refers to a sector or whole economy in an underdeveloped country which is mainly used for large-scale production of export crops normally managed and owned by foreign powers.

Euler, Leonhard

He was a renowned Swiss mathematician who contributed immensely to science of pure mathematics. Some of his propositions were later applied with commendable result in the field of economic theory, the most prominent of which is the application of the theory of distribution based in marginal productivity.

Euler's theorem

It is a mathematical theorem relating marginal to average products. The theorem states that where a function is homogeneous of order n in its arrangements, so that, for example, if b = f(a, z), then $f(\lambda a, \lambda z) = \lambda^n f(a,z)$, the sum of the marginal product of each arrangement times its quantity equals nb.

euro

It is the unit of the single European currency, adopted in 1999 as part of European Monetary Union (EMU) by 11 members of the European Union: Austria, Belgium, Finland, France, Germany, Italy, Ireland, Luxembourg, the Netherlands, Portugal, and Spain. It has a fixed value in terms of each country's domestic currency; for example, approximately 1.6 Deutsch-marks, or 200 Portuguese Escudos.

eurobond

It is a bond issued in a Eurocurrency, that is, a European currency held outside its country of origin. Eurobonds are issued in bearer form, to the investors wishing to remain anonymous.

euromarket

It is a market dealing in Eurobonds and Eurocurrencies, i.e. securities and currencies held in European countries other than their country of origin. There are large Euromarkets in several centres in Europe like Frankfurt, London, Paris, Brussels, Rome, etc.

European Bank for Reconstruction and Development (EBRD)

It is an international bank founded in 1990 to assist in the transformation of the countries of Central Europe and the erstwhile Soviet Union to market economies.

European Commission

It is the main executive body of the European Union. The commissioners are appointed by the governments member countries of two each by larger and one each by smaller members. The Commission takes decisions by majority vote.

European Economic Community (EEC)

It is the European common market set up in 1958 by the original six members of the European Coal and Steel Community (ECSC). These were Belgium, France, Germany (West), Italy, Luxembourg, and the Netherlands. The EEC was combined with the European Atomic Energy Community (EAEC) in 1967 to form the European Community (EC).

European economic integration

It denotes the process by which various countries of Europe are becoming more closely linked, particularly in trade and finance. This is partly the result of natural economic developments. Trade has increased mainly because of the rise of intra-industry trade, which is increasingly important as industrialised countries saturated close together and financial links have been fostered by the general move to ambition of exchange controls and financial deregulation.

European Free Trade Association (EFTA)

An association of European countries with free trade between them, established in 1959.

European Union (EU)

It is the name given to the former European Community (EC) since 1993. The EU was formed with twelve members: Belgium, Denmark, France, Germany, Greece, Italy, Ireland, Luxembourg, the Netherlands, Portugal, Spain and the United Kingdom. Austria, Finland, and Sweden joined in 1995. Ten more countries, including the Czech Republics, Hungary, and Poland joined in 2004.

ex ante

It means as viewed in advance. The ex ante value of a variable is what the person or organisation responsible expects it to be. An individual's ex ante saving, for example, is the amount he/she intends to save. Ex ante is opposite to ex post, meaning as viewed after the event. Ex ante plans may not get carried out as individuals may save more than they intended if the goods they meant to buy are not available, or may save less if their incomes fall unexpectedly.

excess demand
It refers to a situation when the quantity of a good demanded exceeds the quantity supplied. In markets where a market maker maintains the price by buying all supplies offered and supplying the demands of other market participants, excess demand can be directly measured.

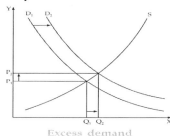

Excess demand

excess profits
These are profits which are larger than the writer regards as normal. There is no objective definition of excess profits. The views that profits are excessive are normally based on comparisons with the rate of return on capital xpected in other industries.

excess supply
It is a situation where at the existing price the quantity of a good or service supplied is greater than that demanded. In markets where a market maker stabilises the price by meeting all other people's offers to supply and their demands, excess supply can be measured directly.

exchange It refers to the following:
1. Trading one good or asset for another. This usage appears in the exchange of contracts between the buyer and seller of land/buildings.
2. The money, from its use in trade. Money is a medium of exchange rate which is the price at which one currency can be traded for another.
3. Also a place where trading is carried on. Shares are traded at the stock exchange.

exchange control
It is a system under which holders of a national currency require official permission or approval to convert it into other currencies. Exchange control may apply to all holders of currency, or some holders. Non-residents, are usually exempt from it.

exchange rate
It is the price of one currency in terms of another. This can be quoted either way round. If one pound is worth two dollars, one dollar is worth 50p, or half a pound; it is necessary to check which system is being used, i.e., direct or indirect. Some types of exchange rate are explained below:
(i) A par exchange rate is that agreed between governments, or registered with a central authority like the International Monetary Fund (IMF).
(ii) A market exchange rate is the actual price on foreign exchange markets.
(iii) The real exchange rates compare the relative prices of different countries' products.

excise duty
It is a tax levied on the consumption of particular goods. These may be levied government revenue, and are often levied at higher rates on goods whose consumption is believed to have adverse effects on public health, such as liquor public order, or the environment. Excise duties on alcoholic drinks, tobacco, and petrol are widely used for both purposes.

exclusion
It is the legal right and practical ability to prevent others from using a good. If a good is a private good it must be possible to exclude others from using it is reasonable cost. If it is impossible or unduly expensive to exclude others from using a good, it cannot be sold, and thus can only be provided by a body or an organisation.

ex dividend
It is the sale of shares where the vendor retains the right to a dividend already declared but not yet paid. This is opposite of cum dividend, where the sale includes the right of the purchaser to receive a dividend already declared but not yet paid.

ex post
It is the value of a variable as it appears after the event that is what actually occurred. Ex post is opposite to ex ante, which means looking at things before the event, i.e. ex ante concerns people's plans.

exercise price

It is the price at which an option gives the right to buy or sell shares, bonds commodities, or currencies. The option will only be exercised if this price is more favourable to the party holding it than the market price. A put option will only be used to sell assets if the exercise price is higher than the market price.

exit

In economics, it refers to the following:
1. Departure of a firm from an industry. This will normally occur if a firm is making losses and sees no prospect that the market will recover. If the the second-hand value of the firm's assets is higher, the exit is easier. Employment protection legislation or other public regulations may hinder a firm wishing to discontinue part of its business while continuing to trade.
2. The preferences of leaving unsatisfactory situations. In this sense, it can apply to selling shares, changing jobs, or migration between areas or countries.

exit price

It refers to the price below which firms will leave an industry. This is likely to be somewhat below the break-even price, as sunk costs cannot be avoided by exit.

exogenous expectations

These are expectations which are not explained, but are taken as fixed by some exogenous or external forces. This is a convenient assumption in small economic models.

expected value

It is the mean of the distribution of the values an economic variable is expected to take. If p_t is the price of a good at time t, its expected value can be written as $E[p_t]$. To specify the time when an expectation is held, the expectation held at time t-1 can be written $_{t-1}E[p_t]$ and the expectation held at time t-n can be denoted by $_{t-n}E[p_t]$.

expenditure

It refers to spending, by consumers, investors, or the government. Consumer expenditure is restricted to purchasing real goods and services. Acquiring assets or making transfer to others by individuals is not taken as expenditure. Government expenditure on real goods and services, but government interest pay- ments and transfer payments to individuals, e.g. pensions, are considered government expenditure.

expenditure switching

It is a policy intended to divert an existing level of expenditure from one outlet to another. Tariffs or import quotas could be used for example, to divert existing spending from imports onto home-produced goods. This is at variance with expenditure changing policies, intended to increase or decrease total spending.

expenditure tax

It is a suggested alternative to income tax, taxing expenditure in place of income. Its supporters argue that it would tax people on what they take out of the economy rather than on what they would put in. A system of allowances in respect of special occasions of major expenditure, such as marriage, and major illness is considered necessary.

exploitation

It means taking unfair advantage of somebody. It takes various forms as paying women workers less than men for equal work, deploying child labour, taking undue advantage of illiterate people, etc.

exponential

It may be a mathematical function with the property that it is equal to its own first derivative. It may be defined as:
$e^x = \exp(x) = 1 + x + (x^2/2!) + (x^3/3!) + ... + (x^N/N!) + ...$ where N! denotes N factorial = $N(N-1)(N-2) ...(2)(1)$. If this series is differentiated term by term, the same series is obtained; every term equals the derivative of the term following.

export control

The restriction of exports by governments. It is less common than export promotion, but can occur in a number of special cases. These are advanced means used in making them to countries which they regard as unfriendly.

export credit

It is the system of selling exports on credit rather than for cash payment. Exports of commodities and consumer goods are frequently financed by trade bills, or short-term credit. These are normally payable in 3 or 9 months, giving the buyer time to manufacture, pack and ship goods and distribute them for resale, thus providing the money to pay the bills. This is also known as packing credit.

Export Credits Guarantee Corporation (ECGC)

It is a government department responsible for encouraging Indian exports by insuring exporters against risks. These include both the risk of default on the part of export customers and the risk of loss through the imposition of import licensing or exchange controls by the importers' governments. Export credits may be for any period up to 5 years; the premium charged may constitute an implicit subsidy if they fail to reflect the full cost of risks.

export-led growth

It is growth in which exports increase faster than other components of national expenditure. This can occur either because incomes abroad are growing faster than at home, or because domestic products are becoming more competitive in world markets, through lower prices, better quality, increased variety, etc.

export promotion

It denotes the following:
1. A strategy for promoting economic development in developing countries. This involves running an open economy, relying on foreign markets to allow export-led growth.
2. Government activities to help sell exports by providing export incentives at home, and various forms of practical assistance for exporters abroad.

exports

Goods and services produced in a country and sold to non-residents, i.e. in other countries. Visible exports are goods sent abroad; invisible exports are services sold to non-residents. Some invisibles, for examples, air and sea transport, are services performed abroad. In the case of service such as bank insurance the location of the service is not defined. Export of capital means making loans to non-residents or buying real assets located abroad.

export subsidy

It refers to a subsidy to exporters, so that the price per unit received by the producers of exports is higher than the price charged to foreign customers. Direct export subsidies are prohibited by international agreement, but other government measures with similar effects are quite common. Exporters may be allowed refunds on tariffs on their inputs, subsidised credit, preferential access to ordinary credit in an economy, or assistance with their capital costs or training costs.

external balance

It is a sustainable pattern of transactions with the rest of the world. There are no capital movements on current account, since otherwise foreign exchange reserves would become exhausted if there was a current account surplus.

external diseconomy

It refers to a cost arising from an economic activity. For example, factories pollute the atmosphere or rivers, and traffic using crowded roads inflicts delay on other vehicles and health damage on pedestrians. External diseconomies can be controlled by prohibiting some polluting activities and taxing others. However, a complete stopping thereof is difficult and even impossible.

external economy

It is a benefit arising from an economic activity which does not attract charges or costs. For example, farms, hills and externally attractive buildings give pleasure to the general public who cannot normally be charged for the privilege of looking at them.

externality

It is a cost or benefit arising from any activity which does not accrue to the person or organisation carrying on the activity. External costs or diseconomies are damage to other people or the environment, for example, by radiation, river or air pollution, or noise, which does not have to be paid for by those carrying on the activity. External benefits or economies are effects of an activity which are pleasant or profitable for other people who cannot be charged for them, for example, fertilisation of fruit trees by bees, or the public's enjoyment of views of gardens, hills, greenery, etc.

F

face value
It is an alternative term for the nominal value of stocks and shares. A share of the face value of $10 - may be quoted in the market at $100 - or even more. The term is also used in connection with the token coins, the face value of which is generally greater than the value of the metal in the coins.

factor cost
It can be defined as the value of goods and services at the prices received by sellers. This is the market price paid by purchasers, minus any indirect taxes, plus any subsidies provided by the government. Factor cost is called so because the value of output at factor cost is the amount available to pay for bought-in inputs and for the services of the factors of production used.

factor endowment
It implies a country's stock of factors of production. The term endowment is rather misleading. So far as land is concerned, its area and location, and the minerals under it are given by nature; but the quality of the land can be improved by irrigation, fertility resources reflect effort put into improving them.

factor incomes
These are incomes derived from selling the services of factors of production. In the case of labour, this means wages, plus the part of the incomes of the self-employed, which is a reward for their own labour. Income from land is rent, including part of the incomes of the self-employed, and part of the imputed incomes of owner-occupiers of houses.

factoring
It means buying goods for resale without further processing. Debt factoring is buying debts due from another business's customers and collecting them.

factor mobility
It refers to the ease or difficulty with which factors of production can move between users.

factors of production
The resources of a society consist not only of the free gifts of nature, such as land, forests and minerals but also of human capacity both mental and physical, and of all sorts of man-made aids to further production, such as technology, equipment, tools, machinery and buildings. There are following categories of factors of production: (i) All those free gifts of nature such as rivers, forests, minerals, etc. called by economists as land; (ii) All human resources, mental and physical, both inherited and acquired, which economists call labour; (iii) All those man-made aids to further production, such as tools, machinery, plant and equipment, including everything man-made, which is not consumed for its own sake but is used in the process of making other goods and services, which economists call capital. (iv) The entrepreneur is the one who takes risks by introducing both new products and new ways of making old products. He organises the other factors of production and directs them to produce various types of goods and/or services.

factor-price differentials
The term refers to the situation where a factor of production is having two separate prices, for example, the price of labour between capitalistic wage-based production and family-based production activities.

factor-price equalisation
The term is used for the export of products of the abundant factors which increases the demand for its services and makes them relatively less abundant. The import of products with large amounts of scarce factors makes those factors less scarce in the domestic market. Exports will raise the price of the abundant and cheap factor while imports will reduce the return to the scarce and expensive factor, leading to the equalisation of factor prices. This is also known as the Factor Price Equalisation Theorem. It was given by the Swedish economist Bertil Ohlin.

factor-price-frontier
It is a term given by Paul Samuelson and it relates to the negatively sloped trade-off between the wage rate and the rate of profit in growth theory. Cambridge School economists preferred the title, 'wage/rate of profit frontier, John Hicks referred to the same notion as the wage frontier. In conditions of equilibrium, the elasticity of the factor price frontier is equal to the ratio of the shares of output going to the two factors.

factor productivity

It refers to the value, at constant prices, of the output of a plant, a firm, or an industry per unit of factor input. The factor concerned may be a particular factor only, such as labour or land. Productivity is often used to mean labour productivity that is output per unit of labour employed, which may rise or fall for a variety of reasons.

factor reversals

The term refers to one of the assumptions of the Heckscher Ohlin approach to international trade, which states that the production functions for commodities are different in the ratios in which they use factors of production and that a commodity which uses a higher ratio of labour to capital than another will do so at all possible relative factor prices.

fair trade

The term is used to refer arguments for the use of protection to help domestic producers compete with imports whose suppliers have some cost advantage to come to equal terms of trade. There is no straightforward method by which aspects of comparative advantage, such as cheaper labour or cheaper power in one country than another, can be distinguished from 'unfair' cost advantages, such as exports subsidies.

finance

Broadly speaking, it means capital in monetary form that is the form of funds lent or borrowed, normally for capital purposes, through financial markets or institutions. In common parlance the term is applicable to fund, almost any source which is used to undertake any kind of expenditure.

financial assets

They are money and claims, as distinct from physical assets such as land, buildings machinery or equipment. Financial assets include money, securities giving a claim to receive money, such as bills, bonds, and shares giving indirect ownership of the physical and financial assets of companies.

financial deregulation

It refers to the removal or relaxation of regulations affecting the type of business firms may undertake, the type of firms permitted to deal in particular markets, or the terms on which dealing is allowed. Financial deregulation has been in vogue in recent years in many countries. Regulations which have been relaxed include controls on the interest rates at which banks can lend or borrow, controls on operations by banks outside their country of registration, etc. Besides, there have been relaxations in prime lending rates, etc.

financial economies

A large firm can offer better security and is, therefore, in a position to secure better and easier credit facilities both from its suppliers and its bankers.

financial futures

They are futures contracts in currencies or interest rates. Futures contracts, like forward contracts, commit both sides to a transaction on a future date at a pre-arranged price, but futures contracts can be traded only in future markets.

financial innovation

The term is used for changes in financial institutions, financial instruments, or business practices in the financial sector. Today's familiar practices, including the use of cheques, cash and credit cards, debit cards, electronic fund transfers, futures and options markets and derivatives were all innovations when they were introduced.

financial intermediary

It is a firm whose main function is to borrow money from one group of people and to lend it to another one. Financial intermediaries are able to operate profitably because of the economies of scale in collecting savings from many sources and making them available for large loans, and in handling information about large numbers of small debtors or the risks of lending to single large borrowers.

financial markets

These are the markets in which financial assets are traded. These include stock exchanges for trading company shares and government debt, the money market for trading short-term loans, the foreign exchange market for trading currencies, and a number of specialised markets trading financial derivatives.

financial planning

It is an act of deciding in advance the financial activities necessary for a firm of a nation to achieve its basic objectives.

financial ratios

They are ratios between various items in a company's accounts and the market value of its shares. These include the price-earnings (P/E) ratio, that is the ratio of the market price to earnings per share, and the price-dividend (P/D) ratio, that is the ratio of the market price to the latest dividend paid per share.

financial sector

It refers to the part of the economy concerned mainly with lending and borrowing, either long term or short term. This includes banks, non-bank financial intermediaries or savings and loan associations as well as merchant banks, insurance companies, mutual funds, pension funds, etc.

financial statement

It refers to the statement which is prepared by a business concern at the beginning of the year. This is an income statement or trading and profit and loss account (statement), which is prepared by the firm, company or enterprise in order to know the profit or loss earned/incurred during a specified period and position statement or balance sheet which is prepared by a business concern on a particular date in order to know its financial position.

financial year

The year used as an accounting period by any organisation. This can coincide with the calendar year, but frequently it does not. It is usually taken as 1st April to 31st March of the next year. In view of the need to prepare and audit accounts at the end of each financial year, it would be very inconvenient for the accountancy profession if all companies' financial years were to coincide.

firm

It is the basic unit of decision-making in a decentralised economy. The theory of the firm models on how a firm would behave given the assumptions about its objectives, which may include profit maximisation, avoidance of risks, and long-run growth. Many firms are run by sole traders, and others are partnerships, but larger firms are usually organised as companies.

first derivative

It is the rate at which the value of a function increases as its argument increases at any point, if this is defined. In a graph, the first derivative of a function is its slope.

fiscal drag

The tendency under progressive tax systems for the proportion of incomes collected in taxes to rise under inflation. This results from the fact that the threshold at which income tax becomes payable, and the thresholds for the application of higher tax rates are fixed in money terms.

fiscal illusion

It refers to a situation in which the benefits of particular government expenditure have been clearly identified by recipients but the costs are not, being widely dispersed over a period of time and population.

fiscal neutrality

It refers to the aim of devising a fiscal system which does not cause distortions in the economy. For example, if the tax system allows firms to write off some types of equipment faster than others with a similar actual life, this tends to divert investment into the types of equipment benefiting from more generous allowances. Fiscal neutrality aims to avoid this type of perverse incentive.

fiscal policy

It is an instrument of microeconomic policy. It has been very popular with modern governments to influence the size and components of national product, employment, industrial production, prices etc. J.M. Keynes used the term fiscal policy when referring to the influence of taxation on savings and of Government investment expenditure financed by loans from the public. Keynes looked at fiscal policy as one form of state action as a balancing factor. According to Arthur Smithies, the term 'fiscal policy' refers to a "policy under which a government uses its expenditure and revenue programmes to produce desirable effects and avoid undesirable effects on the national income, production and employment." Fiscal policy is the use of taxation and government spending to influence the economy. This may work through changing tax rates or the rules about liability to tax, or through changes in government spending on real goods and services or transfer payments.

fiscal tools

These are tools which can be classified in many ways: (i) One based on the division between automatic and discretionary measures; (ii) The automatic tools which are built-in stabilisers, government expenditure, taxes, insurance and welfare schemes, and agriculture support prices.

fiscalists

The term refers to those who believe that fiscal policy has been the most important means available to the government for influencing the level of economic activity.

fiscal stance

It is the tendency of the tax and spending policies embodied in a government's budget to expand or contract the economy. This involves comparisons with a normal budgetary position. It is argued that a government's fiscal stance cannot be judged purely from its actual spending and tax revenues, as these are affected by fluctuations in activity.

fiscal year

It refers to the year used for accounting purposes by a government. In the UK, for example, the fiscal year runs from 6 April to 5 April. The US budget year runs from 1 October to 30 September.

Fisher's ideal index

It refers to an index which has been based on a formula devised by the American economist Irving Fisher. It is intended to be a "true index", i.e. the Laspeyre's index giving an upper limit and the Paasche index a lower limit to this "true" index. It is in fact an index of the geometric means of the Laspeyre's and Paasche indices.

fixed assets

These are permanent investments, acquired for the purposes of use in the business over a long period and are not held for the purpose of making profit on resale. Examples are land, building, machinery, equipment, etc.

fixed capital

It is one that can be used in production over and over again. Machinery is fixed capital. There is gradually a wear and tear of the fixed capital as well. So after a certain time, which may be several years, fixed capital also has to be replaced.

fixed exchange rate

It is a system in which a country's exchange rate remains constant. Normally this means that the exchange rate between the country's currency and some other currency or basket of currencies remains within some small margin of fluctuation around a constant par value. A fixed exchange rate cannot be established by mere policy statements by the government or central bank issuing the currency.

fixed factors

They are factors of production which cannot be withdrawn from a firm even if its output falls. Factors may be fixed because their use is essential if a firm is to stay in business at all.

fixed-interest security

It is a security whose return is fixed, up to some redemption date or indefinitely. The fixed amounts may be stated in money terms, or indexed to some measure of the price level.

fixed investment

It is the investment in durable capital equipment, which is expected to last for a long period, and is written off over several years. This is distinct from investment in stocks and work in progress, which are goods expected to be used up quickly, and not depreciated at all.

fixed throttle policy

It refers to a policy which is associated with the name of professor Milton Friedman of steadily increasing the money supply by three to five per cent per annum so as to support non-inflationary economic growth.

floating currencies

These are currencies, whose value is set by the free movement of supply and demand.

f.o.b. (free on board)

The term is used for goods shipped where the price is not including shipping or insurance charges. An f.o.b. quotation implies that the exporter will deliver the goods free on board a ship in accordance with the contract at the port named; he pays all expenses up to that point. F.o.b. includes costs of production and transport to the port of embarkation, but does not include the costs of freight and insurance in getting them to their foreign destination. Free on board is contrasted with cost, insurance and freight (cif), the value of goods on arrival at a foreign port, which includes freight and insurance.

Food and Agriculture Organisation (FAO)

It is an agency of the United Nations (UN), responsible for problems of agricultural production and nutrition. It conducts research, provides advice, and promotes education and training in productive techni- ques in agriculture and allied activities like fishing and forestry, in the distribution of their products, and in nutritional standards.

food stamps

These are documents issued to poor families in the US to entitle them to obtain cut-foodstuffs free or at reduced prices. This is a working example of the use of vouchers, a method of ensuring the use of public assistance for an approved purpose. These documents help in the provision of basic foodstuffs to poor people.

food subsidies

These denote subsidies to the sale of foodstuffs, which allow the price paid by the consumer to be below the amount received by the vendor. Food subsidies have been adopted in various countries. They virtually increase the value of money of farmers, and decrease the cost of living for the poorest members of society, who spend the largest share of their incomes on food.

footloose industry

The term is used for an industry where there are a few advantage in any particular location, so that small differences in cost can lead to large shifts in location. This is distinct from extractive industries tied to particular inputs, services industries that need to be close to their markets, and industries with large sunk costs.

forced saving

It refers to a situation when consumers are prevented from spending a part of their income on consumption. This occurs in a period of rising prices accompanied by a corresponding rise in personal incomes.

forecasting

It is the production of estimates of future economic events. This includes events which have already occurred, but the official version of the facts has not yet been published. Economic forecasters rely on some standard techniques such as the use of econometric models based on published statistics of past events.

foreclosure

It can be defined as taking over by a lender of a mortgaged property, because of failure by the borrower to comply with the conditions of the mortgage, including failure to make interest and amortisation payments by the due dates. Foreclosure is usually only resorted to by lenders when considerable arrears have arisen, and normally requires authorisation by a court.

foreign direct investment (FDI)

It is the acquisition by residents of a country of real assets abroad. This may be done by remitting money abroad to be spent on acquiring land, constructing buildings, offices, hotels, etc. mines, or machinery, or buying an existing foreign business. Inward foreign direct investment is acquisition by non-residents of real assets within a country. Once a country has real assets abroad, if these make profits which are ploughed back into expanding enterprises, these are shown in the balance of payments as receipts on current account balanced by an outflow on capital account.

foreign exchange reserves

They are liquid assets held by a country's government or central bank, for the purpose of intervening in the foreign exchange market. These include gold or convertible foreign currencies, e.g. US dollars for countries other than the United States, or yen for countries other than Japan, and government securities denominated in these currencies. Foreign exchange reserves can also include balances with international institutions, notably the International Monetary Fund (IMF) and World Bank.

foreign investment

The acquisition by residents of a country of assets abroad. These assets may be real, in the case of foreign direct investment, or financial, in the case of acquisition of foreign securities or bank deposits. Foreign investment may be made by the state or the private sector, and foreign securities required may constitute private or government debt.

forex markets

These are foreign exchange markets including forward foreign exchange markets.

forward contract

It refers to a contract in which a price is agreed for commodities, securities or currencies to be delivered at a future date. A forward contract is made with an identified counter-party, and the individual or firm entering into a forward contract may be to the risk that the counter-party may fail to carry out their side of the bargain.

forward exchange

It refers to an operation in exchange whereby a rate is fixed in advance for the purchase and sale of one currency in terms of another. It is in addition to a 'spot' rate. Exchange for current exchange transactions is the rate at which forward exchanges are carried on and are called Forward Rates of Exchange.

forward integration

It is the inclusion of 'downstream' activities in the same firm which uses or distributes the products of an 'upstream' activity. An example of this is the ownership of petrol pumps or gas filling stations by oil companies. Forward integration is usually adopted to improve efficiency by better co-ordination of the different levels of production.

forward market

It is a market in which forward contracts are entered into, that is contracts for the delivery of commodities, securities or currencies at some future date.

forward price

It is the price at which commodities, securities, or currencies are to be delivered in a forward contract. The forward price and the spot price, that is the price for immediate delivery, may be different and the same commodity may have different forward prices for delivery at different dates.

franchise

It refers to the system by which independent firms are authorised to use a common business system. This may include the use of a brand name, designs, patents and operating systems teaching skills and provision of equipment, training, capital or credit by the franchiser. This system gives the advantages of incentive for the operating firms and economies of scale in research, development, and advertising for the franchiser.

free enterprise

It can be defined as an economy in which the initiative for production and consumption decisions is with individuals, firms and companies. This is contrasted with a planned economy in which firms and individuals have to conform to rules set by the government, and the companies literally owe their very existence to laws.

free entry

It is the absence of any obstacle to new entrants to a market. Barriers to entry may be legal or economic. Legal barriers include monopoly rights for an incumbent, exclusive possession of necessary patent rights by an incumbent, or licensing of entrants. Economic barriers include difficulty in getting raw materials, low margins of profit, etc.

free exit

It means absence of obstacles to leaving a market. Difficulties over exit may be economic or legal. The main economic barrier to exit is comprised of sunk costs, which cannot be recovered by leaving a market. Thus, the firms will only stay in lines of business which they would not enter if they were not already engaged in them, given what they now know. Legal barriers include employment protection laws and redundancy costs that keep workers in existing jobs who the employers would not now take on.

free good

It is a good which is not scarce, so that its availability is not an effective constraint on economic activity. A good is not a free good merely because its market price is zero, but it may in fact be scarce, be underpriced by the market because of a lack of enforceable property rights over it. A really free good has a shadow price of zero.

freehold

It refers to land or property held for use by the owner without obligation to any landlord. Freehold is in contrast with leasehold, where the owner of land is entitled to ground rents and reversion of the property at the end of the lease, and may be entitled to impose restrictions on the use of the property.

free lunch

It is a policy or combination of policies which produces advantages without any offsetting disadvantages. There is an adage that "there is no such thing as a free lunch". Any policy normally has some adverse side effects. For example, tariffs benefit some domestic firms but bring a disadvantage to consumers. It may be possible to find a combination of policies.

free market

It refers to a market in which people buy and sell voluntarily, without legal compulsion. Neither the quantities traded nor the prices at which trade takes place are subject to control by third parties. However, the participants have to conform to laws concerning health and safety, weights and measures, labelling requirements, and the like. The essential point about these rules, however, is that they lay down what traders must not do, e.g. misrepresenting the weight or quality of their product.

free market economy

It is a system of economy where all major economic decisions such as what to produce, how to produce, how much to produce, when to produce are taken by the impersonal market forces of demand and supply and market mechanism. In a free market economy majority of economic activities are organised through free markets, in which the parties choose the quantities and prices traded without central direction. This is distinct from a centrally planned economy in which a substantial majority of economic activities are carried on through central directions to people and firms as to what they must buy and sell, and at what prices. Very few economies are either totally free-market-based or centrally planned; most have substantial elements of each.

free port

It is a seaport or airport where national tariffs are not levied. This is intended to encourage inward trade, as goods can be shipped in and out without having funds tied up in tariff payments and free from the administrative expenses involved in claiming tariff drawbacks when goods are re-exported.

free rider

It refers to a person or organisation who/ which benefits from a public good, but neither provides nor contributes to the cost of collective provision. Thus, they ride free on the efforts of others. The free-rider problem means that many public goods are underprovided, or have to be provided by governments which can collect taxes to pay for them.

free trade

It is a policy of unrestricted foreign trade, with no tariffs or subsidies on imports or exports, and no quotas or other trade restrictions. Free trade regime applies to most goods, though there may be exceptions, for example, agricultural goods or military equipment. It has usually been interpreted as applying only to trade in goods and not in services, but a similar policy is now applied to trade in services. In free trade, no effort is made to protect the domestic industries from foreign competition.

free-trade agreement

It is a treaty between a group of countries concerning setting up a free-trade area. Such a treaty normally contains exceptions for particular products, and transitional arrangement for the early years of the agreement.

free-trade area

The term is used for a group of countries with free trade between them, but retaining independent tariffs systems on trade with non-members. There are several free-trade areas, for example, the South Asian Free Trade Area (SAFTA) and the North American Free Trade Agreement (NAFTA). The free-trade arrangements must apply to a substantial proportion of trade, but some sectors such as agricultural products or defence equipment may be exempted from the free-trade provisions.

free-trade zone

It is an area of a country where national tariffs are not applied. This is intended to encourage industries which rely largely on producing goods for export using large quantities of imported inputs. Having the inputs duty-free saves interest costs or having money tied up by tariffs, and avoids the administrative expense of claiming tariffs drawbacks on the exports.

frequency distribution

It is a function describing the distribution of random drawings of a variable. If the variable, a, can take values over a continuous range from a minimum or a maximum of b, the frequency distribution will be f(a). The integral of f(a) from x to b, must be 1.

frictional unemployment

The term can be defined as the unemployment that would exist due to the reason that as people change jobs because some sectors of the economy grow and others contract, it is not practicable to dovetail precisely, leaving old jobs and starting new ones. At times of full employment, frictional unemployment may form an appreciable portion of total unemployment. Under conditions of high unemployment its, contribution is almost negligible, except in sectors which are facing localised labour shortages.

fringe benefits

These are benefits, other than pay, bonuses, and pensions, provided for employees by their employers. Such benefits may include company cars, sports facilities, subsidised canteen facilities, health care or insurance, free or subsidised accommodation or cheap mortgages. Employers provide fringe benefits to improve the health, morale and thus the performance at work of their employees; to strengthen loyalty to the firm; and to reduce their own and their employees' joint tax liabilities.

front-end charge

It is an initial fee made by the management of an investment or unit trust, or life insurance policy. This is calculated as a percentage of the initial sum invested, and is distinct from and in addition to any annual management fee based on the value of the assets managed.

full cost pricing

It refers to the practice of setting prices so as to cover what average cost would be at a normal rate of production, plus a conventional mark-up. When output is low, actual average costs exceed those when output is normal, as fixed costs have to be spread over a lower output level.

full employment

It is a situation when every worker available for employment has a job. It is very unlikely that this can ever be achieved, even when there is general excess demand in labour markets. Some forms of unemployment probably cannot be reduced to zero. These include frictional unemployment, which is a situation when people leaving jobs in declining sectors of the economy have not yet obtained a job in the expanding sectors.

full employment budget

It is the government's budget as it would be if the rates and rules for taxes and expenditure stayed the same, while national income was at full employment level. If the actual level of national income is lower than this, tax receipts tend to be lower and government spending on unemployment and other means-tested benefits may be higher than with full employment.

function

It is a relation between two or more variables. If b is a function of a, written b = f(a), when the value of the agreement a is known, the function tells us how to find the value of b. If b is a single-valued function of a, for each value of a there is only one value of b. In the linear function b= xa+y, for example, or the quadratic functions, however, there may be more than one value of b for any given a, or there may be no real values of b.

functional income distribution

It is the distribution of income between the owners of the various factors of production. Wages accrue to labour, rent to landlords, and interest, dividends, and retained profits to capital of companies. The incomes of the self-employed pose a problem for functional income distribution, as they often contain elements of the rewards of labour, land, capital, and entrepreneurship; disentangling these is a matter of convention.

fund flow statement

It is a statement of sources and application of funds - a technical device designed to analyse the changes in the financial condition of a business enterprise between two dates.

fundamental disequilibrium

It is the condition of the balance of payments under which the original rules of the International Monetary Fund (IMF) allowed countries to devalue their currencies. No formal definition of fundamental disequilibrium was ever produced, but it was widely assumed that it meant severe balance-of-payments problems.

funding

It refers to the conversion of government debt from short-term forms, or bills, to long-term forms, or bonds. Some economists regard it as a form of monetary policy, since bills are more liquid than bonds, and are a part of the bank's liquid reserves, whereas bonds are not. The monetary authorities may sell long-term secu- rities to the public, thus raising the long-term rate of interest. They may then use the funds so acquired to reduce the supply of short-term securities, which is known as funding.

futures contract

It is a contract to buy or sell a good, share or currency on a future date, at a price decided when the contract is made. A futures contract entails for both parties the right as well as the obligation to trade. It is in contrast with an option, which confers only the right to trade on one party and only the obligation on other. Futures contracts can be used to reduce risk by traders who have to hold a lot of shares or some goods and want protection against a low price, or who know they are going to have to buy and want protection against a high price.

futures market

It refers to a market organisation through which futures contracts are traded. These contracts commit both parties to buy and sell shares, commodities, or currencies on a future date at price fixed when the contract is made. To ensure that both parties will be able to carry out their side of the bargain, the actual contracts are entered into by both sides (i.e., buyer and seller) and the market organisation which requires both parties to make margin deposits with it of a given percentage of the market of a contract.

G

gains from trade

The term is used for the improvement in welfare possible as a result of countries trading with one another, as compared with having autarkic economies. Gains from trade arise from two principal sources: (i) differences, in proportions of labour of various types, and (ii) stocks of capital.

galloping inflation

It is the name given to rapid growing inflation, such as that which was characterised by Germany and several other European countries just after World War II when prices rose so rapidly that money quickly lost its value and people resorted to the system of barter. In recent years, the increase in the price of petroleum and allied products by oil producing countries has caused a galloping inflation round the world.

gambling

It means taking on bets at less than actually fair odds. On the assumption that the gambler understands the odds, one of the possible reasons for being willing to gamble: is that the gambler may have a non-concave utility function, with marginal utility increasing over some range of incomes.

game theory

It is the modelling of economic decisions by games whose outcome depends on the decisions taken by two or more agents - each having to make decisions without information on what choices the others are making. Game theory distinguishes between one-off games and repeated games, where reputation established through earlier games affects the conduct of subsequent ones.

gamma stocks

The term is used for shares of relative small companies, in which trade on the London Stock Exchange was not very frequent. This was part of a system of classification of shares which has now become redundant.

gazumping

It is the practice of raising the price of a home after accepting a deposit from a prospective buyer, who is told by the real estate agent to pay the increase or miss out on the sale. A person may engage a solicitor, arrange finance and incur expenses such as a value's fee. The practice becomes more common when the housing market has been buoyant and buyers possess little resistance against smart operators.

GDP deflator

It refers to a price index used to assess whether there has been a real rise or fall in gross domestic product (GDP) from one financial year to another. GDP at current prices is divided by the GDP deflator to obtain an index of GDP at base-year prices.

gearing

It is the ratio of a country to its equity. Gearing or leverage as called in the US, is the ratio of a country's debt to the part of its capital owned by shareholders. High gearing of leverage means high reliance on debt financing.

general agreement on tariffs and trade (GATT)

It was an agency of the United Nations (UN), based in Geneva (founded in 1948) to promote international trade. By 1995, it had over 100 members, including most leading trading countries. GATT successfully concluded several rounds of multilateral negotiations to reduce world tariffs, but was not able to prevent the spread of non-tariffs barriers to trade. It has now been replaced by World Trade Organisation (WTO).

general agreement on trade in services (GATS)

It is an international agreement on trade in services which was arrived at in 1994 as a part of the Uruguay Round of Negotiations under the General Agreement of Tariffs and Trade (GATT). The GATS was very limited in scope and was a long way from providing for world-wide market access and 'national', i.e. non-discriminatory treatment for foreign providers of services.

general agreement to borrow

It refers to an agreement made in 1962 by the Group of Ten (G10) countries to extend international credit. The agreement is a misnomer, as the countries actually agreed to lend via the International Monetary Fund (IMF).

general equilibrium

It denotes the approach in economics of considering all markets in an economy simultaneously. For general equilibrium, all markets must be in equilibrium, and no change of actions in any market must take place. General equilibrium is distinguished from the partial equilibrium approach, in which some part of the economy is considered, neglecting what is happening in other markets.

general human capital

The term refers to skills and qualifications of value in a wide range of occupations. This clearly applies to general skills such as literacy and numeracy. General human capital is distinct from the forms of human capital, such as medical, legal or technical skills or qualifications, which are of value only in particular occupations.

generalised system of preferences (GSP)

It is an agreement by members of GATT (now the World Trade Organisation, WTO) to grant market access to the exports of developing countries subject to preferentially lower tariffs than the normal level. GSP agreements were made by some European countries and Japan in 1971-72, by the US in 1976.

Giffen's paradox

It is a concept that states that there are certain goods for which the negative income effect is so strong that it can outweigh the positive substitution effect. The individual consumers will buy less of a good if its price falls, and more if it rises.

Giffen good

It is a good for which quantity demanded falls when its price falls. This can in theory occur when: a Giffen good must be interior and also have poor substitutes. A fall in the price of a good increases real purchasing power. In case the good is interior the income effect of this rise in real income is negative. The substitution effect of a price fall cannot be negative, but if the good has poor substitutes, the positive substitution effect is small.

gift tax

It is defined as a tax on gifts between the living or inter vivos. It is in contrast with a tax on transfers, of wealth by inheritance. A gift tax is designed to counter the loss of revenue from inheritance taxes through people transferring their wealth to their relations or friends while still alive.

gild (or guild)

It is an association established during the Middle Ages to protect the interest of members of the same craft and to ensure that new members reached a certain standard of competence before being admitted as full members.

gilt-edged security

The term refers to a fixed-interest security issued by the government. Gilts may irredeemable consoles; long dated, with 15 years or more in maturity; medium-dated, with 5 to 15 years in maturity; or short-dated, with under 5 years for maturity. Gilt-edged securities are considered extremely safe from risk of default.

Gini coefficient

It is a statistical measure of inequality. If b, is the income of individual x, for example, the Gini coefficient is half the expected absolute difference in the incomes of any two individuals x and y chosen at random, as a proportion of the mean income.

Glass-Steagall act

It refers to a US law passed in 1933 prohibiting banks from acting both as lenders and as investors in companies. This Act forbids universal banking in the US, whereas such banking is common in other countries including Germany.

globalisation

It can be defined as the process by which the whole world becomes as single market. It means that goods and services, capital, and labour are traded on a worldwide basis, and information and the results of research flow readily between countries. The rise of cheap sea transport and the telecommunication contributed to the process of globalisation. Cheap air travel, mobile phones, the telephone, and the computer, together with the rising importance of multinational companies and general relaxation of controls on trade and international investment, have strengthened the process.

global maximum

It refers to a value of a function as high as or higher than that for any other values of its arguments. The sufficient condition for a maximum of function of a single argument, in terms of a zero first and negative second derivative, depicts only that the function takes local maximum.

gold

It is a precious metal, widely used both as a form of money and for jewellery and other ornamental purposes. Gold was used in these other ways before its use as money and the invention of coinage. Gold coinage has been in general circulation since long. The monetary use of gold is now confined to holdings of gold bullion by central banks as a part of their foreign exchange reserves.

gold account

It is one of the accounts in the balance of payments of company. Non-monetary gold account items refer to while the gold account deals with monetary gold.

golden handshake

It is a provision of an executive's contract giving entitlement to a large bonus on leaving a firm's employment before retirement.

golden parachute

It refers to a financial compensation package which is designed and negotiated threat of displacement or takeover. If, in adverse circumstances, the top executive gets displaced or he/she finds it necessary to go, the individual descends to earth with the dignity of his golden parachute.

golden rule

It depends on the rule that an economy can maximise its consumption if the rate of growth is equal to the marginal product of capital. Suppose that on steady-state growth the capital-output ratio is s; with a growth rate of r, a proportion sr of output must be invested.

gold points

The term is used for the values of exchange rates under the gold standard at which it becomes profitable to ship from one country to another. For example, if the dollar rose relative to the pound sterling (£), a firm holding sterling with a dollar payment to make will buy gold from the Bank of England, ship it to New York, and sell it to the Federal Reserve Bank of dollars.

gold standard

It refers to the following:
1. A system for fixing exchange rates by the central bank or government of each country making its currency freely convertible into gold at a fixed price. Under this system, the par value of exchange rates is set by the amount of each currency that can be obtained for a given quantity of gold.
2. A monometallic standard in which the value of the monetary unit is fixed in terms of specified weight and purity. As pointed out by Robertson, "Gold standard is a state of affairs in which a country keeps the value of a defined weight of gold at an equality with one another."

gold sterilisation

The term describes a situation where gold increases in the balance sheet of the central bank, and it discounts securities to leave the total volume of member-bank reserves unchanged, considering that the foreigners hold their funds in the form of deposits with the commercial banks. This policy requires no stabilisation fund and therefore, is termed as "gold sterilisation".

Gompertz s-curve

It is a curve that describes the process of economic growth. In the early stages, growth is slow. Once the process gets underway, it becomes faster and faster like all geometric growths, but it ultimately slows down. Finally, the curve asymptote and flattens out.

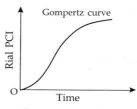

Gompertz s-curve

goods

1. Things people prefer more of rather than less. Thus, income, leisure, safety, security, profits, etc. are goods, while pollution, risk, losses, etc. are bads.
2. Economic assets taking a tangible physical form, such as houses, or clothes. These are contrasted with services, such as transport,

which cannot be stored, or banking, insurance, etc. which have no physical embodiment.

Goodhart's law
It is the observation by professor Charles Goodhart that when an empirical regularly starts to be exploited as a basis for economic policy, it is liable to break down.

goodwill
1. In economics, it is an intangible asset representing that a business is worth more than its tangible assets. This is usually due to the acquired skill, know-how and trade contracts of its staff. Goodwill is not normally included as an asset in balance sheets.
2. In business, it is the probability that the old customers will resort the old place. It is the attractive force, which brings in customers. Goodwill is the prosperous business beyond the intrinsic value of net assets.

gosplan
It is a Russian term used for the State Planning Commission in the USSR. It has been responsible for working out production plans passing them on the relevant organisations for execution.

Gossen's laws
These are laws developed by Hermann Heinrich Gossen. The 1st law states that the pleasure obtained from each additional amount consumed of the same commodity diminishes until satiety is reached. The 2nd law holds that once a person has spent his entire income, he will have maximised his total pleasure from it in case the pleasure or satisfaction gained from the last item of each commodity bought is the same for each commodity. The 3rd law denotes that a commodity has a subjective value, and the subjective value of each additional unit owned diminishes and eventually reaches zero.

government debt
It is debt owed by the government at any level. It is necessary to net out any debt owed by one level of government to another, such as central government debt held as financial reserves by local authorities. Government debt may be measured gross or net, when some firms or individuals are indebted to the government, e.g. through local authority mortgages.

government expenditure
It refers to spending by government at any level. It is necessary to net out payments by one level of government to another, for example, central government grants to local authorities. Government expenditure is comprised of spending on employment in state services such as administration, defence and education.

gradualist monetarism
It is the policy of stabilising inflation by gradually decreasing the growth rate of the money supply until it approaches the real growth rate of the economy. This is distinct from the rational view that with a pre-announced and credible commitment to lower the growth rate of money rapidly, stable prices could be achieved by means of a 'short sharp shock', with little delay and at no greater cost in unemployment than is possible by a gradual monetary squeeze.

grant-in-aid
It is a government grant to state or local government. These grants are used to ensure that public services can be maintained in poorer states or times of depression.

gratuity
It is a kind of retirement benefit, viz. a payment which is intended to help the workers after their retirement, whether the retirement is the result of superannuation, of some physical disability or under voluntary retirement scheme (VRS).

great depression
It refers to the worst depression in living memory. At present, this position is still conceded to the world depression in the early 1930s, though the global financial crisis of 2008-09 also shook the world. The great depression is believed to have contributed to the rise of Hitler to power in Germany and thus to the Second World War.

greenfield development
It denotes a factory erected on a previously undeveloped site, as contrasted with extending or converting an existing plant. Greenfield development allows firms to avoid the congestion and pollution problems of the areas around many old sites.

green pound

It refers to the exchange rate for the pound sterling which is used for converting agricultural prices agreed under the Common Agricultural Policy (CAP) in terms of the European unit of account into domestic prices.

Gresham's law

The Chancellor of the Exchequer under Elizabeth I, Sir Thomas Gresham enquired about debased coins in 1558 and came to the conclusion that "bad money drives out good money". This has come to be known as Gresham's Law. Alfred Marshall defined this law thus, "Whenever the specific value of a certain class of coins exceeds their currency value, the coins will begin to go into the melting pot or be exported." Money refers to debased, clipped, or worn out legal tender such as coins and paper notes. Thus, when fullbodied and debased coins circulate together, people have a tendency to hoard the good any try to pass on the bad ones as medium of exhange. They may even melt the full-bodied coins for bullion in order to export it or use it for jewellery. This actually happened in some countries which were on silver or gold standard.

gross domestic product (GDP)

It is one of the main measures of economic activity. Gross implies that it is calculated without subtracting any allowance for capital consumption; domestic measures activities located in the country regardless of their ownership.

gross fixed investment

It is the total amount spent on fixed investment, before making any deduction for depreciation of the existing capital stock. This is different from net fixed investment, which is gross fixed investment minus an estimate of capital consumption.

gross national product (GNP)

It is a major measure of national economic activity. Gross indicates that it is measured without subtracting any allowance for capital consumption, while national implies that it includes residents' incomes from economic activities carried on abroad as well as at home, and excludes incomes produced at home but belonging to non-residents.

gross

It is an indication that something which could have been subtracted, has not been subtracted. The word appears in economics in a variety of contexts: (i) The gross weight of a product includes packaging; net weight is gross weight minus the weight of any packaging. (ii) Gross investment is total investment spending, before making any deduction for capital consumption, which is subtracted to get net investment.

group of seven (G7)

It is an informal group of leading industrial countries, whose leaders meet periodically to discuss economic problems and policies. The group includes members, namely Canada, France, Germany, Italy, Japan, the United Kingdom, and the United States.

growth rate

It is the proportional or percentage rate of increase of any economic variable over a unit period, normally a year. If a variable measured over discrete time intervals grows from 1 to 1 + a, this is a proportional growth rate of a, or a percentage growth rate of 100a.

guarantee

It is a promise that if a good is unsatisfactory it will be repaired or replaced, or that if a loan is not repaid the guarantor will repay it. Some guarantees are legally enforceable.

H

hammer price
It refers to a price which is calculated according to the rules of the UK stock exchange and many other countries. It represents the market value of a security at the time of the default of a member firm.

hard currency
It refers to the following:
1. A currency which is convertible into other currencies, and whose price in terms of other currencies is expected to remain stable or rise. This is in contrast with a soft currency, which is not convertible into other currencies.
2. A currency which is having a continuing high level of demand, relative to supply in the market for foreign exchange. Currencies of stable industrialised nations are generally included in this category while those of underdeveloped countries and of the Eastern Bloc are not.

hard landing
It refers to the difficulty of ending a period of excess demand and inflation without starting recessionary trends. It is difficult to judge exactly how much fiscal and monetary restraint is needed to stabilise effective demand t a high level and inflation at a low level.

hard loan
It is a loan on normal market terms relating to interest, including a risk premium appropriate to the borrower's credit rating, the maturity date, the currency in which interest is paid, and when repayments are due. This is opposite to soft loan, which is generally given at a concessional rate of interest.

harmonisation
It is the idea that the taxes and regulatory rules in countries belonging to economic blocs should not diverge too widely. If capital and labour were perfectly mobile between countries, the members of common markets would have to adopt identical tax and regulatory regimes.

Harrod-Domar Model
The term refers to the models given by the two economists Ray F. Harrod and E.D. Domar - the two pioneers in the field of model. Economic growth and growth theory have been deeply affected by their contribution. Domar discovered that investment would have to rise quickly enough to absorb all the savings which rising incomes made variable. This gave him the equation: $\Delta L/I = Sx$. which states that the rate of growth of investment $(\Delta L/I)$ must for all employment, be equal to the proportion of income saved S, multiplied by the capital output ratio, x.

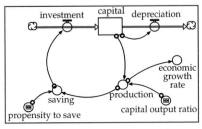

Harrod-Domar model

Hayek's theory
Hayek takes the help of the concepts of natural and money rates of interest to explain his theory of business cycles. In this theory, the interest rate which is the result of changes in the savings is known as the money rate of interest, while the natural rate of interest is the marginal productivity of capital.

hedging
1. A transaction that limits the risk associated with market price fluctuations for a particular investment position. A hedge is accomplished by taking offsetting positions in the ownership of an asset or security through use of derivatives such as buying or selling futures contract or an option to cover risk exposure in the cash market.
2. Activities designed to reduce the risks imposed by other activities. If a business has to hold stocks of a commodity, it runs a risk of making losses if the price falls. This loss can be avoided by hedging, which involves selling the good forward, that is for delivery at an agreed price on a future date, or by selling in the futures market.

heteroscedasticity
It means having different variances. Data are heteroscedastic if their variations are not consistent with being random drawings from

the same population. This is distinct from homoscedasticity, where the data appear consistent with being random drawings from the same distribution.

heterotheticity
It is the property of a family of curves, that they differ in shape as well as scale. The isoquants for an industry where larger firms find it economical to use more capital-intensive techniques than smaller firms must be heterothetic.

Hicks Hansen diagram
This is a diagram that shows that the economy is in equilibrium with the rate of the interest of and a level of income of Y. The IS curve shows all those combinations of the rate of interest and the rate of income at which savings and investment would be equal and for the LM curve we can discover what the transaction demand for money is. We then deduct this from the total amount of money available. This tells us what level of the rate of interest has to be if all this money is to be held for speculative purposes.

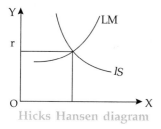

Hicks Hansen diagram

Hicks' neutral technical progress
It is the technical progress where, with any given factor proportions, the average and marginal products of all factors increase in the same proportion.

high-powered money
It refers to money of forms that qualify it to be used as commercial bank reserve assets. Such money is 'high-powered' in the sense that if the commercial banking system maintains a reserve ratio of a, an additional £1b of high-powered money allows total deposits to extend by £(1a)b.

high-tech
It is modern jargon for processes involving the use of advanced technology. High-tech is mainly associated with a wide range of industries, including aeronautics, atomic energy, chemicals and pharmaceuticals, computers, cell phones, military equipment, digital TVs, cameras, telecommunications, etc.

hire purchase (HP)
It refers to the following:
1. The system by which goods are made available to the buyer for immediate use, but payment is made by instalments. HP may or may not require some downpayment. Instalments are spread over an agreed period, and until the final instalment is paid the goods remain the property of the seller, who can reclaim them if payments are in default.
2. A procedure which is used for purchasing goods under which the purchaser pays a deposit on receipt of the goods followed by a number of instalments until the debt gets cleared. The goods do not become the property of the purchaser until the last instalment has been paid. In other words, we can say that, it is a system in which money is paid for goods by means of periodical instalments with the intention of ultimate purchase.

histogram
It is a diagram representing the distribution of a variable, where information is about discrete ranges of values. Areas in the diagram are proportional to the number of observations in each interval.

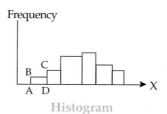

Histogram

historical cost
It is the system of accounting in which assets are valued and depreciation allowances are calculated for terms using the prices paid for assets when they were first purchased, acquired or built. The great merit of this system is that it uses prices based on actual market transactions. Any other method of accounting for assets involves using valuations which are not based on market.

hoarding
It refers to the act of holding money. If the desire to hoard increases the result will be that money incomes will fall. Conversely, if there occurs a fall in the desire to hold money, incomes will rise.

holding company
It is a company which is having control over a number of other companies, through ownership of a sufficient proportion of the latter's common stock. A holding company is concerned with control over the financial, managerial or marketing functions of its subsidiaries, and thus performs more of a supervisory role.

homotheticity
It is the property of a family of curves that their shapes are all the same. If a family of indifference curves or isoquants f(a,b) is homeostatic, the gradient db/da at any point depends only on the ratio of b to a and not on their absolute size.

Hoover's theory
This theory, given by Hoover, suggests an alternative to Weber's theory. According to Hoover, transport costs do not increase in strict proportion to distance. The unit cost of transporting goods actually decreases with distance, partly due to economies arising out of greater distance covered and partly due to the use of more efficient forms of transport, e.g. railways instead of roadways, water transport instead of rail transport. Hoover also introduces another variable, the trans-shipment town, where goods and materials are transferred from one mode of transport to another mode (e.g. from rail to sea). Thus, he also took into account the off-loading and on-loading costs at trans-shipment points. Hoover came to the conclusion that, given the declining marginal cost of transportation per unit of distance and the trans-shipment costs, the most favourable location for the firm can be near to either the market for finished goods or the market for input. He, thus, negates Weber's theory of locational triangle, except where the trans-shipment point lies inside the Weberain triangle.

horizontal equity
It is the view that people in similar circumstances should be treated equally and that differences in needs should be reflected by differences in treatment. Applying this concept to the tax system, for example, it would appear unfair to tax two similar workers at different rates.

horizontal integration
It means combining two or more enterprises at the same stage of production. This may allow cost savings, if there are economies of scale in any of the processes involved, or if it is possible to avoid duplication of effort, for example, in raising loan, hiring labour or in research and development.

horizontal merger
It refers to a take-over bid whose acceptance is opposed by the directors of a company. A bid be opposed because the directors feel that the company is better off independent, largely motivated by concern for their own job security, or because they expect a higher offer either from the present or a rival bidder.

hot money
It denotes the following:
1. Money in bank balances or liquid securities which is liable to rapid removal to other countries if the holders suspect that the currency will depreciate. An inflow of hot money makes a country's balance of payments situation look satisfactory.
2. Money which gets transferred rapidly from one financial centre to another to take advantage of differences in short-term interest rates or to escape the financial risks of devaluation.

households
It can be defined as all the people who live under one roof and who take, or are subject to others taking for them joint financial decisions.

Hume's law
Hume was the first economist to suggest the connection between exports and imports. He developed the price-specific mechanism to show how an increase in exports would lead to an increase in imports, the mechanism by which his law operated was not prices but changes in income.

hundis
Hundis are indigenous negotiable instruments written in a vernacular language. These are mostly like bills of exchange in form and substance. Sometimes these are like promissory notes.

hyperinflation

The term denotes very rapid inflation. It is sometimes reckoned to set in when price increases exceed 50 per cent per month. Such rapid inflation not just makes money useless as a store of value, but also seriously affects its use as a medium of exchange.

hysteresis

It means dependence of the equilibrium position of a system on what happens during the process of dynamic adjustment. It damages the traditional distinction between comparative statics and dynamics. Comparative statics considers the new equilibrium of the economy after a change in some exogenous variables.

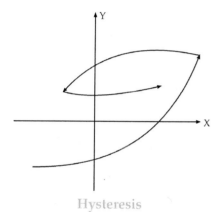

Hysteresis

I

idiosyncratic risk
It is a type of risk which affects each individual case largely independent of others. This could apply to the risk of an individual dying, of a building/house catching fire, or due to an accident, during any period.

idle balances
The term refers to money that has been withdrawn from circulation and held as a store of wealth. Keynes identified it as speculative demand for money. He argued that money would be idle as to the future price of financial assets.

illiquidity
It refers to the following:
1. The property of not being easily turned into money. Some assets are illiquid because there are no markets where they can easily be traded, e.g. unsecured loans to bank customers. Other assets are illiquid because while they can be traded, there is no demand for them.
2. The property of having illiquid assets. A business may have problems over meeting its obligations because, although it believes itself to be solvent, its assets are not liquid. If its own view of its solvency were shared by credit institutions it would be able to obtain liquidity on credit, but the information which leads it to feel solvent may not reach others easily.
3. Lack of liquidity in a specific asset, or in a portfolio of assets held by a transactor. Being the obverse of liquidity, the condition has been always a relative one.

immiserising growth
It refers to the possible but improbable case where an increase in economic output within a country results via repercussions through trade to a situation where its economic welfare gets diminished. The term denotes circumstances in which foreign demand has been price inelastic, and yet there is a high marginal propensity to import. The growth in real output is able to induce a demand for more imports.

immobile factors
They are factors which do not move ready between sectors, regions, or countries when relative rewards or job opportunities get changed. Immobility of labour between occupations may be due to lack of qualifications, or absence of adequate information on job opportunities.

immobility
The term is used in context of factors of production which cannot easily be, moved either (i) from one location to another, or (ii) from one type of employment to another.

imperfect competition
It is an important market category wherein individual firms exercise control over the price, to a small or large extent, depending upon the degree of imperfection present in a case. Control over price of a product by a firm and so the existence of imperfect competition can be caused either by the absence of good number of firms or by the product differentiation. Imperfect competition has several sub-categories: (i) Monopolistic competition where a large number of firms produce somewhat different products which are close substitutes of each other; (ii) Oligopoly, under which there is competition among the few firms producing homogeneous or identical products.

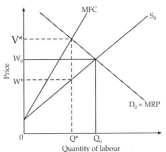

Imperfect competition

imperialism
According to Marxist or socialist thought, it refers to a foreign policy which seeks political and economic control over backward areas to guarantee the home country an outlet for idle savings and surplus manufactured goods in exchange for important raw materials in adequate quantities.

implicit contract
It is a situation when people or firms expect to have continuing dealings with one another, and so need to agree the terms on which these

will take place, but a formal or explicit contract between them is either impossible or impracticable. The difficulties which make implicit contracts preferable to formal legal contracts arise from uncertainty about the future.

implicit costs
Also called imputed costs they are theoretical costs in the sense that they go unrecognised by the accounting system. These costs may be defined as the earnings of those employed resources which belong to the owner himself.

import control
It refers to administrative restriction and allocation of imports. This may be imposed for balance-of-payments reasons, to reduce spending on imports, or due to industrial policy reasons, to protect domestic producers of import substitutes.

import deposit
It is a requirement to place a blocked deposit in advance with the central bank as the condition for obtaining foreign currency to pay for imports. Such a deposit has the effect of imposing a tax on imports, as well as of reducing the money supply in circulation.

import licence
It is a permit from the government to import particular goods. The requirement for import licences may be intended to (i) protect domestic producers from competition; (ii) improve the balance of trade by restricting imports; and (iii) facilitate government control over dangerous materials such as explosives. Import licence is a licence which is of the nature of an authorisation by the government and used to be acquired by the potential importers.

import quotas
These are quotas that limit the quantity of the commodity that may be imported into the country in a given period. Once the limit is reached, no further imports are possible.

import restrictions
It refers to the restrictions on the quantity or types of goods imported into a country, through the use of tariffs or quotas.

import substitution
It is a strategy for the industrialisation of developing countries, of concentrating initially on replacing imports by domestically produced substitutes. This has the advantage that it is already known what markets exist for the products, but its disadvantage is that as the imports most easily made up the decrease, further progress becomes ever more difficult.

imported inflation
It is inflation due to increases in the prices of imports. Increases in the prices of imported final products directly affect any expenditure-based measure to counter inflation. Increases in the prices of imported fuels, materials, and components raise domestic costs of production, and lead to a spurt in the prices of domestically produced goods.

imports
The term is used to describe the following:
1. Goods and services bought by residents of a country but provided by non-residents. They are of mainly two types: (i) visible imports are goods physically brought into the country; (ii) imports of services, or invisible imports, may involve the supplier entering the country, or residents going abroad to enjoy the services of airlines, hotels, steamers, treatment of some disease or entertainments.
2. Goods or services obtained for consumption or industrial use by one country from another, some taxes or duties are levied on imported goods which are called import duties. There are import restrictions to correct balance of payments. Imports are a must in the modern day world.

incentives
It is a system of wage payment, which offers an inducement in the form of a bonus to encourage workers to maintain a high level output. Opportunity of promotion too is a type of incentive that may be offered to a worker. Incentives also refer to rewards or penalties designed to include one set of people to act in such a way that they produce results that another set of people want. As rewards for good results, incentives can include higher pay, higher designation, better working conditions, better job security, better promotion prospects, or simply prestige. As penalties for poor results, incentives may take the form of lower pay, poorer promotion prospects, even demotion or sacking.

incidence of taxation

It is the distribution of the real burden of taxation. The distinction between direct and indirect taxes is based on the assumption that the real burden of direct taxes falls on the person, firm or company responsible for paying them, whereas the real burden of indirect taxes can be passed on to somebody else, usually a firm's customers as in the case of sales tax or value-added tax.

income

In economics, the term refers to the following:
1. The amount that can be spent consistently with being able to maintain the same level of spending in the future. It is defined as permanent income.
2. The amount an individual can spend in a period while leaving his or her capital unchanged. For an individual with neither assets nor debts, personal income can be defined as receipts from wages, or earned income, plus receipts from transfers, such as pension. Taxable income is this income minus any deductions allowed.
3. A macroeconomic aggregate, equal to the sum of individuals earned and unearned incomes, the undistributed profits of companies, and property income accruing to the government. National income does not include transfer payments, which merely transfer part of the national income from one set of individuals to another.
4. The receipts of firms or companies from sales or payments of interest and dividends by other firms. These appear as the income side in income and expenditure accounts:
(i) income distribution is concerned with the shares of total income going to different groups.
(ii) functional income distribution looks at the shares of different types of income, for example, wages and profits.
(iii) the income effect of a change in price is the change in demand for a good whose price has altered which would have resulted if prices had stayed the same.
(iv) income support is government payments to keep people's incomes up to some prescribed minimum level, in the event of illness, old age, disability or unemployment making them unable to earn for themselves.

income distribution

It implies the way in which total national income of any country is distributed among the households on the socio-economic basis. Income in this case means the flow of money or goods of an individual, and a group of individuals of a firm over some period of time.

income effect

The damage in the demand for a product due to a change in income of the consumer is termed as the income effect on demand for that product.

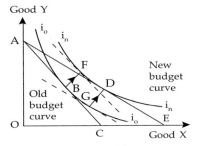

Income effect

Income effect is the part of the response in the demand for a good to a change in its price which is due to the rise in the real income of consumers resulting from a price decrease. Income effect is normally positive, except for interior goods, for which it is usually negative.

income elasticity of demand

Income elasticity may be defined as the degree of responsiveness of quantities demanded to a given change in income. The income elasticity of demand can be measured by the formula:

$$e_p = \frac{\dfrac{(Q_2 - Q_1)}{Q_1}}{\dfrac{(Y_2 - Y_1)}{Y_1}}$$

where Q_1, stands for quantities demanded before the change in income; Q_2 stands for the quantities demanded after the change in income; Y_1 stands for the income before the change; and Y_2 indicates the income after the change. Income elasticity of demand is the ratio of proportional increase in quantity demanded to proportional increase in income, with all prices held constant. A luxury is a good with an income elasticity of demand in excess of unity, viz. a higher proportion of income is spent on luxuries as income rises.

income expenditure model

It is a simple Keynesian model which shows the determination of the equilibrium level of national income. Under the assumptions of a fixed capital stock, labour force and technology on one hand, and rigid wages and prices and, therefore, expectations, on the other, it describes the static equilibrium in which the supply of real national output is equal to the quantity of national output people wish to buy.

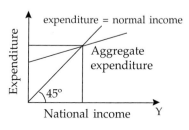

Income expenditure model

income redistribution

It is the use of taxation in government spending, and controls to change the distribution of real incomes. Under a stable policy, taxation may be more or less progressive, government spending programmes may be generally available, or may be targeted or means-tested to try to concentrate benefits on the relatively needy.

income support

The term denotes payments by the state to bring people's incomes up to a socially acceptable level. Such payments are made to various groups, including the old, the sick, the handicapped, the underprivileged, and the unemployed. Making such payments is justified on equity grounds.

income tax

It refers to the following:
1. A tax on income, it is normally zero on some bands of small incomes, both on equity grounds and because of the expense of collecting tiny amounts of tax. It is then proportional up to some upper limit; income beyond this taxed income is calculated after deducting various allowances, housing loan interest payable, charitable donations, responsibility for dependents, medical insurance, superannuation contributions, etc.

2. It is the most important single tax which plays an important role in the fiscal regimes of all countries. In most countries it is levied on taxable income of individuals at progressive rates. Income has been widely recognised as being a suitable base for taxation on equity grounds. Income tax is a direct tax as it is recovered from the person who has to bear it.

incomplete markets

These are actually situations where certain goods or services cannot be traded because there is no organised market on which to trade. Markets may be incomplete due to various reasons. One reason may be that the goods concerned have not yet been invented (especially in technology) so that no contract involving them can be specified.

increasing function

A function whose value increases as its argument increases. If y = f(x), y is increasing function of x if and only if dy/dx ≥ 0 for all xy is a strictly increasing function of x if and only if dy/dx > 0 for all x.

incumbent capital-output ratio

It refers to a ratio acquired by a firm which is already in stable position in a market. In a fully contestable market, where the goods produced by different firms are homogeneous and there are no sunk costs, there is complete symmetry between an incumbent firm and would-be entrants.

indefinite integral

It is a function whose first derivative is equal to a given function. If g(x) is the derivative of f(x), then (x) + k, where k is any arbitrary constant.

indexation

It is a system by which wages, prices, or the interest and redemption payments on securities are not fixed in money terms, but instead are adjusted in proportion to a suitable index of prices, such as the Retail Price Index.

index number

It is a single number which is given the average value of a set of related items, and stated as a percentage of their average value at some base period. A price index number finds the price of a given physical quantity of each item in the current period. This can be expressed as a percentage of the price of the same quantity in the base period and then weighted average of these percentages can be taken for price relatives to give the overall price index. Index numbers are a very concise and efficient way of providing information.

indicative planning
It refers to planning to promote economic growth by influencing expectations. Indicative planning attempts to combine the advantages of decentralisation and central planning. Growth in an economy may lag because of pessimistic expectations.

indicator
It is a variable used in deciding on the use of some policy instruments. Policy indicators are different from both targets and instruments. Economic policy targets include objectives such as high levels of employment and growth, low and stable levels of inflation, or maintenance of particular exchange rates.

indifference curve
It can be explained by considering the situation of a consumer who wishes to allocate an available amount of income between two commodities, X and Y. The utility, U, or satisfaction the consumer receives from the goods, can be expressed as U= f(QA, QB) where QA and QB are the respective quantities of goods X and Y consumed. An indifference curve is a plotting of points representing various combinations of two goods, for example, X and Y, such that the consumer is indifferent among any combination along a specific indifference curve.

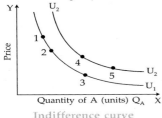
Indifference curve

indirect tax   It refers to the following: 1. A tax on spending on goods or services, for example, sales tax, value-added tax or taxes on alcohol and tobacco. The term indirect tax is used because it is usually assumed that the real incidence of such a tax will not fall on the firm immediately responsible for paying it.

2. A tax paid in the first instance by one person and is then shifted on some other person. Taxes on commodities are indirect taxes.

indirect utility function
It is a function giving utility as a function of income and prices. In a direct utility function, utility may be expressed as an increasing function of non-work income and the wage rate for work performed. It is also denoted as a decreasing function of the prices of goods and services consumed.

indivisibility
It is the existence of a minimum scale at which any technique can operate. This applies to all productive techniques. In many cases the minimum scale is so small that it has no economic effects, but in other cases it is large enough to make the technique unavailable to small firms.

industrial action
The term implies action taken by trade unions or informal groups of workers to bring pressure to bear on employers when industrial disputes have not been settled by negotiation or arbitration.

industrial democracy
It is the principle that all those employed in a firm should have a say in how it is run. This can take various forms. In cases where capital requirements are relatively small, a firm can be owned by those who work in it. In this case, the workers can elect the directors and managers, and thus control all decisions taken.

industrial dispute
It refers to a disagreement between employees and employers concerning pay, working conditions, hours of work, manning levels, job security, etc. Industrial disputes may be settled by conciliation that is discussion; by arbitration through some third party agreed upon by both sides or prescribed by law; by industrial action; or by a court of law.

industrial economics
It deals with the aspects of economics relating to organisation of productive activities. This includes the factors determining which activities are co-ordinated within firms and which through markets; the problems connected with providing incentives within firms to surmount principal-agent problems.

industrialisation

It is the process of moving resources into the industrial sector. This is common in the early stages of economic development, when resources move out of primary production as happened in the case of many countries. Industrialisation was the norm in the advanced countries earlier in their development, and was energetically pursued by many developing countries and by the former planned economies of the ex-USSR and central and Eastern Europe.

industrial policy

It refers to the set of official policies concerning the direction of economic activity to particular parts of the economy. For many years governments were concerned with the division of economies between industry and primary production; the less industrialised countries like India, China, etc. tried to encourage the growth of local industry, while the more industrial countries like USA, UK, France, etc. protected their native agriculture and mines.

industrial sector

It is the part of the economy that is concerned with producing goods without much direct input of natural resources. This is also called secondary sector and is distinguished from the primary producing sector that is agriculture, fishing, forestry, mining and quarrying.

industry

A generic term which refers to the following:
1. A sector of the economy, in which firms use similar factor inputs to make a range of related products.
2. A group of sectors, mainly in manufacturing and construction, typically producing physical goods rather than services.
3. Hard and persistent work.
4. An industry consists of all those firms which are producing the same product. For example, cement industry means all firms, producing, selling and dealing in cement.

industry demand

Industry demand refers to the total demand for the products of a particular industry. However, we can add up the demands of the various firms only if either all the firms produce exactly the same commodity or they should be close substitutes of each other, e.g. the various tooth pastes, boot polishes, etc.

inefficiency

In economics, the term implies not getting the best possible results from the use of resources. This is costly to the economy, as it means either getting lower outputs than would have been possible or using more resources than necessary to get any given results. X-inefficiency, which is also called organisational slack, denotes that enterprises are producing the right outputs, but are using an unnecessary level of inputs.

inelastic

In economics, it means lacking in repulsiveness. Where one variable, a, can affect another, b, the relation is inelastic if a proportional change in a is associated with a smaller proportional change in b, of whichever sign is appropriate. Demand for a good is inelastic if a fall in price produces a smaller proportional increase in quantity demanded.

inelastic demand

It refers to weak response of quantity demanded to price, so that a proportional fall in price produces a smaller proportional increase in quantity demanded. Total revenue thus falls when quantity increases, and marginal revenue is negative.

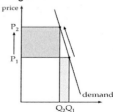

Inelastic demand

inelastic supply

It means low response of quantity supplied to price. The supply of a good or service is inelastic if a given percentage increase in the price at which it can be sold produces a smaller percentage increase in the quantity supplied.

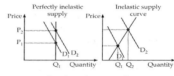

Inelastic supply

inequality of income

It is perhaps the greatest defect of present economic order. It is often seen that the incomes of different individuals differ to a great extent. The differences in incomes are both small and great. When one talks of inequality of income one does not take into account minor ifferences in incomes. It is natural that in a society where individuals have different powers of work, the rewards to individuals in the form of income should be different.

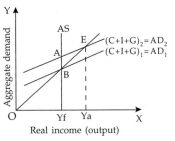

Inflationary gap

inflation

It refers to a persistent tendency for prices and money wages to increase. Inflation is measured by the proportional changes over a period of time in some appropriate price index, commonly a consumer price index (CPI) or a GDP deflator. Due to changes in the type and quality of goods available, measures of inflation are probably not reliable to closer than a margin of 1 or 2 per cent a year, but if prices rise faster than this there is no doubt that it is inflation. Economists have attempted to distinguish cost and demand inflation. Cost inflation is started by an increase in some element of costs. Demand inflation is due to too more aggregate demand. According to Kemmerer: "Inflation is too much currency in relation to the physical volume of business being done." This is what Coburn also means when he defines inflation as, "Too much money chasing too few goods."

inflationary gap

It is the excess demand which has been explained by Keynes in terms of the inflationary gap analysis. The inflationary gap is the gap measured as an excess of aggregate demand over or full employment. Since aggregate demand in the three sector model is equal to household consumption expenditure plus private investment expenditure plus government expenditure (C+1+G), the situation where C+1+G>Yf indicates the presence of inflationary gap in the economy as the total expenditure, viz. aggregate demand is in excess of the full employment level of output or real income Yf. Inflationary gap is a measure of the positive difference between demand that exists in the economy at the full employment level of income and the aggregate supply at the full employment level.

Inflationary gap is also denoted as the excess of the actual level of activity in the economy over the level corresponding to the nonaccelerating inflation level of unemployment. If the inflationary gap is positive, inflation tends to speed up, and the inflationary gap, the faster inflation speeds up.

informal sector

It refers to self-employed in a developing country who are engaged in small scale labour-intensive work like tailoring, food preparation, trading, shoe-repairing, etc.

infrastructure of an economy

The term is used for the following:
1. The underlying capital of a society involving basic amenities for economic development in the country like roads and rail transportation, ports, airports, communication systems, water supplies, electric, power, and other public utilities. The term is also said to include education health, skills, and other available to people for self-development and professional proficiency.
2. The capital equipment used to produce publicly available services, including transport and telecommunications, and gas, power, electricity, and water supplies. These provide an essential background for other economic activities in modern economies.

input-output

It is the study of the flows of goods and services between different sectors of the economy. An input-output table lists all flows of goods and services between sectors of origin and factor services, normally denoted by rows, and sectors of destination, including both intermediate and various types of final use, normally represented by columns.

input-output analysis

It is widely used as an analytical tool in highly developed economies - those which engage in economic planning and - those which rely primarily on the market mechanism. More recently, a number of developed countries like USA and UK too have turned to this new and powerful technique as a guide to important policy decisions.

inputs

These are the services or factors of production and usage of fuels, materials, and intermediate products necessary for a process of production. The relation of output to the use of various inputs is shown by a production function. Inputs may be required in fixed proportions, or may either be substitutable for one another.

inside money

It refers to the following:
1. Forms of money which have been on private sector debt, the prime modern example being commercial bank deposits to the extent that they are matched by bank lending to private sector borrowers.
2. Money which is an asset to the person or firm holding it, but is also a liability for somebody else in the economy. Inside money is distinct from outside money, where the asset of the holder is not balanced by a liability for some other party. Bank balances, for example, are clearly inside money, while gold coinage is outside money.

insider dealing

It implies stock exchange transactions by insiders who are people throwing their positions in or contracts with companies and are able to obtain price-sensitive information, such as profits figures or news of takeover bids, in a more detailed and accurate form, and in particular earlier, than outsiders, who have to rely on published information.

insolvency

1. It can be defined as the inability of an individual or company to pay debts as they fall due. This may lead an individual to become bankrupt, or a company to go into liquidation. In either case, a trustee in bankruptcy or liquidator is appointed by a court to realise the available assets and pay off the debts so far as possible. An individual or business may be unable to pay debts because of illiquidity rather than inadequate assets, i.e. if the assets are in fact sufficient, creditors may eventually be paid in full.
2. The state of being unable to pay one's debts. An insolvent person or company may, after various legal processes, be declared bankrupt, or is able to agree on arrangement with the creditors to discharge his/ her/its debts.

instalment

It is payment of a total sum in regular amounts at intervals over a period, instead of making a single payment. Instalment payments are used in hire/ purchase.

institutional economics

1. It refers to a type of economic analysis which emphasises the role of social, political and economic organisations in determining economic events. This movement flourished in the early twentieth century particularly in the US.
2. The view of economics, which stresses the importance of institutions in determining how economies really work. For example, the rules of land ownership are important in economic development in the developing countries, and the lack of clearly defined and enforced property rights is proving a handicap in the transformation from planned economies to free market economies.

insurance

It refers to the use of contracts to reduce and redistribute risk. In an insurance contract, the insurer accepts a fixed payment, or premium, from the insured, and in return undertakes to make payments if case of insurance of vehicle, the event may be an accident causing damage, events occur. In some life insurance, the event insured against is the death of the insured, or his or her survival to some agreed age.

insurance company

It is used for a company whose activity is providing insurance. This may include life, fire, motor, health, or many other varieties of insurance. Since the premiums for policies are paid regularly and much before claims occur, and in the case of life policies the funds collected accumulate for decades, insurance companies hold large stocks of liquid funds which they invest in the various securities.

insurance fund

It is an investment fund specialising in taking speculative positions in markets, for shares or currencies. This may involve selling short, that is, selling forward shares, commodities, gold or currency which the funds do not actually possess, in the expectation that the price will fall. Hedge funds are perhaps the only form of investment fund which can profit from bear markets, though in practice most do not.

intangible assets

These are assets of an enterprise which cannot be seen or touched. This includes goodwill, patents, trademarks, and copyright. In the case of goodwill, there is no tangible evidence of its existence. There is in all these cases, evidence that intangible assets exist, as they are occasionally bought and sold.

integrated economy

It is a term which refers to a situation when different sectors of an economy, generally the agricultural and industrial sectors, work together efficiently, and have become, for all intents and purposes mutually interdependent.

integration

It is a generic term and carries various meanings in economics:
1. The combination of different economic activities under unified control. This may involve vertical integration, or backward integration, where a business is combined with one using its outputs.
2. The process of finding an integral. For many mathematical functions, there are convenient standard forms, or rules for doing this. For example, the integral of x^α is always $x^{\alpha+1}/(\alpha+1)$.
3. A property of time series, concerning the number of times they need to be different to produce a stationary series.
4. The organisation of economic activities so that national boundaries do not cause any problem. Complete economic integration implies trade in all goods and services, perfect capital mobility, complete freedom of migration, complete freedom of establishment for businesses, and an unhindered flow of information and ideas.

interest

1. It is an amount paid by the borrower to the lender for the use of capital. Interest involves a transaction between those people, firms or institutions who/which have surplus and others who/which are deficit in funds and require them for their own use. The transaction of borrowing and lending money will take place only if those having surplus funds are willing to part with their funds. The willingness to part means or parting with funds is more attractive than holding funds for their own use.
2. Payment for a loan additional to repayment of the amount borrowed. The rate of interest is the extra payment per unit of the loan, normally calculated as an annual rate, e.g. 10% p.a. An interest-bearing security yields interest to the holder; some interest-bearing loans are used as money. Interest payments are made by borrowers to lenders. Simple interest denotes that, where interest is not actually paid out but is added to the principal of a loan each period, the amount added is the same each period. Compound interest implies that where interest is not paid out, the amount to be added to the loan each period is the same percentage of the debt already accumulated. In other words, compound interest includes interest on interest.

interest-rate swaps

These are transactions by which financial institutions change the form of their assets or debts. Swaps can be between fixed and floating-rate debt, or between debt denominated in different currencies.

interim dividend

It is a dividend payment based on interim profit figures for part of a company's financial year. Payment of an interim dividend normally carries a suggestion, but no guarantee that a final dividend payment will follow, though it usually does.

inter-industry trade

It describes trade between countries where exports and imports consist of different types of goods. Such trade is based on differences in factor endowments. Countries export goods where they have relatively large amounts of the factors intensively used in producing them thus, having a comparative advantage and to import goods which they cannot produce themselves.

internal balance

It is a situation where the level of activity in an economy is consistent with a stable rate of inflation. At higher activity levels, inflation tends to rise, and at lower levels, unemployment is unnecessarily high. Maintaining internal balance is one of the objectives of macroeconomic policy.

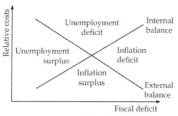

Internal balance

internal economies
It refers to the economies which are available to a particular firm and give it an advantage over other firms engaged in the industry. Internal economies arise from the expansion of the size of a particular firm. Internal economies are more important from the managerial point of view, as they can be affected by managerial decisions of an individual firm.

internal labour market
It is the system by which recruitment for senior appointments in an organisation is mainly from existing employees in lower grade jobs. It is distinct from an external labour market, in which recruitment is mainly by open competition. The major benefits of internal labour markets are that a firm is likely to know more about the strengths and weaknesses of existing employees than about those of outsiders.

internal rate of return (IRR)
It is the interest rate at which the net present value of a project is zero. If the net cash flow on a project starts off negative, and once it becomes positive it remains so, the IRR is unique; but if cash flow at the end becomes negative the IRR may not be unique.

international economics
It deals with that part of economics which is concerned with transactions between countries in the fields of goods and services, financial flows and movement of factors of production. It is mainly divided into two subject areas, pure theory and monetary theory.

international monetary fund (IMF)
It is an agency of the United Nations, founded in 1946 to promote international monetary stability and co-operation. The IMF is financed by quota subscriptions from member countries, partly in gold or convertible currencies like dollar, pound and euro, and partly in their own currencies. It was intended to promote international trade through stable exchange rates and additional international liquidity to enable countries to avoid the need for trade restrictions and exchange controls.

international monetary system
It is the system of foreign exchange markets through which international trade and capital movements are financed, and exchange rates are determined. If there were no national foreign exchange reserves and no world central bank, exchange rates would be entirely determined in the foreign exchange market. Most of the countries have central banks, which hold foreign exchange reserves, which can be used to stabilise exchange rates at least, in the short run. As the long run measures central banks and governments can use the instruments of monetary and fiscal policy.

international money
It is money which can be used in making international transactions. It may be a national currency, provided that it is acceptable to residents of other countries, which is now-a-days likely only with a fully convertible currency. At one time sterling was widely used as an international money, and the US dollar is still widely acceptable; though euro is being preferred.

International money

international payments
The term is used for payments made between residents of different countries, or between residents and international companies or bodies. These include payments for exports of goods and services, payment of property incomes and international transfers for gifts. These are securities, and making the repayment of loans as well as transfers of foreign exchange reserves between central banks

and governments. International payments may be made in a country's own currency in case the foreigners are willing to hold it.

interpolation
It means inserting missing data into a series. This is normally done by assuming that the data grew according to some known set of rule or theory over the period for which data is missing.

intertemporal substitution
It is the extent to which similar goods or services at different times can be substituted. For example, fares at peak periods are higher than off-peak; this can induce travellers for whom off-peak travel is a good substitute for peak-period travel.

intra-industry trade
It refers to trade where goods of the same classification are both imported and exported. In some cases, this is because of seasonal factors. For example, a country may export some fruits in the autumn and import them in the spring. In other cases, the reason is transport costs, e.g., a large country may export goods over one border and import similar goods over another. In many cases, however, intra-industry trade results from economies of scale.

inventories
These are stocks of goods held by a firm or an enterprise. They may be fuel, materials, or components awaiting use in production, work in process, for example, vehicles on assembly lines, or stocks of finished products ready for sale to distributors or final users.

investment
It refers to the following:
1. The process of adding to stocks of real productive assets. This may be through acquiring fixed assets, such as buildings, machinery plant, or equipment, or adding to stocks and work in progress. This is the Keynesian definition of investment: it is a flow concept. Investment goods are designed to be used for investment rather than consumption.
2. The acquisition of financial assets, such as company shares debentures or bonds. Investors are the people who own such assets; 'investments' are the funds/ capital that they apply for acquiring securities, assets, etc.

investment function
The investment function shows as to what determines the level of investment $I=F(i.c)$. Investment depends on the rate of marginal efficiency of capital. Given the marginal efficiency of capital, investment will be lower if the rate of interest is higher and vice versa.

investment incentives
These imply arrangements designed to encourage investment, by increasing its rewards or decreasing its costs. Many such incentives work by means of the tax system. Accelerated depreciation denotes that firms are allowed to write off investments faster than the true rate of capital consumption. This reduces measured profits and thus taxes paid in the early years after an investment is made.

invisible balance
It is the balance of trade in invisibles. This is the excess of receipts from sales of services such as transport, tourism, and consultancy over payments for imports of invisible items.

invisible tariff
The term is used for procedural difficulties the importing country in the rapid determination of the duty or requires marks of origin stamped on the article or in other ways hinders the process of importing.

invisibles
These are international trade in services. Invisible exports are sales of services to non-residents; invisible imports are purchases of services from hotel facilities, banking, insurance, health care, education and repair/ maintenance of equipment as well as various forms of consultancy.

iron law of wages
It is the hypothesis which states that notwithstanding the possibility of upward movements in wages in the short run, wages would inevitably return to the subsistence level in the long run.

irredeemable security
The term is used for the following:
1. A security with no redemption date. Interest on an irredeemable security is payable for ever, but the original sum borrowed is never to be repaid. Securities may also be termed irredeemable if the borrower has the

right, but no obligation, to redeem them.
2. Unlike the usual redeemable securities that mature on the expiry of a certain fixed period - short or long-term the irredeemable security does not bear a time at which capital amount of the security is to be returned or repaid.

IS curve

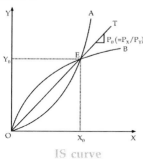

IS curve

It is a curve showing where ex ante savings and investment are equal. This is a condition of equilibrium in macroeconomic models. The IS curve shows those combinations of national income, Y, and interest rates, r, at which ex ante investment, I, will equal ex ante savings, S. It is usually assumed that when income rises, savings rise considerably and investment changes little.

ISLM model

It refers to a model which is an extremely simple example of general equilibrium in macroeconomics. The IS curve shows the combinations of national income, Y, and interest rate, r, at which ex ante savings and investment are equal. The LM curve shows the combinations of Y and r at which the supply of and the demand to hold money are equal.

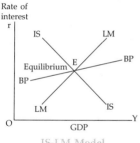

IS-LM Model

Iso-cost line

It is a line used to show alternative combinations of factors a firm can buy for a given outlay.

Iso-product curve

Also known as producer's indifference curve, or isoquant it is an iso-product curve which details the combinations of any two or more inputs which give rise to the same being convex to the origin because of the assumed substitutability of inputs.

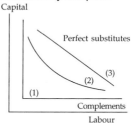

Iso-product curve

issue

It denotes the following:
1. The amount of shares or stock available, or the amount of bank notes in circulation.
2. The process by which new shares are distributed. In a bonus issue or scrip issue, extra shares are given to existing shareholders. In a rights issue, new shares are sold on preferential terms to existing shareholders.

issuing house

It refers to the agency that is entrusted by newly incorporated company for the sale of its new issue or by an existing capital for the subscription of the additional capital that may have been sanctioned to it. Issuing houses do this to earn a commission.

issued capital

It is the part of the authorised capital of a firm which has actually been issued to shareholders. Any authorised but unissued capital remains available for issue when required, for example, to allow executives to take up share options.

J

j-curve
It denotes a model of the delayed effects of devaluation on the balance of trade. Devaluation allows the foreign price of exports to fall and the domestic price of imports to go higher immediately. However, some time is needed, for orders to be obtained and contracts negotiated before the quantity of exports rises and the quantity of imports falls.

jelly capital
The term is used to refer to that capital when it is theoretically assumed that the capital labour ratio can get altered immediately.

Jevons, William Stanley
He was an economist, who in the 1870's put forward a marginal utility theory. Prior to him for over a century, since the times of Adam Smith in the study of the valuation of a product all the emphasis was placed on the cost of production. The other important contribution was the theory of capital, in which his assertion was that the capital should be measured in terms of both time as well as quantity. Jevons is regarded as one of the founders of econometrics. Jevons also advanced sunspot theory in the study of the trade cycles, which is considered more valid. A passing reference of the theory is made in economic analysis because of novelty of its expression than for any scientific accuracy.

job
It denotes the following:
1. A task, as in: "Give us the tools and we will finish the job" and "Finish the job in hand." A jobber carries out tasks for pay on a selfemployed basis.
2. A racket or crime, as in put-up job, or jobbery.
3. Paid employment. Jobs may be full-time or part-time, permanent or temporary.

jobber
The term is used for the following:
1. A dealer in shares or commodities who holds a stock of the assets and trades as a principal. Jobbers are distinct from brokers, who operate in the same markets, but put people who want to buy and sell in touch with each other, and do not trade for themselves.
2. A person who is ever willing to buy or sell securities and who thus makes a market of such securities. Like any other dealer, jobber's intelligence lies in purchasing the share or the security at a lower price and selling the same at higher rate.

job duplication
It denotes a situation when an individual is having more than one form of employment at the same time and therefore is not dependent only on one source of income. It is particularly prevalent in underdeveloped countries especially in the informal sector.

job enrichment
It is an approach, developed by Herzberg, that involves increasing the individual's discretion to select activities and outcomes. The objective of job enrichment to improve efficiency, thus production and human satisfaction by means of building into people's jobs greater scope for personal achievement and recognition.

job evaluation
It refers to an assessment of the prospective job seeker to exactly know the skills, academic and professional qualifications he/she possesses and to match those skills with the needs of job.

jobless growth
It refers to increases in production which is made possible by more and better use of machinery, latest use of technology and innovations, but without an increase in employment.

jobseeker's allowance
It is a term used for the USA's and UK's unemployment benefit. It is an indicator of unemployment in these countries. More seekers of this allowance mean more unemployment and fewer seekers indicate rise in employment.

job splitting
It refers to a practice where two people share the same job for one wage.

Johansen's theory

It is a pure theory of public expenditure that solves two problems: (i) under assumptions of given preferences, and (ii) distribution of income. These are divisions of total output between public good and private good and division of the total supply of private goods between two consumers X and Y. All these solutions are Pareto-optimal because any departure from them involves a loss to either X or Y. The optimum of all such optima is then decided on the basis of a social utility function as a part of the general problem of welfare maximisation. From the implementation point of view, it is far from satisfactory. But, Johansen has tried to remove some of these difficulties. This fact is illustrated with the help of figure given.

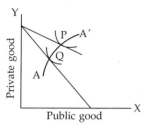

Johansen's theory

joint sector

Apart from the private sector and the public sectors, there is another sector, known as joint sector. When a sector is jointly owned, managed and run by both the sectors, public and private, it is called joint sector. It is a partnership between the two sectors. There has been a lot of controversy with regard to the industries that should be placed under this sector.

joint stock companies

Companies subdivided under two headsprivate and public. Private limited company is one whose membership varies between 2 and 50. It cannot invite the public in purchase of its prospectus. It is exempted from a number of legal formalities, which public limited companies have to undergo before its formation. Private limited company has become extremely popular. If the business is to be within the reasonable proportions, this is an ideal form of business organisation. Public limited company has the minimum strength of seven but there is no upper limit.

joint venture

It refers to the following:
1. A business where the provision of risk capital is shared between two or more firms. This is a method of organisation which is often adopted for projects which are too large or risky for any one firm to attempt alone. The firms joining such a venture may invest abroad to seek local partners.
2. A situation where both public and private sectors have been working together in an economic activity. It is particularly prevalent in developing countries where capital has been very scarce in the private sector and government funds have been often needed so as to develop industry, or banking services, etc.

Juglar cycle

It refers to business cycles of between 9 and 11 years duration which were identified by Clement Juglar of France. He has been credited for being the first to speak of business cycles. He divided business cycles into three phases: (i) prosperity, crisis and liquidation, and (ii) argued that the sole cause of the crisis had been the prosperity phase that preceded it, and that depression always followed the crisis. The maladjustments of the prosperity phase made the crisis and depression inevitable. Standard business cycle theory deals mainly with explanation of the Juglar cycle.

junk bonds

These are bonds issued on very doubtful security. The finances of the firm issuing them are regarded as so insecure that there is serious doubt as to whether the interest and redemption payments promised will actually be made. Junk bonds are thus risky to hold, and lenders will only hold them if they expect a rate of return.

K

Kalecki's theory

According to J.M. Keynes, it is the initial expenditure on investment which results in the operation of multiplier effect. Kalecki tried to improve on the Keynesian theory. He introduced the concept of accelerator, along with that of multiplier, to analyse the swings in business activity. The logic of Kalecki's approach is that changes in investment do not result in increase in income immediately. There is a time lag between investment increase and rise in income. It is due to time lag, i.e. if the investment increases period by period by a fixed percentage, the effect of the second dose of investment overlaps the effect of first dose of investment. This cumulative effect or overlap between the preceding and subsequent investments remain unaffected even if the doses of investment are not regular or uniform and the prosperity keeps on heading towards the boom.

Keynes, John Maynard (1883-1946)

He was a famous British economist. Keynes studied philosophy and economics under Alfred Marshal and A.C. Pigou. He worked as a lecturer in economics at King's College Cambridge. In 1936 his major work of revolutionary importance, General Theory of Employment, Interest and Money was published. No single book on economics till then or thereafter as much has affected the Government policies all over the world. Keynes provided measures for the removal of unemployment. The effectiveness of his ideas, however, was tested and proved only during the later years of the Second World War. He was responsible for the creation of modern macroeconomics.

Keynesian economics

Economic policies advocated by Keynes in the domain of employment were so drastic and different in several respects that these have come to be known as Keynesian economics. His basic postulates are enumerated below:

(i) The economy's functioning when left to its own self normally generates an equilibrium of less than full employment.

(ii) The aggregate effective demand plays a decisive role in determining the level of unemployment.

Keynesian theory

Keynes developed the theory of employment and money in his celebrated work General Theory of Employment, Interest and Money. Keynesian theory of trade cycle is only a by-product of this work. The logic of Keynes' viewpoint is that as investment increases, income in the economy also increases. But this income cannot increase in the same proportion as investment because of consumption increase in income. So long as investment rate remains greater than the rate of increase in income or consumption, economy experiences the condition of prosperity and boom. But eventually, the boom must come to an end because of increasing income elasticity of demand. Slow rate of increase in consumption manifests itself into a fall in prospective rate of profit.

Keynesian unemployment

It can be defined as unemployment due to lack of effective demand for goods and services which people could have been employed to fiscal policy to increase effective demand. This demand-deficiency unemployment is distinct from classical unemployment, where wage rates are too high relative to productivity for employment, to be profitable.

kina

It is the standard unit of the currency of New Guinea. It is subdivided into 100 toeas.

kinked demand curve

It is a demand curve as it would appear to a firm which expected that if it raised its price, rivals would not follow suit, whereas if it cut its price, rivals would also do so. The demand curve would thus appear more elastic for price rises than price falls.

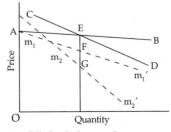

Kinked demand curve

Klein, Lawrence R.

He was an economist who in 1980, was awarded the Nobel Prize in Economics for pioneering the design construction application of large scale econometric models and applied econometric over its development to his work. His important work includes The Keynesian Revolution (1947), An Econometric Model of the United States 1929-1952 (1955) and The Economics of Supply and Demand (1983).

know-how

It is practical economic knowledge, enabling firms to achieve results. Some of this is technical in nature, and can in principal be made in private property the use of patents, although these may be difficult to enforce. However, much practical know-how takes forms such as modes of organisation, professional standards, or systems of incentives, which cannot be privatised by patents.

kobo

Sub-unit of the currency of Nigeria. It is worth one hundredth of a Naira.

Kondratiev

It refers to a long wave in economic activity and is named after its discoverer. Over a period of fifty or sixty years, one could find evidence of a long general upswing in the economy, followed by a similar decline, and again a rise.

kopek (or copeck)

It is a functional unit of the Russian currency. It is worth one hundredth of a rouble.

kurtosis

In it a measure of humped flow frequency distribution is compared to a normal distribution with the same mean and variance. The kurtosis of a variable a with mean μ can be measured by $K = E(a-\mu)^4$. A distribution with $K > 3$ is slim and long-tailed, with more weight in its centre and extremes and less at medium distances from the mean than a normal distribution.

kyat

It is the standard unit of the currency of Myanmar (Burma), it is subdivided into 100 pyas.

L

labour economics

1. It deals with the study of the nature and determinants of pay and employment. It emphasises the role of institutions in determining the pattern and speed of adjustment in the labour market.
2. The aspects of economics concerned with the supply and demand for labour. It includes factors affecting the participation rate, wage rate and bargaining, organised labour, training, hours and conditions of work, practices concerning hiring, redundancy and labour turnover, among other things.

labour force

It refers to the number of people available for work. It is affected by many factors. The population of working age is affected by the school-leaving age and the size of higher education system, which keeps down the number of young workers, and the retirement age and pension system, which keeps down the number of older workers.

labour intensive

A process or technique of production in which the emphasis is more on employing large number of workers rather than wider use machines, technology, etc. It is distinct from capital intensive.

labour market

The term implies the processes by which workers and employers are brought into contact, and wages and conditions of work are decided. Some of these involve formal institutions, e.g. contacts between workers and employers may be arranged by employment exchanges or agencies, either public or private. Wages and conditions of work are often decided by negotiation between trade unions representing workers and associations representing employers. The hours and conditions of work, and other facilities like compensation are frequently subject to legal regulation.

labour mobility

It is the mobility of labour from one place to another, from one firm to another, or from one industry or sector to another.

labour supply

It is defined as the total number of hours of work that a population has been willing to supply which is a function of (b) size of population able and willing to work; and (c) number of hours worked by each individual.

labour theory of value

It is the theory that states that the value of goods or services is determined by the amount of direct and indirect labour inputs needed to produce them. This view does not take into consideration the role of scarce natural resources of production, and the fact that the cost of using capital goods depends not only on the labour used to produce them but also on the interest rate.

labour

It refers to human beings as a factor of production. The labour supply consists of all who are able and willing to work, including the self-employed and unemployed as well as employed workers. Labour varies in its levels of skills and qualifications.

Laffer curve

It is a curve showing the relation between tax rates and revenue raised, named after its inventor, Arthur Laffer. If any activity is taxed, revenue starts from zero with a tax rate, and rises as the rate is increased. However, the tax tends to discourage the activity, so that at some point the total revenue raised turns downwards.

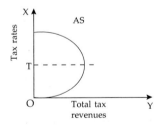

Laffer curve

Laffer curve also refers to an illustration of the thesis that there exists some optimal tax rate, shown in the diagram above, which maximises government tax revenues. The thesis could be expressed in terms of either personal or corporate taxes and it proposes that taxes above the optimal rate discourage production and hence results in lower revenues. These arguments represent an aspect of supply side economics.

laissez-faire
It can be defined as the following:
1. A policy of complete non-intervention by governments in the economy, leaving all decisions to the market. If there were perfect markets everywhere, with no externalities, and we were indifferent to income distribution, *laissez-faire* would be the best policy. However, there are numerous market imperfections and distribution.
2. A policy of non-interference by the state in economic affairs. The underlying philosophy is that man is moved predominantly by self-interest and that there exist certain immutable laws which produce a natural harmony.

land
It is one of natural resources as factors of production. Land is used in economic activity in a variety of ways, viz. for growing crops and rearing animals; for extracting minerals. Attributes provided by nature can be changed by human activities, for example agricultural land can be improved by fertilisers and drainage, or ruined by erosion. Land comprises all kinds of natural fertility of the soil, mineral wealth, climate, etc. and is distinct from capital which has to be produced. Ricardo considered land to be fundamentally different from the other factors of production in three ways: (i) land is a free gift of nature; (ii) land unlike the other factors is strictly limited in supply; and (iii) production in land is peculiarly subject to the law of diminishing returns.

law of demand
Law of demand states that the amount demanded of a commodity and its price are inversely related, other things remaining constant, i.e. if the income of the consumer, prices of the related goods and tastes and preferences of the consumer's demand for the good increases, its quantity demanded increases.

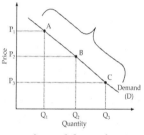
Law of demand

law of diminishing marginal productivity
The term states that one cannot be certain that marginal productivity will be diminishing over all ranges of output, but there is no reason to doubt that in the end the addition of more and more units of a variable factor to a fixed will cause marginal productivity to decrease.

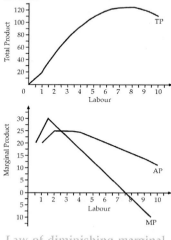
Law of diminishing marginal productivity

leads and lags
The term implies the ability of traders to bring forward or defer the timing of transactions. If a company's currency is expected to be devalued, importers have a strong incentive to buy now before import prices rise, and exporters have a strong to delay selling goods, or delay converting the foreign exchange they get for them, as it is expected soon to be worth more.

leapfrogging
It implies a process which is also known as the wages spiral. It is held to be an independent cause of wage and price inflation by those who believe in cost-push inflation theories.

leasing
It is the practice of hiring items of equipment, rather than buying them outright. This enables firms to manage with less capital than they would need if all their equipment had to be bought. It also shifts to the owners the risk of

obsolescence; this will be reflected in the rentals demanded.

least cost combination
It is a concept that tells that the efficient combination of factors, which the entrepreneur should employ, depends on the marginal productivity and price of the various factors.

legal monopoly
It refers to a situation when private-owned firm is granted an exclusive right by government to operate in a particular market, in return for which government may impose standards and requirements regarding the quantity and quality output, geographic areas of operation and the prices or rates that are charged.

legal tender
It refers to forms of money which a creditor is legally obliged to accept in settlement of a debt. It is necessary to have some rules on this so that it is clear when debts have been defaulted on. What the rules should be is often a matter of convenience. Coins and bank notes are legal tender, with some exceptions, for example small denomination coins are not legal tender in large amounts, and nobody is legally obliged to give change, so that large notes are not legal tender for small amounts.

lender of last resort
The term refers to the function of providing liquidity for the banking system at times of crisis. This is one of the duties of the central bank. In the event of a run on the banks or other financial panic, the central bank should be willing to lend to sound banks or other financial institutions in order to avoid a general collapse of the financial system.

Leontief paradox
It is the observation by Wassily Leontief that despite being the world's most capital-rich country, the US appeared on average to have exports that were slightly more labour-intensive than its imports. This appeared to be paradoxical because the Heckscher-Ohlin models of international trade led people to expect that US exports would be capital-intensive and its imports would be labour-intensive.

leverage
It is the ratio of a company's debt to its equity, that is to the part of its total capital owned by its shareholders. High leverage or gearing means high reliance on debt financing. The higher a company's leverage, the more of its total earnings are absorbed by paying debt interest, and the more variable are the net earnings available for equity shareholders.

liabilities
It refers to the items on the debit side of a balance sheet. These include unpaid bills from suppliers, unpaid taxes, insurance or other payments due within the year, and secured and unsecured debts of various sorts. The net equity value of the firm is included as a liability to make the total equal to total assets.

liability
The term denotes the following:
1. The legal obligation to pay debts. Unlimited liability means that the individual or company concerned must make the payment if their assets permit, otherwise they can be made bankrupt or liquidated. Unlimited liability normally applies to individuals, and firms trading as sole traders or partnerships.
2. The legal obligation to make some payment. This includes payment of compensation to employees injured at work, or to customers injured by defective products, if any, or paying other people's debts if one has guaranteed them and they default.

liberal trade policy
It is a trade policy aimed at allowing a country's residents to take part in international trade with the minimum of interference. This involves the reduction of tariffs the relaxation of rules, and quantitative controls by tariffs.

liberalisation
It is a programme of changes in the direction of moving towards a free-market economy. This normally includes the reduction of direct controls on both internal and international transactions, and a shift towards relying on the price mechanism to co-ordinate economic activities. In such a programme, less use is made of licences, permits, quotas, limits and price controls, and there is more reliance on prices to clear markets.

licensing

It means allowing another firm, for payment, to make use of a patent, trademark, brand, etc. This is a method of profiting by a patent without investment on the scale necessary to exploit an innovatory idea for oneself. The other possibility would be to sell the patent to somebody who could afford to exploit it.

linear programming

It is a mathematical procedure for finding the maximum or minimum value of a linear objective function, but subject to linear constraints. Where only small numbers of variables and constraints are involved, it is possible to proceed by assuming every possible set of the constraints to hold exactly and solving this as a system of simultaneous equations.

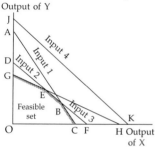

Linear programming

liquidity constraint

It denotes the fact that it is not always possible for individuals or firms to borrow as much as they would like to. Individuals, who have their own expectations, may prefer to consume now and pay later, in case they expect that in the future their incomes will be higher or their needs will be less than they are now.

liquidity preference

It refers to the factors determining the amount of money people want to hold. In Keynesian monetary theory, liquidity preference is affected by three main considerations: (i) the volume and motive of transactions; (ii) people's expectations concerning movements in interest rates, or the speculative motive; and (iii) their degree of uncertainty about the future, or the precautionary motive.

liquidity ratio

It refers to the proportion between a bank or other financial institutions' holdings of liquid assets and its total liabilities. Minimum liquidity ratios may either be imposed by law or convention, or be adopted voluntarily as a matter of commercial prudence.

liquidity trap

It is a situation in which real cannot be reduced by any action of the monetary authorities. This is liable to arise if prices are expected to fall. If general price falls are expected, holding money will produce an expected real gain equal to the expected rate of inflation.

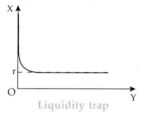

Liquidity trap

listing

It implies agreement by a stock exchange to allow a company's shares to be traded at the stock exchange. This requires the company to comply with the exchange's requirements as regards the information provided to investors.

loan

It is defined as money lent, which has to be returned, usually with interest. Loans may be secured, that is backed by collateral, which the lender can sell to get his/ her money back if the borrower fails to pay, or may be unsecured in which the lender holds no tangible security. If a debtor cannot pay all debts in full, unsecured creditors rank below secured ones where it is expected that the conditions will be strictly enforced.

loanable funds

These are funds that are determined by a theory of matching of the rate of interest with the need to equate the demand for funds for investment with the supply of available savings. This was popular in pre-Keynesian thinking, when the level of national income was taken as fixed by long-term supply-side factors.

loan-loss reserve

It is a reserve fund held by a financial institution which believes that some of the loans it has made are liable to turn into bad or doubtful debts, but does not know, or does not wish to specify, which of its debtors are likely to default.

loan portfolio
It refers to the collection of loans held as assets by a financial institution. Such institutions hold loan portfolios for two main reasons: (i) their total assets are often too large for it to be practicable to lend to only one borrower; and (ii) a number of loans are safer than one large one, especially if the borrowers have a degree of spread, either geographically or by industry.

local maximum
It implies a value of a function which is higher than at any nearby value of its argument, or set of values of its arguments. It is a necessary condition for a local maximum of y = f(x) that $dy/dx = 0$; provided this is satisfied, it is a sufficient condition for a local maximum that $d^2y/dx^2 > 0$.

local minimum
It is a value of a function which is lower than at any nearby value of its argument, or set of values of its arguments. It is a necessary condition for a local minimum of b = f(x). It is a sufficient condition for a local minimum that $d^2b/dx > 0$.

location quotient
It is a statistical measure of the extent to which a particular economic activity is overrepresented or underrepresented in the economy of an area compared to its representation in the economy as a whole. The location quotient can be calculated as follows: E_{ia}/E_{in} where E_{ia} denotes the percentage of economic activity accounted for by activity i, and E_{in} shows the percentage of national economic activity accounted for by activity i. This ratio may then be multiplied by 100 and expressed as a percentage.

lock-out
The term refers to a situation arising out of industrial dispute which occurs when employers refuse to employ their workers unless they agree to accept the employers' terms. A strike may take place when workers demand higher rates of pay.

logarithmic scale
It is a scale on a diagram where distances represent the logarithm of a variable. Log scales are used particularly in diagrams with time on the horizontal axis, and some real or nominal variable such as GDP or the price level on the vertical axis. The slope of a curve in such a diagram shows the proportional growth rate of the variable, and a constant proportional growth trend is represented by a straight line. The horizontal axis shows time, and the vertical axis shows the real GDP of an imaginary economy 1 uses a natural scale; 2 usage a logarithmic scale. It is assumed that the economy has alternating booms, each lasting five years, and slumps each lasting two years.

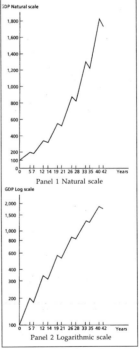

Panel 1 Natural scale

Panel 2 Logarithmic scale

Logarithmic scale

log-rolling
It describes the co-operation between representatives in national or local legislatures to support other member's bids for public money in return for some support for measures to benefit their own constituents.

Lorenz curve

It is a graphical representation of inequality. Personal incomes, in a country, for example are arranged in ascending order, wherein the cumulative share of total income is then plotted against the cumulative share of the population. The slope of Lorenz curve is proportional to per capital income at each point of the population distribution.

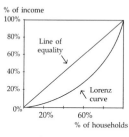

Lorenz curve

loss

It refers to the result of a business operation where expenditures exceed receipts. Business losses either arise internally, through failure to produce something that the market will buy to cover production expenses, or externally, through failure of others to pay bills due, or to repay debts. The effect of losses is to reduce a business's capital.

lump of labour

It refers to the view that there is a fixed total amount of employment available. If this were true, it would be correct to believe that limiting hours worked would create more jobs, and making the elderly retire early would create jobs for the young.

luxury

It is a good or service the consumption of which at any given price rises more than in proportion to an increase in income. The income elasticity of demand for a luxury is thus more than unity. A luxury is therefore a good on which richer people spend a higher proportion of their incomes than do poorer people. For example, cars, air conditioners, microwave ovens, diamonds, etc. are luxuries.

M

M0
It denotes the narrowest definition of money supply. This includes notes and coin in circulation, and bank's till money and balances with the central bank.

M1
It is a less narrow definition of the money supply. M1 includes notes and coin in circulation plus private sector current accounts plus deposit accounts transferable by cheque, etc. It also includes currency outside the RBI's demand deposits of commercial banks, and other checkable deposits.

M2
It refers to broad money and includes notes and coin in circulation plus non-interest-bearing bank deposits plus building society deposits plus National Savings accounts. In the US it includes M1 plus money market deposit accounts, balances in money market mutual funds, and savings and time deposits of under $100,000.

M3
It is a variety of alternative broader definitions of broad money as M1 plus assorted other deposits at banks and other financial intermediaries.

macroeconomic policy
There are different levels of macroeconomic policies. At the top is macroeconomic policy itself, which includes any measure directed at influencing such macroeconomic variables, as the overall levels of employment, national income and prices. One branch of macroeconomic policy is demand management, which seeks to influence macroeconomic variables by working through aggregate demand. Another branch of demand management is fiscal policy while the second branch consists of the monetary policy.

macroeconomics
It studies the macro aspects of economics, connecting the determination of aggregate and average figures in an economy. It considers what determines total employment, output consumption investment in raising productive capacity, and how much a country imports and exports.

majority shareholder
It is used for a shareholder who owns a majority of the voting shares of a company. Such holding gives control of the appointment of the company's directors, and gives them the final say on company policy.

malleable capital
It refers to an assumption about the nature of physical capital which is used in neoclassical economics. It denotes that the materials incorporated into a particular machine may be instantly changed into a different machine at a small cost.

managed trade
It implies international trade conducted in accordance with plans outlined by government bodies. It is the natural mode of trade for planned economies, but is not convenient for market economies. The governments in market economies have sufficient powers to prevent trade which they do not approve of, but they have no adequate means of including private firms to supply exports that they have promised that their country will provide.

Manoilescu argument
It is a concept which was developed by the economist Manoilescu regarding the infant industry and is based on the empirical observation that the average wage in the manufacturing sector in a developing country exceeds that in the agricultural sector though labour productivity may be similar. The manufacturing industry has been at a disadvantage vis-à-vis imports and, therefore, it should be compensated by a tariff on manufactured goods.

margin
It is a proportion of the value of a transaction which traders have to deposit to guarantee that they will complete it. Buying shares on margin means contracting to buy them without actually putting up the full cash price immediately.

marginal
It is the effect per unit of a small change in any variable. The term is used in different ways, such as marginal costs are in addition to total cost from a small increase in output, per unit of the increase. Marginal revenue is the effect on total revenue of a small increase in sales, per unit of the increase, allowing for any effect of a small increase in the activity

on total social costs, per unit of the increase, including any externalities like rise in cost of transportation, etc. as well as direct costs to the producer.

marginal benefit
It is the additional benefit from an increase in any activity. This is the addition to total benefit resulting from a unit increase if it varies discretely, or the addition to total benefit per unit of the increase, if it varies continuously.

marginal cost
It can be defined as the additional cost from an increase in an activity. This is the addition to total cost resulting from a unit increase if it varies discretely, or the addition to total cost, per unit of the increase, if it varies continuously. Marginal cost may be short-run, when only some inputs can be changed, or long-run, when all inputs can be adjusted.

Marginal cost

marginal disutility
It refers to the extra disutility which is resulting from a small change in some variable.

marginal efficiency of capital (MEC)
The term implies the highest interest rate at which a project could be expected to break even. This depends on the immediate profits expected from operating the project, and the rate at which these are expected to decline through reductions in the real price of the output, or increase in real wages and fuel and materials costs.

marginal firm
A firm which could just be included to enter an industry by a small rise in profitability, or would just be induced to leave the industry by a small worsening in market conditions.

marginal land
It denotes land on the margin of cultivation.

Such land would become just worth farming if output prices rose slightly, to leave some profit or benefit to the cultivator of that land or would go out of cultivation if prices fell slightly.

marginal product
It defines the addition to output from a small increase in any input, per unit of the increase. Marginal physical product measures this in physical terms, not taking into account any effects of the change in output on the price at which it can be sold.

marginal productivity of capital
It is the extra value of potential output, at current prices, resulting from a small increase in capital, per unit of the extra capital. This is distinct from the marginal efficiency of capital (MEC), which is the highest interest rate at which a project can be expected to break even.

marginal propensity to withdraw
It refers to the change in withdrawals (W) because of one additional unit of income (Y) which may be written as follows: MPW=ΔW/ΔY.

marginal revenue
It is defined as the increase in total revenue when the quantity sold increases by a small amount, measured per unit of the increase in sales. If the seller is a price-taker, marginal revenue is equal to price.

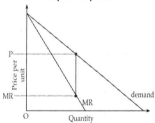

Marginal revenue

marginal revenue product
It denotes the addition to total from a small increase in any factor input, per unit of the increase. This takes account both of the effect of the extra input in raising the quantity produced.

marginal utility of money
It is the amount by which an individual's utility would be increased by a small addition to

their money holding, per unit of the increase. It is assumed that other assets held do not undergo an increase or decrease, so that the extra money represents a net increase in total wealth. In considering particular goods, it is convenient to assume that the marginal utility of money is constant.

marginal values

These refer to functional relations - the independent variable A determines the dependent variable Y and we wish to know what would be the change in B if A changed by a small amount from its present value. The solution is referred to as the marginal value of B and is given various names depending on what economic variables A and B stand for.

market

It refers to the following:
1. A market economy which plays a dominant role in co-ordinating decisions. The formed in markets convey information and provide motivation for decision takers. Market forces are the supply and demand factors which determine prices and quantities in a market economy. An efficient market is one where prices reflect all available information about the goods.
2. A place or institution in which buyers and sellers of a good or asset meet. A market was originally a building, which is still the case for some goods, for example, cattle, fruit, and vegetable or textile markets.
3. A network of dealers linked physically by telephone and computer networks, and institutionally by trading rules and conventions.

marketable security

It is a security which can be sold in a secondary market. This is contrasted with a non-marketable security, for example, National Savings Certificates which are not marketable, and can only be turned into cash by selling them back to the post office on maturity.

market access

It implies the freedom to sell in a market. Market access may be denied for natural or institutionally imposed reasons. Natural obstacles include distance and inability to meet the requirements of customers, while institutional obstacles include legal restrictions on entry, tariffs and quotas, and public procurement rules excluding possible suppliers.

market equilibrium

It is the situation when supply and demand in a market are equal at the prevailing price. The equilibrium price is determined by supply and demand.

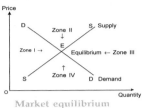

Market equilibrium

market failure

The term is used for describing the view that the market does not provide a panacea for all economic ills. There are various ways in which an unregulated market may fail to produce an ideal state of affairs. Major sources of market failure are monopoly, externalities, and income distribution.

market forces

The forces of supply and demand, which determine equilibrium quantities and prices in markets. Market forces are distinct from the regulations of the government and monetary authorities, which are able to modify the outcome of unrestricted market processes.

marketing

It is the process of getting customers to buy a firm's product. It involves making arrangements for distribution and advertising current products. It also covers market research to discover likely customer reaction to potential new products, and whether possible modifications to existing products would improve their usefulness and appeal.

market prices

In economics, it is the method of measuring national income at the prices customers actually pay. It takes into consideration Gross Domestic Product (GDP) or any other national income accounting any indirect taxes and subtracting any subsidies.

market sharing

The producers in an oligopolistic industry join by agreeing to eliminate price competition, but the new entrants in the industry must be given a reasonable share of the market. It is termed as market sharing.

market structure

It refers to the pattern of market shares in an industry. It is concerned with how many firms there are, and how they vary in size. Two common measures used in describing market structure are: (i) the N-firm concentration ratio and (ii) the Herfindahl index.

mark-up

It is the excess of the selling price of a product over the cost of making or buying it. The mark-up on any product has to cover the overhead of the firm, as well as providing a profit margin.

Marshall-Lerner condition

The term denotes a condition for devaluation to improve a country's balance of trade. Suppose that trade between two countries is initially balanced, and that country devalues by a small proportion p. If exports are in perfectly elastic supply in each country, domestic price and levels do not change, and the price elasticity of demand for imports is α in country X and β in country Y, the balance of trade changes as follows: In terms of country X's currency, Y's imports prices rises by p, and the quantity imported falls by αk, spending on imports rises by $(1-\alpha)p$. Export prices stay the same in φ's currency, but they fall by p.

Marxian economics

It is an alternative form of economics based on the theories of Karl Marx. It includes the labour theory of value, and a theory of exploitation by which surplus value is appropriated by capitalists; which has been extended to cover exploitation of less by more developed countries.

maturity

It refers to the date when a security is due to be redeemed. The further any security is from maturity, the more its market value is liable to fluctuate if there are changes in the rate of interest; the nearer to maturity, the more stable its market price.

means-tested benefits

These are benefits which are available only to claimants whose income or assets fall below some limit. These are distinct from universal benefits, which are available to everybody in particular categories, e.g. based on age, regardless of income or assets. The argument for means-tested benefits is that the cost of providing universal benefits is very high, so that they have to be kept small.

MERCOSUR
(Mercado comun del sur)

It is a Latin American common market agreed in 1991 by Argentina, Brazil, Paraguay, and Uruguay.

mercantilism

It is a belief in the merits if balance of payments surpluses to increase the money supply and stimulate the economy, and advocacy of protectionism to achieve this. Critics argue that in the long run mercantilist policy is self-defeating.

merchant bank

It is a bank dealing mainly with other firms rather than the general public. Merchant banks engage in a variety of specialist activities, including financing foreign trade by accepting bills of exchange, providing hire/purchase and industrial finance, underwriting new issues, etc.

merger

It means the uniting of two or more formerly independent firms into a single unit.

migration

It refers to the movement of people between regions or countries. Immigration and emigration are usually used for migration into and out of countries. Migration may be temporary, with the intention of returning in the future, or permanent i.e., for settling abroad, or migrants may have decided between these alternatives at the time of migration.

minimax

It is the lowest value of a set of numbers, each found by taking the maximum of some further set. The minimax is a useful concept in game theory.

minimum

It is the lowest value a function takes for any

value of its arguments. A minimum may be local or global. For example, $b = 1 + a^2$ has a global minimum of $b = 1$ when $a = 0$; there of a which gives a lower b.

minimum efficient scale
The minimum level of any activity at which all known economies of scale can be enjoyed. In some cases, there is no finite level of output at which further cost savings cease. For example, this is the case, when marginal cost is constant and fixed costs can be spread over an ever larger output.

minimum wage
It implies, a minimum level of wage paid down by law, for workers in general or for some specified type. Its supporters believe that it prevents the exploitation of ignorant or vulnerable workers. Opponents of a minimum wage hold the opinion that it either must be slow as to be ineffective, or will destroy jobs, especially if exceptions are not allowed for handicapped or inexperienced workers with abnormally low productivity.

minority shareholder
It refers to a shareholder who owns only a minority of the voting shares of a company. The vast majority of shares is in fact held by minority shareholders. A minority shareholder can always be voted down by the majority if that majority is united, but usually there is no single majority shareholder.

mismatch
It refers to differences between the skills and location of unemployed workers and available job vacancies. These help to explain why unemployment exists at the same time as unsatisfied demand for labour. Mismatch may happen because the location and skill patterns of new entrants to the market, i.e. those finishing education and immigrants, do not match the pattern of those leaving the labour market through retirement or emigration.

mixed economy
It is defined as an economy with a mixture of state and private enterprises. Some economic activities are carried on by private sector comprising individuals or firms taking independent economic decisions, co-ordinated by markets, while others are carried on by

organisations under state ownership and control, with some degree of centralised decisions taking.

mix of policies
It denotes the use of policy instruments in combination. If a government has only one objective, it will usually be possible to achieve it using only one policy instrument. If more than one policy instrument is available, and use of each involves adverse side-effects which increase more than proportionally as they are used more, it may be profitable to use a mix of policy instruments to reduce these side-effects.

modulus
The size of a number, in the sense of its distance from zero. The modulus or absolute value of a real number a (symbol a) is the difference between a and zero, regardless of sign.

monetarism
It is the school of economics that believes that the quantity of money is the main determinant of money incomes. It is often combined with the view that markets tend to clear; and that people form rational expectations.

monetarists
The term describes a group of economists called monetarists led by the American Nobel Prize-winning economists who believe that the money supply is a key economic magnitude that exerts a strong influence on their macroeconomic variables. They hold that there is close relation between the money supply, on the one hand, and income employment and the price level, on the other.

monetary overhang
It implies that part of the money supply that people are holding merely because they have not been able to spend it. In an economy with repressed inflation, people hold more money than they really want, because shortage of real goods and services make it impossible to spend it as they would wish.

monetary policy
It refers to the use by the government or central bank of interest rates or controls on the money supply to influence the economy. The target of monetary policy may be the achievement of a desired level or rate of growth in

real activity, the money supply, the price level, the exchange rate, or the balance of payments. Methods of monetary policy include establishing the interest rate, sales or purchases of securities like bonds to control the money supply, and changes in CRR, SLR, etc.

monetary system

It is the system by which an economy is provided with money. It is possible for a small country simply to use some other country's money, but most countries choose to provide their own.

money

It refers to the following:
1. Short term for monetary policy. Thus, cheap money means that loans are cheap and easily available; tight money or dear money means that loans are expensive and difficult to obtain.
2. A medium of exchange and store of value. This may consist if physical objects, i.e. notes and coin; or of book or computer entries, that is bank deposits. Money was originally a physical substance such as gold or silver, which was valued for its own sake before it came to be used as coinage. Coins and notes are now usually tokens, whose intrinsic value is below their face value.
3. A synonym for wealth in general. Easy money is earnings which are quick though not necessarily legal. Black money is unaccounted for wealth accumulated through tax evasion or other illegal means.

money at call and short notice

It denotes the most liquid assets after cash. Money is lent to other banks and non-bank financial institutions (NBFCs) such as discount houses, repayable on demand (call) or at up to 14 days notice (short notice). These are secured loans, bearing interest, usually at low rates.

money illusion

It means mistaking nominal for real changes. People may interpret rises in their own wages, or the prices of goods and services they sell, or assets that they own, as real gains rather than as part of a general process of price and wage inflation.

money laundering

It is the use of often complex series of trans-actions to conceal the ultimate source of money holdings. It is widely used to camouflage receipts from illegal activities, including drug trafficking, corruption, fraud, and tax evasion.

money market

It refers to the market for very short-term loans. For example, in lending money for very short periods, overnight, transactions costs are quite large relative to the interest that can be earned, so transactions in the money market are usually for large amounts.

money multiplier

It is a formula relating changes in money supply to changes in income. It relates an initial change in some form of money to the change in the money level of national income which will ultimately result.

monitoring

The term is used for the process of checking whether individuals or firms are actually behaving as they should. This is applicable to seeing whether laws imposed by the government are being obeyed; whether instructions issued by regulatory agencies to firms are being complied with; and if orders by employers to their employees are actually being carried out.

monopolistic competition

It is a form of market structure in which a large number of independent firms are supplying products that are slightly at variance with the point of view of buyers. Thus, the products of the competing firms are close but not perfect substitutes because buyers do not regard them as identical. This situation arises when the same commodity is being sold under different brand names, each brand being slightly different from the others.

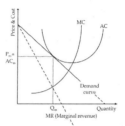

Monopolistic competition

monopoly

It is defined as a market situation with only one seller. Monopoly can be of various types: (i) a natural monopoly exists when the monopolist's sole position is due either to the exclusive possession of some essential input or to the existence of eco-nomies of so great scale that no entry by competitors is possible, (ii) a statutory monopoly exists when the entry of competitors is forbidden by law, (iii) bilateral monopoly means that as well as there being only one seller, there is also only one buyer in a market.

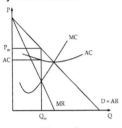

Monopoly

monopoly policy

It refers to government policy towards monopolies. It is motivated partly by a belief that monopoly may lead to inefficient use of resources, and partly by a desire to promote a more equal income distribution than tends to result if some firms have monopoly power.

monopsony

It is defined as a market situation with only one buyer. Unless the supply is perfectly elastic, a monopsonist has an incentive to exploit the fact hat a reduction in the quantity bought will reduce the price.

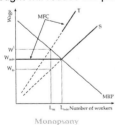

Monopsony

moral hazard

It refers to the danger that if a contract promises people payments on certain conditions, they will change their conduct so in order to make these conditions more likely to occur. For example, moral hazard suggests that if

possessions are fully insured, their owners are likely to take less than adequate care of them than if they were not insured.

moratorium

It is a suspension of the obligation to repay debts, and may apply to the principal, interest, or both. It may apply to all debts or only to particular types of debt. The payments are only deferred and not waived. The object is usually to give time to arrange to refinance the obligations of some particular debtors.

mortgage

In economics, it refers to a loan using a real asset, such as a house or other buildings, as collateral. If the interest and redemption payments are not made, the lender or mortgagee can foreclose on the collateral, i.e. he can take t over and sell it to repay the loan. Mortgages can be for any period: between 10 to 25 years.

most favoured nation (MFN)

The term is used to denote a country with rights under a trade agreement. An MFN clause stipulates that imports from the partner country will be treated no less favourably than imports of similar goods from any other country. In the case of tariffs, MFN treatment means no other foreign goods face a lower tariffs than those from the partner country.

moving average

It is a time series obtained from the original series by averaging the figures for a number of consecutive periods. For example, suppose that a_y is the original series for years $y = 1, 2, ..., N$. A moving average b_y can be calculated by averaging a_y for a number of periods centred on y, say $y - 2$, $y - 1$, $- y + 1$ and $y + 2$.

multicollinearity

It refers to the problem which arises in multiple regression when the explanatory variables are not themselves independent. This makes it difficult to fit significant coefficients to explanatory variables which are related to one another.

multilateralism

The term refers to the belief that international economic relations should be conducted on the basis of equal treatment for all non-nationals. It applies both to trade, where multilateralism denotes multilateral trade rather than preferential arrangements within trade blocks, and to international capital movements.

multilateral trade
It is trade carried on between a group of countries where there is no need for trade between any pair of countries to balance. This follows naturally if all countries in the group have convertible currencies.

multiple equilibrium
It refers to the possibility that equilibrium is not unique. The conditions for equilibrium are that no agent desires to act differently, given his/her expectations of the reactions of all other agents on the system. These conditions may be satisfied at more than one set of values of the relevant variables in macroeconomics.

multiple exchange rates
It is the system by which a country's currency has more than one exchange rate with any foreign currency. The rate which applies to any transaction may depend on the holder of the currency, or on the purpose for which it is being used.

multiplier
It refers to the following:
1. A formula relating an initial change in spending to the total change in activity which will result. The multiplier is applicable in an economy in which supply is elastic, so that activity is determined by demand. It is a type of calculation rather than any particular formula.
2. A mathematical device used in dealing with constrained maximum and minimum problems.

multiplier-accelerator model
It is the model deriving economic fluctuations from the integration of the multiplier and the accelerator. The multiplier makes output rise following a rise in investment, and the accelerator makes investment increase.

mutual fund
It is a financial institution which holds shares on behalf of investors. Investors buy shares, in the fund, which use their money to buy shares in companies. An investor, selling back the units gets the proceeds of selling a fraction of the fund's portfolio. In the UK mutual funds are called unit trusts.

N

Nash equilibrium
It is a situation in which two or more agents take decisions on their strategies, and no agent can gain by any change in their strategies given the strategies currently being generally pursued by the others. Such a non-cooperative equilibrium is not Pareto-optimal, and can be improved on by some form of co-operation.

National Association of Securities Dealers Automated Quotation (NASDAQ)
It is a US securities market, originally for over-the-counter securities not listed on regular stock exchanges. It is now a computer-based market, with a system of market makers, and is a strong rival to the New York Stock Exchange.

National Bank for Agricultural and Rural Development (NABARD)
NABARD was set up on 12th July, 1982, with the passing of the NABARD Act. The objectives of NABARD are:
1. It is a re-financing institution for promotion and development in rural areas.
2. It is an apex bank for promotion of agriculture, small scale industries and community services.
3. The bank is a link with the Reserve Bank of India in matters of rural development.
4. It provides direct financing approved by the Central Government.

national debt
It is the debt of a country's government. This may be owed to residents or foreign lenders. In some countries net national debt is smaller than the apparent total, as some government securities are held by other public bodies such as civil service pension funds.

national income
It refers to the following:
1. Any one of the many possible measures, that is, national product, domestic product, gross or net, and stated in either market prices or factor cost. One or other of these is meant when the term is used in general discussions of economic policy.
2. The total income of residents of a country, measured at factor cost after deducing capital consumption. This equals gross national product at factor cost minus capital consumption.

nationalism
It refers to an act by which a government takes over the ownership and operations of an industry, bank or a business previously in the hands of private companies or citizens. The supporters of nationalism believe that it increases productive efficiency by permitting the direct investment of public funds, by enlarging the scale of operations and by coordinating operations more effectively.

nationalised industry
It implies an industry whose ownership has been taken over by the state. Motives for nationalisation vary. In some cases industries were nationalised because they were natural monopolies, such as public utilities, so that public ownership was expected to give consumers a better deal. Some industries were nationalised because of the fact that large subsidies were needed to avoid run-downs in output and employment.

national product
It is the total value of income produced by factors of production owned by residents of a country. This includes income from factors owned by residents but operating abroad, and excludes the value of factors operating domestically but owned by non-residents.

natural growth rate
It is the growth rate of national income which could just maintain a constant unemployment rate. If there is no technical progress and the labour force technical progress at rate p, the natural growth rate is given by $n = g + p$.

natural monopoly
It denotes monopoly based on an overwhelming cost advantage for the incumbent firm. This may be because it possesses some unique natural resource, e.g. a mine tapping the only known deposits of a particular mineral; or due to past capital installations which would have to be duplicated by a competitor, e.g. domestic electricity supply.

natural rate of unemployment
It is the unemployment rate which would prevail in an economy with a constant rate of inflation. This is a function of various institutional factors, including the extent of industrial monopoly, the social security system, minimum wage legislation, restrictions on mobility between occupations, etc.

natural resources
These are factors of production provided by nature, including land suitable for agriculture, mineral deposits, and water resources useful for power generation, transport and irrigation. It also includes marine resources, including fish and offshore mineral deposits. The effective availability of natural resources is influenced by human activities. For example, most agricultural land has been irrigated and fertilised, mineral resources have been surveyed but the accessibility of resources depends on transportation facilities.

natural wastage
In economics, it is the proportion of the labour force who quit their jobs on their own. This includes workers who retire, and those who leave for personal reasons. These vary greatly, including the need to look after children, elderly parents, the fact that a spouse is moving away due to transfer or change of job, taking up a full-time educational course starting some business or venture.

near money
It refers to securities which are very close substitutes for money, including short-dated securities with a government guarantee which are either marketable, or redeemable by the government at short notice.

necessity
In economics, it denotes a good or service whose consumption by an individual, at a given price, rises less than in proportion to increases in their income. The income elasticity of demand for a necessity is less than one.

negative equity
It defines the position of the owner of an asset whose value is less than the amount of debt secured by a mortgage on it. For example, a house owner with a mortgage of $100,000 on a house whose market value is only $70,000 has negative equity of $30,000.

negative income tax
It refers to a proposal to combine income tax and exemptions due to investments in a single system. Under this system, all citizens would report their pre-tax incomes; they would then pay tax if their incomes after deducting any allowance to which they were entitled came above some cut-off level, and would receive payments if their income was below the cut-off.

net
It is an indication that something has been subtracted. The word is used in economics in a variety of contexts. Net price is price after subtracting any discounts, for prompt payment or otherwise; net weight is the weight of a product excluding packaging; while net profit is profit after the payment of expenses like tax, etc.

net economic welfare
It is the concept of a broader measure of economic welfare than income per head. It includes in addition to ordinary measures of income, items such as the cost effort, the value of household production, and services such as child-care and looking after the sick and the elderly, etc.

net exports
These are exports less imports, either in total, or any category of goods and services. It is thus negative when imports exceed exports.

net foreign assets
The term implies the total of assets owned by residents of a country, but situated abroad, minus assets located within the country but owned by non-residents. A country's overseas assets include both foreign direct investment (FDI), holdings of foreign securities, and foreign holdings of domestic assets which include inward foreign direct investment as well as foreign holdings of domestic securities.

net investment
It is net increase in the amount of capital and equals gross investment minus an estimate of capital consumption. Net investment is harder to measure than gross, since, while gross investment is mainly based on actual market transactions in acquiring capital goods, capital consumption is not based on observing market transactions, but is an estimate of the loss of value of the existing capital stock.

net national product
It is defined as the value of the incomes produced by factors of production owned by residents of a country, whether operating domestically or abroad, measured after deducting an estimate of capital consumption.

net present value
It is the present value of a country or an investment project, found by discounting all present and future receipts and outgoings at an appropriate rate of interest.

net profit
It defines the profit of an organisation after all expenses have been taken into account. This can be arrived at either before or after deduction of taxes payable.

net sum
It refers to a sum arrived at after making all the deductions and including the permitted allowances.

network externality
It is an external economy deriving from being connected to other people, e.g. through the telephone system or the Internet. The larger the proportion of the population connected to such a network, the greater the benefits to people.

net worth
It is defined as the net value of an organisation's assets, after deducting any liabilities. Net worth can only be measured reliably if assets are correctly valued, which cannot usually be done simply by using balance sheet figures.

net yield
It can be defined as the interest or dividends on securities, net of tax, i.e. after deduction of the normal rate of income tax, as a percentage of their price. For taxpayers with a personal marginal income tax rate lower than the normal rate, net yield is higher than that reported.

New International Economic Order (NIEO)
It refers to a set of proposals to improve the position of developed countries by changing their terms of trade with their arrangements for borrowing from more advanced economies.

These proposals were originated at the United Nations in 1974, and urged through the United Nations Conference on Trade and Development (UNCTAD).

new orders
In trade, the term denotes the value of orders for goods obtained by firms in those sectors where goods are made to order than made first and then sold off the shelf.

new (neo) protectionism
It is the revival of protectionism, with the support of some additional arguments. These are based partly on the introduction of strategic considerations, and partly on considering the effects of assuming widespread increasing returns to scale in industry.

nominal anchor
It refers to a mechanism for determining the general price level in an economy. The need for equilibrium in markets for goods and factor services determines the structure of relative prices, but this is achievable with any absolute price level.

nominal protection
It is the proportional price increase in imported goods caused by tariff. With a proportional tariff rate r, the price of imports inside the country is (1+r) times their external price. The tariff rate thus measures nominal protection.

nominal variable
An economic variable measured in money terms. Examples include national income data, and price and wages levels. Nominal variables are contrasted with real variables, which are measured in physical units, such as mobile phones, car productions, etc.

nominee holding
It refers to a shareholding registered in a name other than that of the real owner. This is sometimes done for sheer convenience, for example, when unit trusts/mutual funds hold shares which are ultimately the property of their own unit-holders.

non-discrimination
It means equal treatment for comparable cases. It is at variance with discrimination, which is differences of treatment on irrelevant grounds. In employment, for example,

non-discrimination implies choosing employees without any consideration of sex, race, or religion, for positions where these grounds are not directly relevant to the duties to be performed.

non-inflationary growth
It is growth of economic activity without any tendency to inflation of prices. This is sometimes taken as the ideal target for macroeconomic management. It can be criticised as a target from various viewpoints.

non-linear function
It denotes a function which cannot be expressed in the linear form, x = ay + b. It may be non-linear in the sense of being continuously curved, with $d^2x/dy^2 \neq 0$.

non-marketable debt
It refers to debt where there is no secondary market. The holders of such debt may have to wait until it falls due for redemption, or may be able to get it redeemed by the borrower at any time, but possibly on terms involving some penalty.

non-pecuniary goals
The term refers to those objectives which are pursued by individuals or organisations and are not directly measurable in monetary units. Objectives like power, prestige, professional excellence and status have been commonly referred to within managerial theories of the firm.

non-performing debt
It denotes debt on which the interest and redemption payments are not in fact being made. Non-performing debt is a problem for lending institutions, as they may suffer not merely direct financial loss but also damage to their reputation for sound judgement in selecting borrowers.

non-price competition
It means competition for markets using methods other than price cuts, which may include quality of product, quality of advertising, information and instructions, reliability of delivery dates, durability in use, and after-sales service. Non-price competition is important when there are legal or cartel restrictions on price-cutting.

non-tariff barriers
These are all forms of obstructions to international trade other than tariffs. Non-tariffs barriers have proliferated in recent decades, and they now involve a wide variety of devices, including prohibitions, oppressive and dilatory procedures for the routing and documentation of imports; regulations allegedly for health and safety purposes.

non-tradeable
The term implies goods and services which cannot be traded internationally. There is no direct motive for the prices of non-tradeables in different countries equal. However, given that both have tradable substitutes, there is an indirect connection between their prices.

North American Free Trade Agreement (NAFTA)
It is an agreement reached in 1993 between Canada, Mexico and the United States making the three countries into a free-trade area.

null hypothesis
It refers to the hypothesis that a variable has no effect. For example, in investigating the relation between income and saving, the full hypothesis could be that the income level of an individual does not affect the proportion of income that is saved.

O

obsolescence
It is loss of value of equipment due to changes in techniques or tastes. Equipment may become obsolete because consumers no longer want the goods produced, or because technical progress in other industries leads to redundancy of intermediate goods.

occupational mobility
It is the mobility prevalent in an economy and provides for an interchange of work force from one occupation to another. Occupational mobility is generally less in underdeveloped countries, compared to fully developed countries.

offer curve
It is a diagram showing the willingness of the rest of the world to engage in trade. The offer curve shows the amount of trade that any one country can do at various relative prices. For a small country, the offer curve facing it is a straight line, whose slope is proportional to world relative prices of exports and imports.

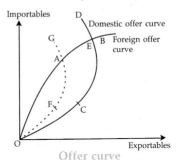

Offer curve

offshore
It refers to a marketing area beyond the regulation of the home country.

offshore fund
It refers to a fund operating in a country which is not the residence of the holder. Use of offshore funds may lead to tax avoidance or evasion.

Okun's law
It is the proposition that in cyclical fluctuations, the ratio of actual to potential real output generally rises by a greater percentage than the fall in unemployment. This effect is due partly to shortrun increasing returns to employment, and partly to a tendency for some workers to drop out from the labour force when sacked.

oligopoly
It is defined as a market situation with only a few sellers, each anticipating the other's reactions. Each firm has a sufficiently large share of the market to need to consider the individual reactions of the others to changes in its price or output. Equilibrium in such a market depends on how each oligopolist forecasts the other's reactions.

oligopsony
It is the situation where there are only a few buyers in a market, who take account of each other's reactions in deciding how much to buy.

ombudsman
The term implies an official responsible for investigating complaints against the administration of institutions. In the UK the use of the ombudsman system started with government bodies, through the Parliamentary Commissioner for Administration; it has since spread to other areas, including banking, finance and insurance.

one sector growth model
It is a model which is used in growth theory. In it a single homogeneous product, which is equally normal as a consumptive or as an investable goods, is produced. An example of this model has been the Harrod-Domar model.

opaque policy measures
These are policy measures where it is difficult to discover what they are, who decides on them, and what they cost. These are opposite to transparent policy measures, where these points are relatively clear.

open economy
It defines an economy which has transactions with the rest of the world. These may include trade in goods and services, movements of capital, transfer of information and technical know-how, and migration of labour.

opening prices
These are the bid and offer prices quoted in stock or commodity markets open on any working day.

open market operations

It means the purchase or sale of securities by the central banks as a means of changing interest rates and the money supply. These operations constitute one of the major instruments of monetary policy.

open position

It refers to a situation when a trader in securities, commodities, precious metals like gold, silver, etc. or currencies, is at risk if market prices rise or fall. It may involve selling for future delivery items not either held or hedged by contracts to buy, in which case the trader will make a loss if market prices rise, or contracting to buy without hedging by contracts to sell.

opportunity cost

It is the amount of other goods and services which could have been obtained instead of any good. If it had not been produced, the resources used in making it could have been used to produce other goods and services instead.

optimisation

It refers to the choice from all possible uses of resources of that which gives the best results. It is often represented by maximising an objective function. Those who are against optimisation argue that there are unlimited numbers of different ways of using given resources.

optimum currency area

It denotes the best area to use a single currency. To see what determines this, we may assume there are two separate currency areas, and analyse the gains and losses from uniting them. The gain is the reduction in transactions costs in respect of trade and financial transactions between them, and the reduction in currency risk affecting such transactions. If such transactions are larger relative to national incomes, the gain is more.

optimum population, the theory of

It is a theory that attempts to define an economically ideal size of population for a country, given the size of natural resources, stock of capital and the state of technical knowledge, etc. which will correspond to the per capita real income that is the optimum or the highest. Increase beyond or decrease below this ideal size will cause only a diminution in the per capita real income of the country.

optimum savings

It is a concept which answers the question, what proportion of income should be saved and invested? There is a tradeoff between present consumption and future growth, viz. more consumption now means a lower marginal utility of consumption but less investment means slower the future.

optimum tariff

It is a tariff which maximises a country's welfare, trading off improvement in terms of trade against restriction of trade quantities. For smaller economies, which cannot affect world prices in the markets in which they trade, the optimum tariff is zero.

option

It is a contract giving the holder the right but not the obligation to trade in a commodity, precious metal like gold and silver, a share or a currency on some future date at a pre-determined price. A put option gives the holder the right to sell at a pre-agreed price. It can be used to reduce risk by somebody who has to hold the actual asset and is worried that its price may fall. It can equally be used to speculate on a price fall. On the other hand, call option gives the holder the right to buy at a pre-agreed price.

option value

It is the value of being able to put off decisions. If one invests in a project at present one's capital is sunk in it. Market conditions may then change in future to make the project more or less profitable. If the decision is deferred, one can invest next year in case the market improves, or abandon the project if the market worsens.

order-driven market

It is an asset market where the role of intermediaries is to match buy and sell orders. In such a market, orders to buy at given prices or below, and to sell at given prices or above, are accumulated until a set time, for example noon daily.

ordinalism

It states that utility levels can only be ranked in ordinal terms.

ordinary share

It is a term for a share in the equity of a company. The US term is common stock. The holder of an ordinary share is entitled to share in any distribution of dividends in proportion to the number of shares held. Ordinary shares usually entitle their holder to vote at company meetings.

Organisation for Economic Cooperation & Development (OECD)

It is an international organisation set up to assist member states to develop economic and social policies to promote sustained economic growth with financial stability. OECD members have been mainly free-market economies like Finland, France, Germany, Greece, Iceland, Ireland, Italy, Luxembourg, the Netherlands, Norway, Portugal, Spain, Sweden, England and Switzerland.

Organisation of Petroleum Exporting Countries (OPEC)

It is an organisation of oil producing countries, set up to coordinate their policies in negotiating with the oil companies. Since 1973, OPEC has attempted to operate a world oil-exporting cartel, setting an agreed price and allocating export quotas. The members of OPEC have included Algeria, Iran, Iraq, Kuwait, Libya, Nigeria, Saudi Arabia, the United Arab Emirates (UAE), and Venezuela. OPEC's members have experienced difficulties in forming a joint monopoly policy, and the real price of oil has fluctuated considerably since the 1970s.

organised labour

It is that part of the labour force that belongs to trade unions. The use of trade unions to negotiate pay, hours of work, and working conditions is widespread, and is believed to obtain better terms from employers than workers could obtain by individual bargaining. Trade unions also assist their members in settlement of disputes over discipline, sick leave, compensation in case of injury or death, or redundancy. Organised labour may also engage and social security systems are arranged for the benefit of workers rather than employers.

organised sector

It can be defined as those parts of the economy which operate through institutions which feed figures into official statistics. It includes firms organised as companies, payments made via the banking system, incomes reported to the authorities, sales reported to the National Insurance authorities.

origin

It is the point on a graph indicating zero for each dimension. A diagram may contain more than one origin. In a two-factor box diagram, the total available amounts of the factors are shown on the two origins. The amounts employed in one industry use one corner of the box as origin, while the amounts employed in the other industry use the opposite corner as origin.

oscillatory function

It denotes a function y = f(a) which has regular oscillations in b as a increases. The trigonometric functions y= cos (a) and b=sin (a) take this form, each fluctuating between an upper limit 1+ and a lower 1 of -1.

outlier

It is an entry in a set of statistical data which lies away from any pattern apparent in the rest of the data-set. The presence of an outlier suggests two possibilities which warrant further investigation.

output

It is defined as the result of an economic process, available for sale or use elsewhere. Where a process produces goods, measurement of output is straightforward. Where a process produces services, measurement of output is difficult. For example, an airport fire crew produces safety even in a year with no fires for them to put out.

output effect

It is the effect of a rise in output on the use of any particular input, holding input prices constant. Where the most economical proportion in which to combine inputs is not constant with the change in the level of output, a rise in output causes use of some inputs to increase proportionally more than others.

output method

It refers to the method of calculating domestic product using information on the net outputs of various sectors of the economy. It is distinct from the expenditure method, which uses information on the expenditures of various sectors of the economy method, which proceeds by adding up the incomes of the various factors of production.

output per hour
It is a measure of output per unit of labour input.

outside lag
It refers to the delay between implementation of a policy and its full or total effect. It generally takes the form of a distributed lag.

outsourcing
It is the practice of buying goods and services from outside suppliers, rather than producing them within a firm. This is widespread among both firms and government agencies. Outsourcing may be used because specialist outside suppliers can apply more specialised skills, and can draw benefit from economies of scale.

over-capacity working
It is production in a firm or an industry above what is normally regarded as its capacity. It is possible because capacity itself is calculated on a conventional basis, which may be inaccurate. By working more than the normal number of shifts it is also possible to boost output temporarily above normal capacity levels in an emergency.

overdraft
It is a negative balance in a bank account, so that the customer owes the bank money. This is normally allowed only by prior arrangement, though a normally reliable customer may be allowed without prior arrangement.

overfull employment
It denotes levels of employment so high relative to the available force that gives rise to excess demand for labour. Difficulty in filling job vacancies causes wages to rise, and labour scarcity results in shortages of goods and services, so prices rise. Such employment thus produces and accelerates demand inflation. Inflation leads to policy reactions designed to slow it; and the effect of inflation on expectations reduces the power of excess demand to elicit higher levels of real activity.

overhead costs
These are fixed costs a business must incur for production to be possible. Overhead may be avoidable in the short run, if output is temporarily cut to zero. Alternatively, overhead costs may be avoidable only in the long run, in case the possibility of future production is given up.

overheating
In economics, the term denotes a level of activity leading to excess demand. High output levels relative to capacity, at least in some important sectors, usually lead to shortages of factor inputs, or sometimes high levels of imports. Overheating produces inflationary pressure internally and a deterioration in the trade balance externally.

overmanning
It is the excessive use of labour in any business. It is not easy to identify, since most business normally employ more than would strictly be necessary to do the work required if everybody was well trained and always present at work. Actual employment needs to take account of the fact that on any given occasion, some varying proportion of the labour force will be under training, on holiday, sickness or other personal reasons.

overshooting
It is the possibility that after a shock to the economy, some variables will move further in the short run than it is necessary for them to adjust in the long run. It may happen due to differences in speeds of adjustment. For example, after some shock it is necessary for a country's exchange rate to be nearly 5 per cent lower than before.

over-stimulation
It refers to the adoption of monetary and fiscal policies that increase the level of effective demand so far that inflation begins to speed up, or substantial balance-of-trade deficits occur.

over-subscription
It is the situation when the number of shares applied for in a new issue exceeds the number on offer. This means that some applications have to be refused, and it is quite likely that when the market opens the shares will stand at a premium over the issue price.

over-the-counter market
It is a market in securities which are not regulated by a stock exchange. The US has the National Association of Securities Dealers Automated Quotation system (NASDAQ).

overtime

It means work in excess of normal working hours per week. Overtime is used by firms when high demand or emergencies make a temporary increase in labour inputs necessary. Overtime is normally paid at premium hourly rates.

overtrading

It means carrying on business on a larger scale than a firm's capital may warrant. This creates a high risk that the firm will be unable to meet its commitments it encounters temporary problems, e.g. delay in obtaining payments due from a debtor.

over-valued currency

It implies a currency whose exchange rate is too high for a sustainable equilibrium in the balance of payments (BoPs). With no capital movements a currency is overvalued if its exchange rate is too high to produce a balanced current account. With autonomous capital movements, a currency is overvalued if its exchange rate is too high to produce a current account deficit that can be financed by a sustainable flow of inward capital movements.

ownership

It refers to the right to exclusive use of an asset. The owner of an asset normally has the right to decide what use shall be made of it, and cannot be deprived of it except by law. The state, however, claims the right to regulate the use of many assets, and to tax income earned from them. But land buildings are subject to planning permission, and rent from them is subject to income tax.

P

package of policies
The term is used for a number of policy measures all introduced at the same time. Governments resort to policy packages for two main reasons: (i) minimisation of side effects; and (ii) uncertainty about the effects of particular policy measures. Any economic policy, such as changing the interest rate, is bound to have side effects which are not desired as well the effects which are wanted and for whose sake the policy is adopted.

paid-up capital
It is the part of the authorised capital of a company that has actually been paid by shareholders. The difference may arise because not all shares authorised have been issued, or because issued shares are only partly paid-up.

panel data
It refers to data collected over a period by repeated survey of individuals or firms. Surveys may proceed by taking a fresh random sample of the population in successive periods, or by selecting a selected panel of respondents and following them over a prolonged period.

paper currency standard
It is also referred to as the managed system, under which currency notes unrelated to any metal with zero intrinsic value circulate with universal acceptability. The value of currency notes as money is derived from the command of the government.

paradox of thrift

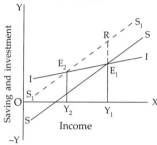

Paradox of thrift

It refers to the view that a rise in the ex ante propensity to save, i.e. the share of incomes that people want to save, may not increase the ex post level of savings and investment in the economy, which may even decrease. Those who hold this view argue that in a depressed economy, attempts to save more from present incomes tend to reduce consumption and thus income levels.

parameter
It is a quantity which is taken as given in any particular piece of analysis. In comparative statics, parameters and indicators may change, but such changes are assumed to be externally imposed, and generated as part of the solution to a problem. The parameters of one piece of analysis may be treated as variables in other contexts.

Pareto-optimality
It is defined as a situation in which no feasible change can raise anybody's welfare without lowering that of somebody else. This applies to reallocation of final goods between different users, reallocation of factors of production to different industries, and changes in the composition of final goods produced.

partial adjustment
It is a process of adjustment where decision-makers aim to remove in any one period only part of any discrepancy between the actual level and their target level of the variables they control. Partial adjustment is adopted for two main reasons: (i) cost of adjustments; and (ii) uncertainty.

partial derivative
It is the derivative of a function of two or more arguments with respect to any argument, holding all the remaining arguments constant. Thus if b = f(a, c), the partial derivative of y with respect to a is the derivative of b with respect to a, holding c constant. This is written $\partial b/\partial a$, or sometimes f_a or f_1.

partial equilibrium
The term implies the method of analysis dealing with some part of the economy, deliberately ignoring possible implications of changes in this part for what happens in the rest of the economy. In studying the effects of changes in the supply and demand for a particular good on its equilibrium price and

quantity, a partial equilibrium analysis ignores changes in the rest of the economy, e.g. due to consequent changes in income distribution. In general equilibrium analysis, the repressions of changes in any one market throughout the rest of the economy are taken into account.

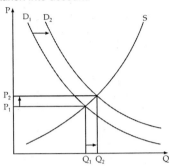

Partial equilibrium

participation rate
In economics, the term denotes the percentage of the population in any given age group who are economically active, either as employees, self-employed professionals, or those unemployed, on the assumption that the unemployed would all work if jobs were available. Participation rates can be found for men and women separately or both combined.

partnership
It is a business which has more than one owner but is not incorporated, the individual partners remaining fully responsible for its debts. Partners need not all be equal. In professional partnerships, it is common for senior partners to get a larger share of the rewards though there may a smaller share of the routine work than junior partners. A sleeping partner has no active role to play.

part-time work
It means working for less than the number of hours per week normal for full-time workers in the country and occupation concerned. This may suit the preferences of either employers or employees or both. Employers may prefer parttime to full-time work because it fits the time pattern of their need for labour, or offers more flexibility. They may also prefer part-time workers if they enjoy less stringent laws than full-time workers. Employees

may prefer it if they cannot spare time for full time job.

par value
It is the price at which a security is due to be redeemed will stand below par if current interest rates are above its coupon yield, and above par if current interest rates are below the coupon yield.

patent
It is defined as a legal device to encourage and reward invention by offering exclusive rights to inventors. In many countries, the inventor of a new product or process can apply for a patent, giving the holder the exclusive rights for a number of years to produce the good or use the process. This right can be used either through their own business, or by charging a licence fee to other users.

paternalism
It is the attitude favouring laws and policies which seek to control people's actions, overriding their preferences for their own good. This is inconsistent with the view taken in welfare economics, that people are the best judges of their own interests.

payback period
It is the period during which a firm requires that it gets back the cost of new equipment in profits if it is to invest. Payback period is not considered an economically rational investment criterion: as it clears a project which brings in 101 per cent of its cost in the initial years and nothing thereafter.

pay control
It refers to the control over wage rates, as part of a prices and incomes policy. As there are thousands of wage rates, no control body could actually determine them all from first principles as pay control has usually been confined to limiting increases, either to some percentage or some flat-rate increase.

payments in kind
It means payment to employees in goods or services rather than money. Welfare economics suggests that in the absence of tax-related motives, it is more efficient to pay workers in money and allow them to choose what to buy.

payments union

It is an arrangement by two or more countries to pool their foreign exchange reserves. Its advantage is that it reduces the total reserves they need to hold, and sets them free to trade with one another without worrying about the effects on their reserves.

payroll

It is a list of those employed by a given firm, company, etc. or the amount paid to them. A payroll tax is a tax on wage payments.

payroll tax

It is a tax on wage payments. In UK, the National Insurance contributions are a payroll tax. Many other countries have similar taxes, which make up a large part of the tax wedge between the costs of employment and wages received.

peace dividend

The term refers to the resources made available for other purposes if a reduction in international tension allows cuts in defence expenditure. In this context, peace denotes a reduction in aggressive intentions towards other countries and/ or fears of aggressive conduct from them, rather than formal agreements with them.

peak

It is the highest point of a fluctuation. Where an economic variable has a trend, it may be necessary to distinguish between a peak in the sense of an absolute local maximum, and in the sense of a maximum relative to trend.

peak-load pricing

It denotes a price structure in which more is charged for units supplied at peak-load periods than for units supplied at others times. The argument for peak-load pricing is that the total capacity needed for, a power, transport system, etc.

pendulum arbitration

It refers to arbitration in which two sides set out their proposal and the arbitrator is required to choose between them. The parties could be employers and trade unions, or firms involved in a commercial dispute. The arbitrators work by spitting the difference between the parties' claims, so that it pays each party to make exaggerated demands.

pension fund

It is a fund from which pensions are paid. Pension funds receive contributions from employers, employees, or both. These funds are then invested to give an income and acquire capital gains until the pensions are paid. Pension schemes may be fully funded, when the fund is actuarially solvent; or they may be partially funded, when the fund relies on the employers to make up the sums necessary to pay for the promised pensions.

pension rights

These are rights to receive pensions, from the state or former employers. The value of pension rights implies the actuarial value of expected pension receipts, given the age and other individual characteristics of the pensioner. What is received in any individual case depends on how long they survive to draw the pension.

per capita income

It is the national income of a country, or region, divided by its population. Per capita income can be calculated per person, counting everybody, using weights to count children of various ages as equivalent to fractions of an adult.

per capita real GDP

It is a country's real GDP per member of the population. This may be calculated using the total population, adults only, or 'adult equivalents', giving children of various ages weights equal to a fraction of an adult. Per capita real GDP is lower than per capita income in a country with net external assets which yield an income, and is greater than per capita income in a country with a lot of internal assets, so that net property income payments have to be made abroad.

percentage change

It is the change in a variable, expressed as a percentage of its previous value. If the variable is a_t, the change is defined as $\Delta a_t = a_{t-1}$, and the percentage change as $100\Delta a_t a_{t-1}$.

percentile

It refers to the values separating parts of a distribution, arranged in order of size. The 90th percentile of the income distribution, for example, is the income level such that only ten per cent of the population have larger incomes.

perfect capital mobility

It is a situation when capital is perfectly free to move between countries. If this happens, the risk-adjusted returns to capital, net of tax, would be equal in all countries. Perfect capital mobility is prevented partly by controls on capital movements, and partly by lack of information about foreign countries.

perfect competition

It is defined as an ideal market situation in which buyers and sellers are so numerous and well-informed that each can act as a price-taker, able to buy or sell any desired quantity without affecting the market price. Very few real world markets are like this, but perfect competition is often regarded by economists as a benchmark with which to compare actual market situations.

perfect equilibrium

It is an equilibrium concept applicable to situations where decisions are made in two or more stages. At every stage, all market participants choose whichever strategy is best for them, given the information they have at hand. At every last but one stage, decisions are taken on the assumptions that market participants cannot now alter the decisions taken at earlier stages.

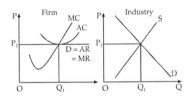

Perfect equilibrium in perfect competition

perfect market

It can be defined as market in which the conditions for perfect competition are satisfied. It denotes a homogenous commodity, and large numbers of buyers and sellers who are well informed about trading opportunities, none of whom receives preferential treatment.

perfect substitute

It refers to a good which is indistinguishable in use from another. If two goods are perfect substitutes, their prices must be the same if both are to be used, i.e. the elasticity of sub-

stitution between them is infinite, and any price difference will lead to all consumers choosing the cheaper.

performance-related pay

It refers to pay related to the output or profits of the employers. This normally takes the form of bonuses over some agreed rate if the firm does well. Pay may be related to the performance of the firm as a whole, that of a division or part of firm.

period of gestation

It refers to the period between the start of an investment project and the time when production using it can start. Owing to the fact that this period is usually quite long, particularly for major investment projects, expectations about market conditions when the project is complete are necessarily very uncertain.

period of oscillation

The length of time it takes an oscillatory function to return to any given point in its cycle. The functions a = a cosa or c = b sina have a period of oscillation of 2π, $t = t_0 + 4\pi$, etc.

periphery

It is an outlying of an economy, with poor communications and sparse population, which hinder its prosperity. The periphery is distinct from the core, central regions with good communications and high population density.

permanent income

It is the amount that an individual can spend consistently with being able to maintain the same level of spending in the future. This is a forward-looking concept, depending on expected levels of earned income, unearned income, and transfers from the state or other individuals.

perpetual inventory method

It is the method of estimating a country's total capital stock, starting from the level of real investment in each past year. Invested is classified by type of capital goods, like buildings, plant and machinery, and vehicles. An appropriate rate of write-off each year, based on the estimated lives of the various goods, is applied to each types of capital.

perquisites

These are payments in kind attached to jobs.

These may be of various forms; e.g., company cars, club membership, and company medical facilities or insurance are common, and there are some idiosyncratic ones, such as company boxes at the opera.

personal disposable income
It refers to personal incomes after deduction of income tax and insurance contributions. This is the sum available to be divided between personal savings and consumption.

personal equity plan (PEP)
It is a system, established in UK in 1986, by which individuals could invest a limited sum each tax year in shares and unit trusts, through a financial intermediary. PEP investments were then free from both income and capital gains tax, subject to a minimum holding period.

personal income distribution
It is the distribution of income between different individuals. It can be measured before or after the deduction of direct taxes and receipt of income transfers.

personal loan
It defines a loan, from a bank or finance company, given to an individual, who is not necessarily required to produce any specific security for it. Personal loans are widely used to finance the purchase of expensive items such as cars and furniture.

personal preferences
These are individual tastes, as regards both consumption and work. No two individuals are precisely the same in their choices between the available goods and services to consume and work to perform. It denotes that it is not possible to find a utility function, which will predict what every individual will do in response to any given set of prices and wages rates.to consume and work to perform. It denotes that it is not possible to find a utility function, which will predict what every individual will do in response to any given set of prices and wages rates.

personal sector
It is the part of a country's economy consisting of households, unincorporated businesses, pension funds, and private non-profit-making bodies serving persons, such as NGOs and charities.

peso problem
It is the tendency in countries having a past history of high inflation for interest rates to remain higher than abroad. This problem occurs where experience of inflation and currency depreciation in the past has led to expectations that the future will be similar.

petro-currency
It denotes the currency of a country heavily dependent on oil exports. The exchange rate of a petro-currency is strongly influenced by the international price of oil.

petro-dollars
It refers to balance of payments surplus of oilexporting countries which were invested abroad, often in US dollars securities.

Philips curve
It is a curve plotting the rate of increase of wages against unemployment. Lower unemployment is associated with greater increases in wages.

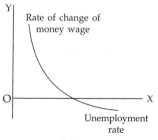

Philips curve

The original Philips curve was named after its inventor. The model has since been extended in the following two days: (i) the rate of inflation is often shown rather than wage increases, on the assumption that wage increases will lead to price increases, and that low unemployment is associated with excess demand, which leads directly to price increases, (ii) the model has been extended to take account of inflationary expectations. Philips curve plots actual inflation against unemployment, with given inflation expectations.

physical capital
It is the capital in the form of physical goods, either fixed capital or stocks and work in progress. Physical capital is distinct from

both financial and human capital. Financial capital includes both cash holdings of firms, and net trade credit extended to customers, while human capital includes both technical know-how, whether embodied in patents or not and the skills of the workforce.

phytosanitary measures

These are restrictions on trade designed to protect the health of humans, animals or plants. While some restrictions on trade are necessary to prevent the spread of diseases like bird flu, swine flu, foot and mouth diseases, etc. There is a danger that restrictions purporting to be phytosanitary will be used to protect domestic producers of the goods concerned.

picketing

In economics, it is the procedure during strikes of placing strikers outside workplaces to inform other workers that they are in dispute, and to attempt to persuade other employees, and those of suppliers and customers, not to enter the premises.

picking winners

It is the idea that governments can promote economic development by selecting particular projects for financial and technical support. Such industrial strategy only promotes economic growth if the government is better than private investors at picking projects likely to succeed.

piecewise linear function

It is a function which consists of a number of linear sections, with different slopes. It is the function relating to income tax payable to taxable income.

Pigou effect

The term is used in the context of argument given by A.C. Pigou that price and wage flexibility could prevent unemployment. If prices and wages fell sufficiently in a slump, full employment would be restored because of the resulting real money supply. In practice, however, nobody relies on such a mechanism. In an economy with money debts, large falls in prices would damage the solvency of many firms, and probably cause the collapse of some financial institutions.

placing

It is sale of shares by company to selected individuals or institutions approached directly, rather than by an issue open to the general public. A placing may be preferred on grounds of lower costs, or because it gives the company a chance to choose its new shareholders.

planned economy

It is defined as an economy in which the government takes all major decisions about what should be produced, how much should be produced and who should get it. This is contrasted with a free market economy in which most decisions are taken by independent individuals and firms. Supporters of a planned economy claim that planning avoids wasteful duplication and unemployment and goods are distributed fairly. The actual process of taking decisions and seeing that they are carried out requires an enormous amount of information and officials to administer the system.

planned investment

It is the amount of investment that firms, companies, individuals, or public bodies intend to make during some period. Actual investment may not correspond to planned investment for various reasons. Fixed investment plans may be thwarted because the arrangement goods required cannot be obtained, as is likely in booms, or because the arrangements for financing the expenditure collapse, as is likely during slumps.

planned savings

The term denotes the amount that individuals, firms or governments plan to save - savings plans not to be carried out for two main reasons. Income may be larger or smaller than expected, and emergencies may arise which require unanticipated spending or prevent spending plans from being carried out.

planning land-use

It means controls by central or local government over the use of land. These are widely used, because of the importance of externalities resulting from land use. Land-use planning is used to keep activities causing where they are believed to be particularly harmful.

plough-back

It refers to the system of financing investment in firms by retaining profits. It is in contrast with financing investment by borrowing or issuing new equity capital. The advantage of ploughback is that it retains con- trol, and reduces gearing if the firm had borrowed heavily in the past.

point elasticity
The ratio of a proportional change in one variable to that of another, measured at a point. For example, if p is price and q is quantity, the elasticity of demand will be denoted as $(p/q)(dq/dp)$. This is the limit of $(\Delta q/q)(\Delta p/p)$ as Δp and Δq tend to zero in.

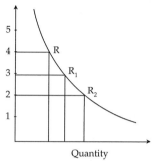

Point elasticity

point of inflection
It is the point where a function changes its curvature. This means that its second derivative changes sign. For example, consider the function $b = ax^3+yx$, for which:
$dy/dx = 3ax_2+y$ and $d^2b/dx^2 = 6ax$.

polarisation
It is the rule followed by the Securities and Exchange Board of India (SEBI) that bodies such as banks and buildings societies must choose either to give independent advice on all brands of life insurance and unit trusts, or confine themselves to selling the products of only one company.

policy co-ordination
It implies to concept that argument that national fiscal and monetary policies would produce better results if countries collaborated. The fiscal and monetary policies followed in each country have effects abroad as well as at home. Each country made less use of policies which were inimical towards other countries than they would choose independently, and more use of policies that benefited the others.

policy instrument
It is a policy measure under the control of the monetary or fiscal authorities. This could be a measure such as a change in the money supply or tax rates, or the imposition of price or quantitative controls. Policy instruments are distinct from policy targets and policy indicators.

political business cycle
It is the theory that some economic fluctuations are due to governments theory of seeking political mileage by expanding the economy in advance of elections.

political economy
It is the original name of what is today known as economics. The name is still used by some circles. Some economists argue that it is actually a better name for the subject, as it draws attention to the political motivation of economic policies.

poll tax
It is a lump-sum tax levied in some countries on every citizen at the same rate regardless of income. A poll tax is necessarily regressive, taking a larger proportion of small incomes than of large ones.

population trap
It refers to a situation where no increase in living standards is possible, because population is increasing so fast that all available savings are needed to maintain the existing capital-labour ratio.

portable pension
It is an occupational pension which allows a person to change employers without loss of pension rights. A pension can be made portable when an employee leaves a firm in two ways. One method may be adopted for the employee's accrued pension contribution to be frozen in the former employer's pension fund until the employee reaches pensionable age, when the fund will pay part of their pension.

portfolio
It implies a set of different assets in the possession of an individual or firm. A variety of assets may be preferred to holding a single type of asset for several reasons. Holding a variety of assets reduces risk, and allows

better returns through a combination of some assets with higher income but poor liquidity, and others with lower income but more liquidity.

portfolio selection
It is the choice of the proportions of different assets which should be held in order to obtain the maximum expected benefit from any given stock of wealth. It largely depends on the characteristics of various assets as well as the objectives of the person or institution holding them. Assets differ in their yield, either in the form of the mean expected income or capital appreciation, and in their riskiness.

positive economics
It is defined as the study of how economic processes work. As it is concerned with what actually happens, it needs a lot of institutional and statistical information. Positive economics is distinct with normative economics, which is concerned with how the economy ought to be run. Positive economics also analyses how economic processes would work given certain assumptions about institutional conditions, e.g. the existence of monopoly or about motivation.

potential competition
It refers to competition from prospective as well as actual rivals. If an industry has constant returns to scale and freedom of entry, potential competition is a powerful deterrent to monopolistic conduct by existing firms, even if the industry currently has a highly concentrated structure.

potential output
It is the output which could be produced with the available labour, capital, and technology. For an individual firm, potential output is the output that could be produced with present capital and technology, having some provision for recruitment of necessary unskilled labour. In some cases, old and inefficient capital equipment could only be used profitably at higher output prices.

pound (£)
It is the UK currency unit; this is often referred to as the pound sterling. The name is also used for the currency units of several other countries, including Cypress, Egypt, Lebanon, and Syria.

poverty
It can be defined as inability to afford an adequate standard of consumption, but this standard is subject to variation between countries and over time. Economists have differed as to whether poverty should be considered in absolute terms, as falling below some fixed minimum consumption level, or whether it should be defined in relative terms, so that poverty means inability to afford what average people have. If an absolute standard is accepted, it can at least be understood that technical progress will eventually lift everybody above the poverty line. If poverty is relative, the poor will be always with us.

poverty line
It refers to an income level supposed to be just enough to avoid inadequate consumption. Where this level stands, depends on numerous factors such as: (i) people vary in their number of dependents; (ii) in the extent to which they are addicted to expensive vices including alcohol and tobacco; (iii) their need to pay interest on loans contracted because of previous over-spending of their incomes; and (iv) their competence at spending such money as they have.

poverty trap
It is a situation when means-tested benefits do not reach people which means that a person does not gain from moving from unemployment into a job, or from obtaining a better-paid job. They may be no better off, or even worse off financially than before, or too little better off to make the extra effort appear worthwhile.
1. An instruction to multiply a number of times. The nth power of x is 1 multiplied by x, n times; n is the exponent of x.
2. A strength in arranging the terms of one's dealing with other firms or people. For example, bargaining power, countervailing power, and monopoly power.

precautionary motive
It is the motive to hold money to provide for the unexpected. This is distinguished from the transactions and speculative motives. The transactions motive on the other hand is to hold money for convenience in transactions which are anticipated, the precautionary motive on the other hand.

predatory pricing

It denotes pricing which are kept low, with the intention of driving rivals out of a market or preventing new firms from entering. It is good for consumers in the short run, but may be bad in the long run if a firm which has used predatory pricing to establish a monopoly position raises its prices.

predetermined endogenous variable

It is a variable in a dynamic economic system which is determined within the system, but by past and not current variables. At any one time, it is thus independent of other variables in the system.

premium

The term is used for the following:
1. A share price higher than the issue price, i.e. a share traded at a price higher than its issue stands at a premium.
2. An addition to interest rates required to compensate lenders for risk.
3. The price paid for an insurance policy. This may be monthly or annual payment, or it is possible to take out a single-premium policy by a lump-sum payment.
4. A suggestion of superior quality, as in premium patrol.

premium bond

It refers to a government security where the interest goes into a fund which provides for lotteries held at regular intervals, in which all bondholders are entered.

prescriptive statement

It refers to a statement about what ought to be, as opposed to a positive statement which is concerned only with facts. In some cases, statements which are formally of one type carry strong implications of the other.

present discounted value

It is the present value of a payment due to be received in the future. If the payment is due p periods into the future and the proportional interest rate is r per period, the present discounted value of a sum A to be received in the future is given by: $v = A/(1+r)^t = A(1+r)^{-p}$.

pressure group

It is defined as an organisation trying to bring about changes in laws or policies. These may be in the interests of its members, or of some wider cause such as the environment.

pre-tax profits

These are the profits of a company before deduction of corporation tax, of an unincorporated business before deduction of other taxes the business has to pay, including value-added tax (VAT), business rates, etc.

price

It is the amount of money one has to pay per unit for a good or service. This is easy to observe for almost all goods and services. In a shop, customers find displayed the price at which as many or few units as they wish can be purchased. For some goods and services, the price may be less easy to observe. The price mechanism refers to the role of prices in organising the production and distribution of goods and services in an economy: the prices people are willing to pay convey information on how they value the effort and inputs needed for production.

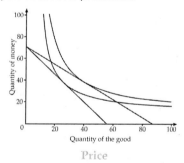

Price

price control

It implies the setting of maximum prices by law. Such control may affect particular markets, for example domestic rents are often subject to special controls, or apply in an economy generally. Since it is administratively not possible to set millions of prices from first principles, price controls have generally worked by covering a limited number of essential goods.

price discrimination

It refers to charging different prices to different customers for the same good or service. It is possible only if the supplier has the monopoly power, and can identify the customer, and if different customers have different elasticities of demand, so that marginal revenue in different markets is equal. There are three types of price discrimination: (i) first-degree price discrimination: it implies selling every unit at the maximum the consumer would pay, so that there is no consumer surplus and the producer takes potential benefits from a good; (ii) second-degree price discrimination: it occurs when producers cannot tell which group the customers belong to, but offer alternative contracts which induce consumers to identify themselves; (iii) third-degree price discrimination: it occurs when sellers can identify different groups of customers.

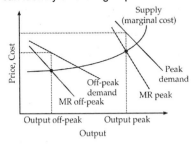

Price discrimination

price-earnings ratio (P/E ratio)
It is the ratio of the current market price of a company's ordinary share to its most recently published earnings for equity per share. A relatively high price-earnings ratio may mean that earnings are expected to grow rapidly, or that they are regarded as relatively safe.

price elasticity
It is the ratio of a proportional change in quantity supplied or demanded to a proportional change in price. The elasticity of supply is $(p/q)(dq/dp)$, where p is price and q is quantity.

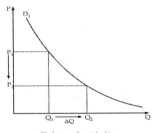

Price elasticity

price fixing
It denotes agreement between two or more firms about the prices they charge. It is considered anti-competitive, and is forbidden by monopoly legislation in many countries.

price index
It is an index number of the prices of goods of some given type. If only one good g is concerned, period 0 is the base period and period t the current period, where p_{gt} is the price in period t, the price index is given by p_{gt}/p_{g0}.

price leader
It refers to a firm whose price changes tend to be followed by other sellers in its markets. It may be by agreement, which is illegal under monopoly legislation in some countries, or by collusion, which is considered anticompetitive but is difficult to prevent.

price level
It is the general level of prices in an economy. This may refer to consumer goods prices, in which case it is measured by a retail price index (RPI), or to all goods produced, including investment and government purchases as well as consumer goods, in which case it is measured by GDP deflator.

price-maker
It denotes a firm which sets the price of a good or security, by offering to buy and sell at announced prices. To effectively act as a market-maker it is necessary to hold a stock of the good, so as to be able to provide it when buying orders exceed selling orders.

price mechanism
It is an expression referring to the role of prices in a market economy in conveying information and providing incentives. The market mechanism is an alternative phrase making the same point. The prices people are willing to pay for a particular good or service convey information about how much they value them, and the prices producers ask convey information about how their inputs are valued. The price mechanism provides incentives for the allocation of resources where their value is highest, and satisfies wants from the cheapest sources.

prices and income policy
The term is used for attempts by government

176

to control prices and income directly, by law. Such policies are different from influencing prices and wages through monetary and fiscal policies, or setting prices by acting as a buyer or seller in particular markets, e.g. at the time of off-take of food grain. There are far too many prices in a modern economy for the task of setting them all from first principles to be administratively feasible. Prices and incomes policies therefore tend to work either by setting some important prices and leaving others to the market, or setting limits to price increases.

price-sensitive information
It is information about a company which could affect its share price. This includes figures on profits, turnover employment, innovations, changes in senior management, or takeover bids.

price support
It refers to government policies to keep the prices of commodities up to some minimum level. This applies mainly to agricultural products, to raise the incomes of producers.

price-taker
The term is used for an individual or firm trading on a market where they do not believe that their transactions will affect the market price. It may be because there are large numbers of traders on each side in a perfect market, or because the individual or firm is a small trader on a market where the price is fixed by a market maker.

price volatility
It denotes the extent to which a price fluctuates. Fluctuations may be measured on any time-scale, from year-by-year to day-by-day or week-by-week. Volatility over short time intervals tends to be lower prices are administered than when they are set in a competitive market.

price war
It means charging low prices to harm competitors' profits. In a price war one or more firms charge prices below those that would maximise their own profits, to inflict losses on rivals.

primary sector
It is defined as the sector of the economy making direct use of natural resources. It in-

cludes agricultural, forestry and fishing, and extractive industries producing fuel, metals, and other minerals.

principal
It denotes the following:
1. The amount lent at the start of loan.
2. A person or firm employing another to act as agent. A person using an estate agent to sell a house, for example, is a principal; the estate agent is the agent.

principal-agent problem
The problem of how a person A can motivate a person B to act for A's benefit rather than following self-interest. The principal, A, may be an employer and the agent, B, an employee, or the principal may be a shareholder and the agent a director of a company.

private company
It is a limited liability company restricted to between 2 and 50 shareholders, not counting present and past employees. Shareholders cannot transfer their shares without the consent of other members, and shares cannot be offered to the general public.

private cost
It implies the cost of providing goods or services as it appears to the person or firm supplying them. Private cost includes the cost of any factor services or inputs bought by the supplier, the value of work done, and the use of land, buildings, and equipment owned by the supplier.

private enterprises
It refers to the system by which economic activity is undertaken by independent individuals or firms, instead of under central direction. Supporters of private enterprises claim that it is generally beneficial not so much, because it is private, as because it is enterprising, which makes for greater efficiency and more technical improvements than centrally controlled firms would produce.

private good
It implies any good or service which if used by one individual or firm is not available to others. Most consumer goods and capital goods are private goods. They are distinct from public goods, where one person's use does not decrease the amount available for others. Services such as radio and TV trans-

missions are almost public goods at times of low usage and almost private goods at peak periods when congestion means that one person's usage reduces the space available for others.

private property
It refers to things which the law recognises as belonging exclusively to particular individuals or organisations. This is distinct from things which are owned by the government, such as public highways, and things which are held to available for use by anybody, for example the works of Shakespeare, Dickens or Kipling and other authors whose copyright has expired.

private sector
It is defined as the parts of the economy not run by the government. This includes households, sole traders and partnerships, companies, and voluntary bodies such as charities and churches.

private sector balance
It is the excess of savings over investment spending by the private sector. It is a national income accounting that identifies that the private sector balance, government sector balance, and current account deficit of the economy must sum to zero.

privatisation
It means the transfer to private ownership and control of assets or enterprises which were pre- viously under public ownership. Privatised assets may have been under direct state ownership, or owned by local authorities. Privatisation is adopted with the aim that assets will be used more efficiently under private ownership, to reduce the power of central authorities, to raise revenue for the government.

probability
It is the likelihood that a random event will occur. This must lie between 0 and 1: probability is 0 if the event is certain not to occur, and 1 if it is certain to occur. The expectations concerning probability may be derived from past experience of how frequently events of this have occurred, or from theoretical models about how the economy works.

process innovation
It refers to the innovation where a product is made in a new and cheaper way. This is different from product innovation, where a new or improved product is introduced.

procurement
It implies government purchase of goods and services. However, the large scale of government purchase makes corruption or inefficiency in procurement a serious drain on government finances. Unless this is necessary on grounds of national security, it is considered a form of protectionism which is an important source of inefficiency. In many countries procurement is necessary to build a stock of food grains, etc.

producer good
It is a good intended for use as a capital good or intermediate product by producers, instead of direct use by consumers. Some goods are both consumer and producer goods.

producer's surplus
It is defined as the excess of total sales revenue going to producers over the area under the supply curve for a good. If the supply curve is perfectly elastic there is no producer's surplus, but if the supply curve is upward-slopping, those productive resources which would have stayed in the industry at a lower price earn quasi-rents.

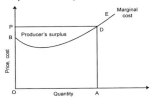

Producer's surplus

product
It refers to the following:
1. The result of multiplication. The product of two numbers, algebraic expressions,vectors of matrices may be indicated by dots, multiplication signs, or simply writing them in sequences.
2. Any produced good that satisfies a necessity.

product differentiation
It is the marketing of generally similar products with minor variations which make them imperfect substitutes for consumers. It may involve real differences in material, design, workmanship, or other aspects of quality.

product innovation
It means innovation where a new or improved product is introduced. It is distinct from process innovation, where an existing product is made in a new and cheaper way.

production
It can be defined as the use of resources to make goods or services which have value. The 'means of production, distribution, and exchange' seek to divide economic activity into changing the physical form of things, changing their location, and changing their ownership. It is not clear how such a classification can apply to services, nor that it is of any economic relevance as applied to goods.

production externality
It refers to an external effect of production, which neither harms nor benefits the person on firm controlling the production. Adverse production externalities include noise, air and water pollution. Beneficial externalities include the public's pleasure from seeing lambs, playing or barley growing.

production function
In economics, it is a function showing the maximum output possible with any given set of inputs, assuming these are used efficiently. The marginal product of any one input is normally positive, but decreasing. If the production function is written as b = f(a, c), where b is output and a and c are inputs, the marginal product of a is $\partial b/\partial a$.

production possibility frontier
It is a diagram showing the maximum output of one good possible with the available resources, given the output of other goods. In a two-dimensional diagram with its origin at the SW corner, the production possibility frontier (PPF) usually slopes down-wards: its slope shows the opportunity cost of each good in terms of the other.

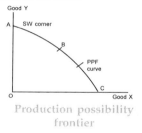

Production possibility frontier

production subsidy
It is a payment by the government to producers of a good or service, at a fixed per unit produced. It is available only to domestic producers and not to importers.

productivity
It can be defined as the amount of output per unit achieved by a firm, industry, or country. It may be per unit of a particular factor of production, for example, labour employed, or per unit of land in agriculture, or 'total factor productivity' may be measured, which involves aggregating the different types of factor.

product liability
It refers to liability for damage caused by a product of the original producer, as well as the immediate vendor.

product life cycle
It is a model of how products go through a series of phases over time. In this model, new products start as small-scale specialities produced by innovators. Initially, the prices are low and the innovators have cost advantages of know-how, equipment, patents, etc. which give them a quasi-monopoly position.

professional body
It refers to the organisation of people with particular professional qualifications. Such organisation may seek to set standards of professional competence, to control entry to ensure that its members to ensure that they also to exclude them if they do not.

profit
It is the excess of the receipts over the spending of a business during any period.

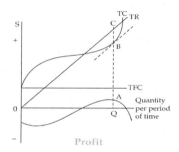

Profit

It includes credit transactions and asset revaluations as well as cash transactions and changes in holdings of real assets. Profits for a period is equal to dividends and profits taxes plus the excess of net assets at the end of the period over net assets at its start.

profit-and-loss account
It is an account of an organisation's receipts and spending over a period. Both sides of the account include credit transactions and asset revaluations as well as cash transactions and changes in holdings of real assets.

profit maximisation
It is the aim of making as much profit as possible for a business. This is a slogan which raises many questions. But the question is over what time horizon are profits to be maximised? Generally, there is a conflict between short-run profits and long-run growth. If the aim is maximising the present discounted value of all further profits, we have to determine what the right discount rate is to use. Profit maximisation is a sensible objective only if the owners are risk-neutral: there is normally a trade-off to be made between risks and mean expected profits.

profit motive
It is the desire for a gain as a motive in economic activity. This motive is widespread. But, it is not the only motive in life for most people. They want a vast variety of things, ranging from a peaceful life, power, friends, honours, the satisfaction of getting things to work, self-respect, and the respect of others that derives from a reputation for hard work and honesty.

profit-related pay
It is the system of making pay a function of the employer's profits, prevalent in many countries. This normally takes the form of additional payments when profits are good, either as a rise in pay scales or as bonuses.

profit-sharing
It means giving employers a share in a firm's profits. It may be done either by profit-related pay, or by enabling employees to become shareholders, by giving them either shares or options to buy shares on preferential terms.

profit-taking
It means selling an asset like shares, etc. in order to realise an accrued capital gain. The holder of any asset has to decide whether to hold on to it or sell it. A sale means that capital gains are realised, which may mean paying capital gains tax.

progressive tax
It is a tax where the revenue collected rises more than proportionally to income. Income tax is made progressive to bring fairness by having exemptions for very small incomes, low rates for the first slice of taxable income, and higher rates for the largest incomes.

prohibitive tariff
It is a tariff set at so high a rate that no trade in the good concerned can take place. Prohibitive tariffs have the disadvantage that they raise no revenue, and make smudging profitable.

proof by contradiction
It refers to a proof which works by showing that considering that a proposition is false leads to a contradiction, i.e. assuming the original proposition is false allows one to prove both same statement and its opposite. Thus, the initial assumption that the proposition was false may not have been correct.

propensity to consume
It is defined as the proportion of disposal income which individuals desire to spend on consumption. The average propensity to consume is total desired spending as a proportion of total disposal income, while the marginal propensity to consume is the proportion of additional income that an individual desires to consume.

propensity to save
It is the proportion of disposal income which individuals do not desire to spend on consumption. The average propensity to give total desired saving is a proportion of total disposal income, while the marginal propensity to save is the proportion of additional income an individual desires to save.

property
It denotes the following:
1. Ownership of assets by private individuals or organisations. The assets may include property and intellectual property such as patents. Property incomes are income derived from such assets.

2. Also the land and buildings. Property forms an important part of a country's capital stock. Property prices are the values of land and buildings, which are liable to large fluctuations.

property company
It is a company whose principal activity is owning and developing property. This may be industrial, commercial, or residential.

property developer
The term is used for an individual or firm which buys property with a view to changing its use, or constructs new property. Property development is inherently risky: because of the liability of the property market to large price changes, as happened during the global recession of 2008-09, and partly because of uncertainty about obtaining planning approval for changes of use and new building.

property income
It refers to income derived from the ownership of property of any sort. It includes rents, dividends, and interest. This is also sometimes known as unearned income; it is contrasted with income from employment.

property lending
It means lending to finance purchases of property. Such lending generally uses the property concerned as collateral, through mortgages on it. Property lending can be very risky if the loans cover a high percentage of the property's valuation because, in case the property prices fall the collateral may be worth less the loan, leaving the borrower with negative equity.

property market
The term is used to denote the system by which land and buildings are bought and sold. There is no central institution for this market, which works through an informal network of estate agents and other specialised intermediaries. The property market is extremely imperfect in the economics sense, as every property is different in location, and properties in close proximity differ in several characteristics.

property portfolio
It is a collection of properties held by a company. This kind of portfolio may be held for income or with a view to development. Property companies hold portfolios rather than single properties to reduce risk, since any particular property may fail to find a tenant.

property rights
These are the rights of an owner over property. These generally include rights to use property, and to exclude others from it. Property rights are not absolute, because the use of assets may be subject to legal controls, such as the need for planning permission for changes in the use of land and buildings.

proportional tax
It is a tax where the revenue collected rises proportionally with income. A tax system could be made approximately proportional by having a uniform rate of income tax with very few exemptions, and indirect taxes like value-added tax levied at similar rates on various goods and services.

prospectus
It is a document provided by a company wishing to sell newly issued shares or debentures to the public. A prospectus must provide information on the aims, past financial history, and capital structure of the venture, and may also contain profit forecasts. Prospectuses have to be lodged with the Registrar of Companies, and there are penalties for not doing so or for making false claims in a prospectus.

protectionism
It is the belief that restriction on international trade is a desirable policy. The aim may be preventing unemployment capital losses in industries threatened by imports, the promotion of particular types of industries improving a country's terms by exploiting its international monopoly power. After the global financial downturn in 2008-09 many countries have started resorting to protectionism.

proxy vote
It is a vote exercised by one person on behalf of another. At company meetings, proxy votes are allowed. Generally, shareholders can nominate some other person to cast their vote, either in some specified manner or at the proxy-holder is discretion.

public finance

It is defined as the study of the financing of government. It includes taxation, spending by public bodies on real goods and services, provision of transfer of incomes by the government, government property incomes, government borrowing and debt, fiscal position and the financial relations between various levels of government.

public goods

These are goods or services which, when provided, are open to use by all members of society. Examples are: defence, law and order, administration, visits to exhibitions, museums, monuments and public parks, etc. As nobody can be excluded from using them, public goods cannot be provided for private profit. Public goods can be and frequently are provided privately, by ostentation.

public interest

It refers to the good of the general public, as contrasted with the particular individuals, firms, companies or institutions involved in a decision. Managers of publicly owned enterprises, or bodies appointed to regulate monopolies, operate in the public interest.

public limited company (PLC)

It is a company registered under the Companies Act. Its name must end in plc. The Act lays down minimum capital requirements, and sets the form for a public limited company's memorandum. Such companies can offer shares and securities to the public with limited liability.

public ownership

It implies ownership of enterprises by the government, or a government-controlled body. It may include direct operation by the central government, as for example, with military establishments or the civil service.

public procurement

It refers to the purchase of goods and services by the public sector, at all levels of government. Public procurement accounts for a considerable fraction of total national expenditure due to state activities in providing defence, law and order, health, education, and other public services. In running an efficient economy, it is imperative to ensure that the considerable sums involved are spent effi-ciently, and that the process of allocating government contracts is free from corruption.

public sector

The team denotes those parts of the economy which are not controlled by individuals, voluntary organisations, or privately owned companies. Public sector includes government at all levels-national and local, government-owned firms and quasi-autonomous non-government organisations.

public utility

It refers to the group of industries providing water, gas, and electricity to both domestic and business consumers. Such businesses are considered as special partly because everybody needs their services, and partly because of economies and their distribution networks.

public works

These are construction projects paid for by the state or central government. These can include both new construction and improvements to roads, bridges, ports, airports, schools, hospitals, government offices, and publicly owned housing. There is almost always a large programme of public works in progress.

pump priming

It refers to the theory that it is possible for the government to bring about permanent recovery from a temporary injection of purchasing power into the economy. It assumes that if incomes are low because lack of confidence in the future prevents investment, a temporary rise in government spending, financed by borrowing rather than tax, can raise incomes through its multiplier effects, which will allow investment to recover.

purchase tax

It is a tax in some countries, charged on consumer goods, at rates varying between goods and over time. It was replaced by value-added tax (VAT) in some parts of Europe.

purchasing power

It defines the amount of real goods and services each unit of money will buy. Purchasing power is the reciprocal of a suitable price index; i.e., if prices go up, the purchasing power of money goes down. Purchasing power is also dependent on consumer tastes.

purchasing power parity (PPP)

It denotes the theory that exchange rates between currencies are determined in the long run by the amount of goods and services that each can buy. In the absence of transport costs and tariffs, if the price of tradable goods were lower in one country than another, traders will gain by buying goods in the cheaper country and selling in the dearer. Thus, relative price levels determine the equilibrium exchange rate.

pure floating exchange rate

It can be defined as floating exchange rate which is set by the market without any intervention by central banks or governments. A pure or 'clean' float is distinct from a managed or 'dirty' float in which there is some official intervention in the foreign exchange market.

put option

It refers to a contract giving the right but not the obligation to sell a good security, or currency on some future date at a price fixed when the contract is first taken out. A put option will only be exercised when the date arrives if the spot market price is below the option price. In case the market price is higher than the option price it will be beneficial to sell on the spot market.

pyramid scheme

It is a financial scheme in some countries of Europe in which investors are offered a high rate of return provided they recruit at least some number of new members. Such schemes are inherently fraudulent as they can only pay the promised return as long as total membership rises fast enough, and once new entry slows down or falls they are bound to default on their promises.

Q

q-ratio

It is ratio which measures the relationship of the market value of physical capital, such as existing plant or other corporate asset, to its replacement cost. This term was derived by Prof. Japes Tobin.

quality control

It is the system for checking the quality of a product. It may be done before it is sold, and/or at earlier stages of production. Where the checking itself destroys or is liable to damage the product, quality control has to work through sampling batches of products selected so that they are expected to have common properties, e.g. those processed on a given date by the same machine.

quality ladder

It is the model of producer development by which firms steadily upgrade the quality of their products. Movements up the quality ladder includes making products more durable and improving their performance, specifications and design. In the process, a product changes from being a cheap line aiming at the lower end of the market - to that catering to higher segments.

quality standards

There are minimum standards for goods, set by government bodies or trade associations. These standards are designed to protect consumers, through ensuring satisfactory levels of durability, electrical safety, fire resistance, etc.

quantity equation

It is an equation relating the price level and the quantity of money. The standard formulation of this is mv=pt, where m is the quantity of money, v is the velocity of circulation, p is the price level, and t is the volume of transactions.

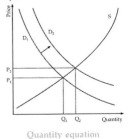

Quantity equation

quantity of money

It is the amount of money in circulation in a country. The quantity theory of money ascribes a major role in determining the price level to the quantity of money.

quarterly data

It is used to imply data for the four quarters of each year, i.e. January-March, April-June, July-September and October-December. Quarterly data are produced for many components of the national income accounts.

quartile

It describes the values such that one-quarter of the observations in a distribution arranged in ascending or descending order lie above the upper quartile, and one-quarter lie below the lower quartile.

quasi-autonomous non-government organisation

It is a form of organisation used when it is desired to provide government finance for an activity without making the day-to-day details of its operations subject to direct political control, and without making government ministers responsible for them.

quota

It refers to the following:
1. A quota for jobs for disadvantaged groups, or that compulsory deliveries by farmers to state marketing organisations would be a minimum. It also means a limit to imports of cars or other luxury goods. In each case, there can be counterarguments that any objective achieved by a quota system could be achieved at lower cost by use of the price mechanism, indirectly if they are fixed on a large scale as this encourages the formation of organisations to share out the market.
2. The share of each member of the International Monetary Fund in its total funds. The quota allocated to each IMF member determines its voting power, the amount of gold or international currency and of its own currencies that it initially subscribes, and its access to various borrowing facilities.
3. Also maximum level of international oil sales allocated to each member of the Organisation of Petroleum Exporting Countries (OPEC) at its periodic meetings.

quotation
It refers to acceptance of a company's shares to be traded on a stock exchange. It is normally subject to providing an acceptable level of information to investors. Market makers are allowed but not compelled to quota prices at which they will buy or sell such shares.

quoted company
It is a company whose shares have been accepted for trading on a stock exchange. This makes it easier to raise capital, as shares once issued are made more marketable as they are quoted on an organised exchange.

quote-driven market
It is a securities market which operates by market makers quoting prices at which they will buy or sell, up to some quantitative limit. Prices are adjusted by the market makers increasing their prices if they run short of stock, or lowering prices if they start accumulating excessive stocks.

R

radical economics
It is a generic name which is used for writing in a Socialist or Marxist tradition, relating particularly to Marxism but adopting and using other sources of ideas such as anarchism, libertarianism, etc.

random sample
It is a sample of a population, chosen by some method which ensures that every member of the population has an equal chance of being picked. A random sample is distinct from a quota sample, where the aim is to have the same proportion of different types, for example the number of workers in the total population.

range
It is the difference between the largest and the smallest observed or possible values of a variable. The range can always be expressed in absolute terms.

rank correlation
It refers to the method of checking the relation between two variables by correlating their orders. It is appropriate if the relation is believed to be monotonically increasing or decreasing, but its form is unknown.

ratchet effect
It refers to a tendency for a variable to be influenced by its own largest previous value. For example, consumption from any given income may be higher, if the previous peak income is higher or the real demanded by trade unions may be an increasing function of the highest real wage previously attained. Variables are stickier in one direction than the other. The ratchet effect may make inflation difficult to stop, if varying speeds of adjustment have developed a situation in which the sum of past peak real incomes of all sections of the community is sufficiently greater than the present total available.

Ratchet effect

rateable value
It is the value placed on buildings for purposes of local taxation. Rateable values were originally supposed to be estimates of the rent which would be paid on a property, but over time have come to bear little relation to this.

rate of interest
In simple terms it is the cost of credit. Any borrower normally has to pay the lender more than the principal originally received. The excess is interest. The rate of interest is the interest which has to be paid for a loan, as a percentage of the principal. It is normally expressed as a rate per annum. If a loan is certain to be repaid, the pure rate of interest compensates the lender for loss of liquidity. If a loan is not certain to be repaid, the rate of interest is much higher than the pure rate of interest. A simple rate of interest does not include interest on interest while compound interest does include it.

rate of return
It is the annual return on a loan as a percentage of its principal. Where interest is paid at intervals other than annual, the annual percentage rate is found by compounding the actual payments.

ratio
It is the result of dividing one number by another. Ratios are widely used in economics to compare securities or institutions, e.g. debt equity ratio. A price-earnings (P/E) ratio is a share price divided by the earnings per share of a company; a reserve ratio is the amount of reserve assets held by a bank or other financial institution divided by its total liabilities.

rationalisation
It is recognition of production in the interests of efficiency or profits. It normally includes non-marginal changes: for example, production may be scattered where it was previously concentrated.

raw materials
They are the products of primary sector industries, intended for use as inputs to production. The main groups of raw materials are agriculture crops such as cotton, and even grains and some vegetables which are used by food-processing industries. Assorted mineral products bauxite ore, etc. used to

make aluminium and raw materials form a decreasing proportion of international trade, but are still very important for many developed countries.

real balance effect
It refers to the effect on spending of changes in the ratio of money balances to income. During inflation, as prices rise, the real purchasing power of the money people already hold goes down. It is expected to make people more likely to save and less likely to spend their incomes.

real business cycle
It refers to the theory that fluctuations in overall economic activity are due to real economic shocks, e.g. variations in the rate of technical progress. It is in contrast with more traditional theories of the trade cycle, which attribute overall fluctuations to many monetary shocks and the inherent dynamic time lags in economic decision-making.

real costs
These are the real resources used up in producing a good or services, or the opportunity costs in terms of other possible outputs foregone. The real costs of a good are distinct from private costs if the inputs are taxed or subsidised or if there are external costs which do not fall on the person or organisation responsible for production.

real GDP
It is gross domestic product divided by a suitable price index, to express it in real terms. The price index used for this purpose is usually the GDP deflator. Since this covers the prices of investment goods and government purchases as well as consumer expenditure, it is more suitable than the Retail Price Index (RPI).

real GNP
It is defined as gross national product divided by a suitable price index, to express it in real terms. The price index used for this purpose is usually the GDP deflator. It covers the prices of investment goods and government purchases as well as consumer expenditure.

realignment of exchange rates
It is a package of changes in exchange rates, negotiated by agreement between the countries concerned. Under the European Monetary System (EMS) from 1980 onwards there were a series of realignments which raised the relative par values of the currencies of countries with low inflation and balance-of-payments (BoP) surpluses, and lowered the relative parties of countries with high inflation and balance-of-payments problems.

real income
It is the income measured at constant prices. It is found by taking money income and deflating by a suitable price index. Owing to continuous changes in the types and quality of goods and services available, measurements of changes in real income become steadily less reliable as comparisons over longer time periods are considered.

real interest rate
It refers to the money return adjusted for inflation. If the nominal interest rate is 80 per cent and the rate of inflation is 80 per cent, the real rate of interest of 80 per cent is given by $(1+r) =(1+i)/(1+p)$. For low interest and inflation rates, the approximation $r \approx i - p$ is fairly accurate. At times when the rate of inflation is changing, the real interest rate can be measured on a forward- or a backward-looking basis.

real national income
It is the national income deflated by a suitable price index. It shows the level of real spending the country can afford. It is affected both by changes in its real productivity and by changes in the terms of trade. For example, if a country's real production grows by 4 per cent, but it imports and exports amounts equal to a quarter of its national income and its terms of trade worsen by 10 per cent, the increase in real national, income is only ½ percent.

real terms
These are attempts to reduce changes in economic variables to changes in quantities. For example, real GDP, is the value of gross national product, measured at current prices, deflated by a 'GDP deflator', or price index.

real variable
It refers to a variable which is measured in physical units of some sort: e.g., the level of employment, or the volume of oil extracted in a year. Real variables are distinct from mon-

etary variables, such as the price level or the annual profits of a firm, and pure numbers or ratios, like elasticities or the percentage of the labour force unemployed.

reciprocity
It refers to the principle of international economic relations by which country A treats the nationals of any foreign country in the same way as that country treats A's nationals. This is distinguished from multilateralism and the most favoured nation (MFN) principle, by which all non-residents are treated equally. Supporters of reciprocity hold that it is both fair and likely to promote market access for one's own exporters; opponents argue that insisting on reciprocity is futile.

recycling
It refers to the reuse of goods which have served their original purpose, e.g. empty bottles, plastic goods or worn-out motor vehicles. Recycling is advocated on both cost-saving and environmental grounds, as it reduces both the need for extractive industries and the dumping of waste products.

redeemable security
It denotes a security which the borrower is due to redeem at some date. This is in contrast with an irredeemable security, where the borrower has no obligation to repay the loan. As a redeemable security approaches maturity, its price dominated by its redemption value, is the amount which is due to be repaid.

redemption date
It is the date on which a security is due to be redeemed by the borrower. It may be a single date, or a range of dates within which the borrower has discretion to choose when repayment will take place.

redemption value
It is price at which a security is due to be redeemed when it reaches maturity.

redemption yield
It refers to the interest rate at which receipts of interest and repayment on a security held till it matures need to be discounted to make their present value equal to its market price.

redeployment
It means shifting of factors of production from one use to another. When labour is redeployed, this can imply that workers no longer needed in one part of a firm found jobs in another part.

redistributive tax
It refers to a tax designed to alter the distribution of incomes or property ownership, generally in the direction of greater equality. Any progressive tax is bound to have some effects of this type. Thus, the term is normally used to denote income taxes with high marginal rates on large incomes, and taxes on inheritance.

reducing balance depreciation
It is the method of depreciating fixed assets by writing off a constant percentage of their remaining value each period. The remaining fraction is then written off when the assets are finally scrapped.

redundancy
It denotes termination of employment without any fault on the part of the employees concerned, because of a nail in the employer's need for labour. Workers in some countries have a right to compensation for redundancy. In many cases, employers make redundancy payments in excess of legal requirements, to include workers to accept offers of voluntary redundancy.

regional aid
It refers to help given by central government for regions with low per capita incomes or high unemployment. It may take the forms of state funds for infrastructure investment, subsidies, or tax allowances to induce private firms to invest in less developed regions.

registered unemployed
It refers to unemployed persons in receipts of unemployment benefits or other forms of income support. It means that they are unemployed in the view of the official agencies responsible for administering benefits.

registrar of companies
The term is used for the official responsible for registering companies, issuing certificates of registration, maintaining a register of companies, and receiving annual returns.

regressive tax
It refers to a tax where the ratio of tax paid to income falls as income rises. The most regressive tax is a poll tax, levied at a fixed rate per person regardless of income. A tax system can be made regressive by having a maximum direct tax charge irrespective of income.

regulation
It implies a rule individuals or firms are obliged to follow, or the procedure for deciding and enforcing such rules. Modern societies have number of regulations. These may be designed to promote public health and safety, e.g. rules on food hygienic, etc. They may be designed to promote competitions and prevent unfair trading practices, e.g. monopolies and mergers are controlled in most societies, and insider dealing is forbidden in many countries.

regulatory capture
It is the tendency of regulators to identify with the interest of the industry they are supposed to regulate. When a public authority charged with regulating an industry in the public interest starts, it identifies the public interest with the interest of producers in the industry.

reinsurance
It is the system by which the issues of insurance policies pass on part of the risk to others, by themselves taking out further insurance policies. Reinsurance normally applies only to claims on a policy or group of policies in excess of some minimum amount.

relationship banking
It means banking on the basis that there is a continuing relation between a bank and a customer. The bank is expected to take an interest in the customer's business, and other ventures offering advice and support when required.

relationship investor
It refers to an investor who is an active participant in business, as well as providing capital. Such participation may be by appointing some members of the board of directors or through informal consultation on a continuing basis. It involves a long-term connection between the investor and the company. A relationship investor is not in the business of selling out to make short-term speculative gains. Relationship investment is opposite to the view that investors should merely hold shares, and let the existing management get on with the task of running a company.

relative income hypothesis
It refers to the theory that savings behaviour is affected by a person's relative position in the income distribution. Thus, at a given level of real income, a person may be relatively poor. The member of the richer community is expected to consume more and save less, as ideas of what constitutes a socially acceptable minimum level of consumption are influenced by habits, tastes and needs.

relative prices
The term is used for the pattern of prices of different real goods and services. It is used in contrast with actual money prices. Two sets of actual prices represent the same of relative prices if it is possible to change one set to the other by multiplying by any constant λ. It has been argued that in any economy the level of absolute prices is mainly set by monetary factors, while the structure of relative prices is set by real factors.

renewable resources
These are resources which are available for use on a continuing basis, for example, wind power and tidal power. These are distinct from resources which are used up when used at all, and must eventually run out. Unfortunately we do not always know whether resources are renewable, which may depend on the intensity of use. For example, forest resources, are renewable if restricted to what is replaced by rainfall and afforestation but can be destroyed by reckless cutting of trees.

replacement cost
It refers to the system of accounting in which the assets of firms are valued and their depreciation allowances are calculated using the costs of replacing their buildings and equipment. Where buildings and equipment can be replaced exactly, it is an ideal accounting method. However, in the case of equipment, owing to technical progress, exact replacements are, at times, not available.

replacement ratio
It is ratio of the income of an unemployed worker as a proportion of income when in work. If this ratio is too high it gives a disin-

centive to accept job offers. For example, allowing for the cost of travel to work and other working expenses, and the value of leisure, a replacement ratio below 1 is needed to maintain incentives. Too high a replacement ratio increases unemployment, but too low a ratio is also not desirable as it inflicts severe suffering by unemployed, and their families.

representative firm
It is the device of considering the behaviour of an industry as if it were composed of a number of equal-sized firms. Where an industry consists of one large dominant firm or firms, surrounded by smaller competitors, the firm does not exist.

repressed inflation
It is a situation in which price wage increases are restrained by official controls. It is liable to lead to a burst if increases when the controls are relaxed, unless policies are adopted to remove excess demand pressure. A major difficulty in ending repressed inflation smoothly is that in conditions of widespread excess demand and controlled prices, nobody actually knows how much excess demand there really is in the market.

resale price maintenance (RPM)
It refers to the fixing by manufacturers of minimum prices at which their products may be resold by distributors. While RPM does not necessarily imply a price-fixing cartel of producers, it does make such a cartel easier to organise.

rescheduling of debt
It refers to a revision of debt contract, by which interest and/or redemption payments are deferred to later dates than those originally agreed. Rescheduling is accepted by lenders because the alternative may be outright default on the debt.

research and development (R&D)
It implies the use of resources to create new knowledge, and to develop new and improved products or more economic methods of production. Research is devoted to discovering new knowledge, development is devoted to bringing new ideas to the stage where production for the market can start.

reserve asset ratio
It refers to a required minimum proportion between banks' reserve assets and their deposits and other liabilities. It may be imposed or varied as part of a central bank's monetary policy to enable it to control total bank lending by using open market operations to control the amount of reserve assets.

reserve currency
It denotes a currency used as foreign exchange reserve by other countries. To be suitable for use as reserves, a currency needs to be convertible, and to belong to a large country which has low inflation. The principal currencies, i.e. currently used as reserves are the US dollar and Euro.

reserve requirements
It refers to the minimum percentage of total assets which banks or other financial institutions are required to hold in money balances, or in some form of liquid assets. The minimum reserve requirements may be used as instruments of monetary policy, or as methods of trying to ensure solvency of banks.

reserve yield gap
It refers to an excess of returns on gilt-edged securities above those on equities. It occurs during periods of high inflation because equities are expected to provide capital gains to compensate for inflation while gilt-edged securities are not.

residual
It refers to anything which cannot be explained in a primary economic relation. For example, it is possible to try to explain the growth in real GDP by increases in the labour force and in the real capital stock. If these were to give a complete explanation of the growth in GDP, it would be equal to the growth in the labour force times the marginal product of labour, which is assumed to be measured by wage rates, and the growth in the capital stock times the marginal product of capital, which in turn is assumed to be measured by profitability.

restraint of trade
It implies a term in a contract that restricts a person's right to exercise a trade or carry on business. Such a term is common, in a business, where the seller agrees not to set up in

competition with the buyer. Most contracts of employment often include a term restraining employees from working for the firm's rivals for some period after they leave.

restrictive practices

The term refers to the following:
1. Practices which affect the efficient use of labour. It includes demarcation of work between different employees, minimum manning levels on the workforce required for any given task, or refusal to co-operate with temporary or unqualified workers.
2. Practices which affect the ability of firms and companies to compete freely in markets for their products and inputs. These practices include discrimination between customers by suppliers, exclusive dealing arrangements, and agreement for collusion to share out markets, either geo-graphically or by products.

retail banking

It means banking involving transactions with the general public. Retail banks collect deposits from individuals and small businessmen, entrepreneurs, etc. and make loans to them. In both cases, the sums concerned may be small. Retail banking is distinguished from wholesale banking, which concentrates on large-scale transactions with other financial institutions or big business houses.

retail sales

It is the part of total consumption expenditure which passes through retail outlets, i.e. shops. Such sales excludes many parts of consumer spending, such as rent, mortgage interest, public utility charges, and insurance.

retained earnings

These are the part of economy profits which is not paid out in taxes or dividends, but is ploughed back into a business. Retained earnings may be used for various purposes, viz. to finance fixed investment, to finance takeovers of other firms, to pay off loans, to extend credit to customers, or increase liquid assets.

retaliation

In economics, it is a policy change made to punish another firm or country for its actions. For example, in a trade war, country X retaliates to quotas on its exports to country Y by imposing quotas on Y's goods. It is, however, difficult to distinguish between deliberate retaliation and policy change which are simply a reaction to a worsening in country X position.

returns to scale

It is defined as the relation between a proportional change in inputs to a productive process and the resulting proportional change in output. If an x per cent rise in all inputs produces an x per cent increase in output, there are constant returns to scale. If output rises by a larger percentage than inputs, there are increasing returns to scale. If output rises by a smaller percentage than inputs, there are decreasing returns to scale.

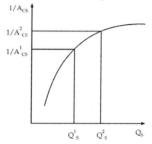

Returns to scale

revaluation

It denotes the following:
1. A rise in the value of a country's currency.
2. A change in the basis of valuing a company's assets in its accounts. It may be necessary because of general inflation, or because of changes in the value of particular assets.

revenue

It denotes the following:
1. Government tax receipts. The Income Tax Department is responsible for collecting direct taxes, and a revenue tariff is a tariff imposed principally to raise income for the government.
2. These are receipts from sales. Total revenue is total receipts, i.e. quantity sold times price; average revenue is revenue per unit sold revenue is the addition to total revenue from a small increase in quantity sold, per unit increase in the quantity.

revolving loan

It refers to a loan which is formally for short periods, but which is habitually renewed. Such a loan would be made, for example, by a bank to a shopkeeper financing stocks on credit. The sales allow the repayment of loans, but it is profitable for both parties to renew the loans to finance the purchase of further stocks.

Ricardian equivalence
The argument given by David Ricardo that individuals' savings behaviour will be affected in the same way by government spending, whether this is financed by taxes or borrowing. The argument is that whatever the government borrows now, it will have to repay in the future, so that future taxes will have to rise.

rights issue
It is an issue of new shares in a company which are first offered to existing shareholders in proportion to their present holdings. Shareholders are entitled but not obliged to take up their rights. Where the issue price is below the market price of the shares, it may be possible to sell the rights.

risk-aversion
The term is used to follow the policy of safer returns, even if they are on average smaller. An individual with decreasing marginal utility of total wealth will get less utility from a prospect with uncertain returns than from a safe project with the same mean expected returns. Such an individual will refuse actuarially fair gambles, and has risk-aversion. It is sometimes characterised by saying that the individual values mean returns but dislikes variance.

risk-capital
It is capital which the owners are willing to invest in equity in new and untried projects, where there is a recognised chance that they will lose it. Venture capitalists are desirous of taking these risks if they expect that their successes will make sufficiently large profits to keep their average return positive, in spite of some losses.

risk-free security
It is a security which is free of the various possible sources of risk such as the default. It is thought to be absent in the case of government debt. A second risk is that the market high price may be low at the time when a security has to be sold; this risk is high for

securities with a long time to go to maturity, and shrinks obligation is risk-free if the holder has the option to have it redeemed at any time.

risk pooling
It denotes combining two or more risky projects, with returns which are uncertain but not perfectly correlated. The expected sum of the returns to such projects is not as dispersed as the expected returns on the separate projects. Insurance companies work by pooling the risks on a number of separate projects.

risk premium
It is the extra return required to induce a risk-averse individual to undertake a project with uncertain returns. If the mean expected return on a project is r, and the individual is difference between this and another project p with certain return, the risk premium, will be equal to the proportional extra return required to induce the individual to engage in the risky project. For a risk-neutral individual the risk premium is zero.

risk sharing
it implies contracts which shift risk from one party to another. Suppose a firm wishes to finance a risky project. If it uses its own money, it bears all the risk itself. Hence, it issues equity capital to finance a certain percentage and of the project and the risk is borne by whoever buys the shares. It sets up a new limited liability company, and buys its debentures which bear fixed interest, while other people buy the shares, all the risk is transferred to the new share-holders, unless the project does so badly that the new company defaults on its debenture interest.

risk taking
It means engaging in any risky activity when a safer alternative was available. It applies to many situations, e.g. trading on one's own account rather than working for an employer, making unsecured loans rather than secured ones, betting, or failing to insure one's home.

roll-over of loans
It denotes allowing borrowers to renew loans when they fall due to repayment, rather than actually paying them off. Some cases of the loans have been used to finance profitable transactions, such as buying goods for resale:

the borrower could repay the loan, but has good prospects of profit from similar further transactions if the loan is renewed.

royalty

It is the share occurring to the landlord from the exploitation of a resource in his property. Generally, it is the payment of the use of a property covered by a copyright, patent or similar claim.

rules-based policy

It refers to a policy which operates according to published or recognised rules. This may extend to rules about how the policy will change if circumstances alter. It is distinct from discretionary policy, where the authorities are expected to use their discretion about what changes should be made in policy instruments. The argument for rules-based policy is that it makes it easier for other economic agents to predict how the policy-makers are going to behave.

running yield

It denotes the interest on a stock as a percentage of its current market price. For example, if stock yields $9 per annum interest and its price is currently $100 the running yield is 9/100 per cent.

Rybczynski theorem

It is a proposition concerning the results of increasing only one factor of production. The proposition, named after its originator, relates a two-good, two-factor economy with constant returns to scale, and economic growth due to an increase in one factor of production, holding other factors and techniques constant.

S

sacrifice ratio
It is the ratio between the amount of unemployment needed to reduce inflation and the achieved. As per demand inflation models, a 1 per cent increase in demand when activity is high has more effect in increasing inflation than a 1 per cent fall in demand has in decreasing inflation when activity is low.

saddle point
It is a point at which a function of two variables takes a maximum for movement in some directions and a minimum for movement in other directions.

salary
The term refers to the remuneration of almost all non-manual, i.e. executives and professionals and some manual employees in exchange for the supply of labour services.

sample
It refers to a random selection of examples of a class of objects, whose characteristics are used to infer those of the whole class. Sampling is used where it would be impossible or too costly to examine all the class. A sample may simply be picked at random from a list of possible cases.

saving(s)
It can be defined as:
1. The excess of income over consumption. Savings are a way of acquiring assets, and for the economy as a whole it is the only way since while individuals may gain or lose through inheritance or gambling, these cancel out on aggregation. The average propensity to save is the ratio of savings to income; the marginal propensity to consume is the proportion of any addition to income that is saved.
2. Savings are many different through related concepts, concerned with acquiring assets and ways of holding them. Savings refer to stocks of assets and ways of holding stock of assets. Saving up for things means acquiring assets temporarily, with the intention of spending them at some time in the future. Small savings are the assets of people who are assumed not to have many. National Savings Certificates (NSCs) are government securities issued through post office with their income and capital value guaranteed but the amount any individual can hold is rationed.

Say's law
This law states that the proportion that 'supply creates its own demand'. The argument is that in an economy with fully flexible prices and wages, factors of production could always find employment and goods could always be sold. Equilibrium with involuntarily un-employed labour and involuntarily held stocks may not occur. There seems no logical flaw in this law, if full price and wage flexibility could be achieved. The problem is that lack of perfect information makes prices and wages somewhat sticky, which means that involuntary unemployment can exist.

scarce currency clause
It is a provision in the original rules of the International Monetary Fund (IMF) to deal with the problem that its stocks of any one particular currency might run out. The clause provided that if the IMF ran out stocks of a country's currency, it could be declared a scarce currency, upon which members would be entitled and expected to discriminate against the country's goods in their trade policies.

scarcity
It is defined as the property of being in excess demand at a zero price. It denotes that in equilibrium the price of a scarce good or factor must be positive. At first sight one might expect that a good or factor that was never scarce would not be counted as economic goods at all. Some factors of production are counted as economic goods, because it is not known in advance whether they are going to be scarce.

scatter diagram
It is a diagram depicting the relation between two characteristics of a number of subjects, which may be individuals, firms or countries. Each point marked on the diagram shows an observation of the two characteristics, and the income of individuals, measured on the two axes.

screening
It is the action taken by uninformed parties to include other people with private information to act so as to reveal it. It can be done by second-degree price discrimination, where

people are offered a choice of contracts, and information about their characteristics can be inferred from which contracts they choose.

search unemployment

The term implies unemployment which occurs while an unemployed worker searches the job market for an acceptable job offer. In some occupations, workers may leave one job voluntarily because search for another is more efficiently conducted while not working. In many professional occupations this does not ever take place because being unemployed is itself a handicap in attractive offers: workers who want better jobs can search unemployment occurs if they do not simply apply for any job and accept any offer.

seasonal adjustment

It refers to adjustment to correct for seasonal variations in economic variables. Seasonally adjusted figures for gross domestic product (GDP) or its components are believed to give a better impression of cyclical movements in the economy than unadjusted figures. Seasonal adjustment is liable to produce including figures if anything happens to change the pattern of seasonal variation in the economy.

secondary market

It is the market for resale of shares and is distinct from the market for new issues, i.e. the vast majority of dealings in shares is in secondary markets. The existence of a liquid secondary market for shares is an important factor in making them saleable as new issues. If people wish to buy newly issued knew they could not sell them readily but had to retain them permanently, they would be reluctant to risk buying them in the first place.

second-degree price discrimination

The term is used for price discrimination where customers are offered a choice of possible contracts, so that they depict information about themselves through their choice of contract. Airlines, for example, offer lower fares to passengers who are willing to book in advance and travel at particular times. It is assumed that business travellers are willing to pay more to fly than tourists.

second order of magnitude

It refers to effects which are so small that they can be neglected for practical purposes.

Economic models often approximate actual functions by local linear approximations.

sector

It refers to a part of the economy. Sectors can be delimited in several different ways. One way is the bodies organising expenditures, whereby the economy is divided between the public sector, that is the government at various levels and government-controlled bodies; the corporate sector, which is companies.

secured loan

It is a loan where the creditor has a claim on some particular part of the debtor's assets in the event of default. This is distinct from an unsecured loan, where the lender has no right to take over any particular asset if payments are not made when due. In the event of the borrower going bankrupt secured creditors rank before unsecured creditors for any available assets. Secured loans, are safer than unsecured loans.

securitisation

It refers to the packaging of numbers of non-marketable assets, such as mortgage loans, into boundless which are marketable. Individual mortgages are usually not marketable because there is too much idiosyncratic risk in dealing with any one of them.

security

These are instruments including government debt, company shares, and economy debt. Securities may be registered, where legal ownership depends on the entry in a register, normally run by a bank, and the paper is merely evidence of ownership, or in bearer form, where ownership is conferred by possession of the document.

segmented market

It is a market where there is contact between different customers, or different suppliers. If different customers do not know the prices that others are paying, or are unable to resell goods and services to them, it is easy to discriminate in the prices charged or level of services offered to different parts of the market.

self-correcting system

It implies a system where deviations from any initial position lead to reactions which tend to return the system to equilibrium.

Such a system is self-stabilising, and will return to equilibrium without any assistance from the monetary or fiscal authorities.

self-employment

It refers to work carried out as a business, rather than an employee. The self-employed persons are responsible for their own tax, national insurance, and insurance, whereas those employed by others can leave these matters to their employer.

self-financing

It means financing a business without resource to borrowing or share issues. A business can only be started on a self-financing basis by those with some initial capital. The business can expand only by ploughing back profits into the business. The advantage of self-financing is that it combines safety with control. A self-financed business can be run without worrying about creditors or shareholders. The main disadvantage is that an entrepreneur's initial capital and profits give him/her full advantage to be taken of possible econo-mies of scale.

self-regulation

It is a system where the approach of government to regulating a sector of the economy lays down general objectives, but entrusts the task of devising and enforcing detailed rules to a body representing those engaged in the sector. This establishes the fact that people within the sector are abler than the outsiders in diagnosing problems and devising realistic methods of control. The danger of self-regulation is that it will operate too much for the protection of established firms in the sector, and too little in the interests of consumer protection.

sell

It denotes the following:
1. To part with any good, service, or asset for money. Where the asset concerned is a foreign currency, selling for dollars is the same as buying dollars with rupees.
2. To persuade somebody else to buy. Selling costs are expenditures on advertising or other methods of persuasion.

seller's market

It is defined as a market in which conditions are much better for sellers than for buyers. If sellers are scarce and buyers are numerous and are under strong pressure to satisfy their requirements, the prices will be high and that conditions of sale will be favourable for sellers.

selling costs

These are costs incurred in the process of selling products. These costs cover items such as the costs of advertisements on hoardings or the media, exhibiting at trade fairs, or employment of representatives or door-to-door salesperson.

sensitive sectors

These are sectors of economy which are particularly concerned about loss of market and jobs through competition from imports. The term applies particularly to sectors where developing countries have a comparative advantage. Agriculture, iron and steel, and basic chemicals fall in this category.

sequestration

It refers to the following:
1. A procedure by which assets can be temporarily frozen by court order.
2. A term used in the US for monetary cuts in the budget proposed under the Gramm-Rudman-Holings law on the deficit.

series

It is a sequence of numbers defined by an initial term and a rule for getting from each term to the next. For example, in the arithmetic progression x, x+y, x+2y, etc. the first term is a, and the rule for getting to the next is to add a constant b to the previous one, such a series can be continued indefinitely.

service flows

It refers to the services endered by durable consumer goods. These services count as consumption when they are bought, but items such as furniture, refrigerators, cars, microwave ovens, ACs, etc. give services over years and often decades. But in the case of housing national income accounts follow the procedure of treating their income in later years.

service industry

It is industry comprised of the parts of the companies that provide services. These may be to individual consumers, for example, medical treatment or entertainment, or to business, for example, computing, engineering, or legal work. In some cases, such as hotels, combination of goods and services is provided.

services

These can be defined as economic goods which do not take a tangible and stroable form. In some cases, these require the physical presence of the customer, as for example, medical treatment or live entertainment.

settlement

It is the actual performance of a contract to pay for or deliver goods, securities, or currency. Owing to the documentation involved, and postal and clerical delays, many bargains are not carried out immediately, but some time is allowed. It may take the form of having a set date for completion of all contracts made during a given period, or of rol-ling settlement, where each bargain is allowed specific time.

settlement risk

It denotes the risk that other parties may fail to fulfil their side of bargains. Delay in settlement may merely cause inconvenience, but complete failure to settlement could cause severe losses.

shadow prices

These are relative prices of goods, services and resources which are proportional to their true opportunity costs for the economy, taking account made choices in order to optimise their situations subject to a set of prices proportional to the shadow prices for the economy, the results would be Pareto-optimal, that is, perfectly efficient.

share buybacks

It refers to the practice of companies with good current profits but poor investment opportunities returning capital to their shareholders by buying in some of their own shares. Buybacks benefit shareholders by reducing their income tax bills.

sharecropper

The term refers to a tenant who pays rent fixed as a share of crops produced rather than an agreed amount of money. This system is relatively common in backward regions and developing countries.

shareholder

The term is used for a person or company

holding shares in a company. The ultimate say over control of a company lies with its equity shareholders, who can change the management either by using their votes at company meetings, or by accepting take-over bids.

share option

It is an option to buy shares at a pre-arranged price, granted as an incentive to company directors or employer. Share option only be exercised if the option price is below the market price at the time.

share price

It refers to the price at which share can be tried. It is not any single amount as even for widely traded shares the offer price at which market makers willing to sell shares is higher than the bid price at which they are willing to buy.

shark repellent

The term is used for contracts entered into to make a company unattractive to potential takeover bidders. For example, contracts may be made with directors, entitling them to large payments on loss of office, or giving them options to buy critical parts of company assets, or the company's shares, at low prices.

shell company

It is a company which does not trade, but has a legal existence, and possibly some non-trading assets. It may include a credit rating, and the right to carry forward losses for tax purposes.

shock

It denotes an event which is different, to an important extent from what people expected, or from what they could reasonably have expected given the information available to them. Actual economic events, like goods prices, share price, or income levels, are seldom exactly what people expected.

shortage

It is a situation when the demand for a good or service exceeds the available supply. It can only occur if price is not adjusted to clear the market. If there is a sudden spurt in the demand or fall in the supply of a good, law or social convention may prevent the price from rising far enough to clear the market, thus creating a shortage.

short position

It refers to a contract to sell, goods or securities, delivery, for future in excess of the amount a firm or individual actually holds. The holder of a short position depends on being able to produce or buy sufficient goods or securities to be able to fulfil the contract. At the time of delivery, if spot market prices are lower than the contract price, the holder of the short position will be able to buy the goods at this lower price, and will make a profit.

short run

In economics, it refers to a period in which some things cannot be changed, which could be changed given more time. For example, in the short run, a firm can buy more materials or fuel, and can hire more unskilled workers, but does not have time to introduce new technology, build new plant or to recruit and train more skilled workers or managers.

short-termism

It refers the conduct of a business with too much regard to short-run as compared to longer-run results. For industry, this means spending too little on research and development, staff, training, and investment in projects with a long lag in bringing in profits.

shut-down price

It denotes a price so low at which or any lower price a firm prefers to shut its plant down rather than continue production. At prices just above the shut-down price the firm will usually be making a loss, but provided that the market is expected to recover, the firm does not plan to leave the industry permanently.

side-payment

It implies a payment made by one or more parties in an agreement to other parties, to include them to join the agreement. For example, in a group of firms, each has a profitable plant, they calculate that if one plant were closed and its output shifted to the remaining plants, total costs for the group would be lower and thus total profits would increase.

silicon valley

The area of Southern California containing a major concentration of computer and information technology business. This is frequently cited as an example of the tendency to geo-graphical specialisation, caused by external economies resulting from the proximity of similar businesses.

simple interest

It is the system by which repayment of a loan after x periods requires payment of a sum equal to the principal plus x times the interest payable for a single period. If the principal is P $(1+xr)$ is required. As x increases, the proportional rate of return to the lender goes down, as the proportional return for the x+1th periods is $rp/[(1+xr)p]$, which is a decreasing function of x.

simulation

It is the use of quantitative models, normally mounted on a computer, to mimic the working of an economy. Simulation provides assumptions about how an economy works, and is often used to see how models respond to changes in these assumptions.

simultaneous equations

It implies a system of two or more equations relating two or more variables. A solution to such a system is a set of values of the variables for which each equation is satisfied. In general as many variables as independent equations are needed for a system of simultaneous equations to be solvable.

single currency

It is a currency used by two or more countries. However, it is to decide how the amount to be issued is determined. This may be by agreement between two or more national central banks, or by commissioning a single supra-national institution to issue the currency. If a single currency is issued independently by more than one national authority, e.g. Euro in many European countries, without any agreement between them, it is likely that too much of it will be issued.

single market

It denotes the unified European market created in 1992 by the European Act. This was supposed to be achieved through the removal of all barriers to movements of goods, labour and capital between member countries of the European Community.

single-picked preferences

It is an assumption about the pattern of individual preferences. This is where any quality of a good or situation can be described by a numerical index, any individual has a unique most-preferred level of the index, and the valuation put on the good declines as the index departs from the preferred value in either direction.

size distribution of firms
It is the number of firms of various sizes. Size can be measured in various ways. For example, employment, turnover, and stock exchange capitalisation are common measures of size.

skewness
It is a measure of distributions, showing whether large deviations from the mean are more likely in one side than the other. In a symmetrical distribution, deviations either side of the mean are also likely. Positive skewness means that large upward deviations are more likely than large downward deviations, and thus, the sum of cubes of deviations from the mean is positive. Negative skewness means that large downward deviations are more likely than large upward ones; and thus the sum of cubes of deviations from the mean is negative.

slack
It implies unused or under-used resources. Organisational slack occurs when firms or government bodies have more employees, material equipment or buildings than they really need. Most organisations contain some amount of slack, but when demand varies, it is difficult to distinguish slack from necessary reserve capacity.

slump
It is a prolonged period of abnormally low economic activity and abnormally high unemployment. This is usually accompanied by a tendency for prices to fall, or at least to rise more slowly than usual, and by a fall in the relative prices of primary products.

Slutsky equation
It refers to the equation showing how the effect on demand for a good of a change in its price can be decomposed into the substitution effect, which depicts the effect of a change in relative prices at an unchanged level of real income, and the income effect,

which shows the effect of a change in real income holding prices constant.

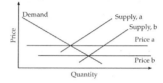

Slutsky equation

Smithsonian agreement
It defines an agreement reached in 1971 to try to restore a Bretton Woods-style of pegged exchange rates. The agreement got its name from the location of the conference at which it was reached, in the Smithsonian Institute in Washington, DC.

snake in the tunnel
It is an expression for an agreement by a group of countries in a flexible exchange rate system to interfere in the foreign exchange market to hold their currencies closer to each other than the normally permitted maximum deviation. The general limit is the tunnel, the closer limit is the snake.

social benefit
It refers to the total benefit from any activity. It includes not only benefits accruing directly to the person or firm conducting the activity, but also external benefits accruing to other people who cannot be charged for them.

social charges
These are taxes on employment, levied on employers and employees. Social charges are levied in many countries, to pay for various social benefits such as unemployment insurance and pensions.

social cost
It is the total cost of any activity. It includes not only private costs which fall directly on the person or firm conducting the activity, but also external costs.

Social cost

socialism

It can be defined as the idea that the economy' resources should be used in the interests of all its citizens rather than allowing private owners of land and capital to use them as they see fit. Socialism marked by voluntary co-operation, central planning, and the use of the market to be egalitarian in principle, though not necessary in practice. The use of planning rather than prices in running the economy makes the actual measurement of inequality difficult, and individuals can be as corrupt as in a capitalist economy.

social overhead capital

It is used for capital goods of types which are available to anybody, hence, social; not tightly linked to any particular part of production, hence overhead.

social safety net

It refers to a system of available payments in cash or in kind which will keep people's income from falling below some socially accepted minimum level. This needs to cover old age, sickness and disability, and unemployment.

social security benefits

It describes the state payments designed to assure all residents of a country of minimum living standards. These benefits are typically provided to those who are over retirement age, and those unable to support themselves through disability, illness. The benefits cover the recipient and any dependents, especially children. Social security benefits may be paid for by contributions from workers or their employers, or both.

social services

These are the parts of social security requiring individual contact rather than cash payments. People's minimum consumption needs can be met by cash payment to those who do not have sufficient incomes, through pensions and other benefits. Some citizens, are in need of personal assistance with managing their lives as well as cash handouts. Personal social services indeed requires advice and supervision for those on probation, advice and assistance in dealing with children with special needs and supervision of peoples in homes, etc.

soft budget constraint

It is a limit to spending by some public body where those supposed to be subject to it hold the opinion that the consequences of breaching it will not be serious. For example, the managers of state-owned firms may argue that if they suffer losses, or make smaller profits than they have been instructed to, the state will meet the firm's losses and not sack them.

soft currency

It refers to a currency which is not convertible into other currencies, or whose value in terms of other currencies is expected to fall. It is distinct from a hard currency, which is freely convertible into other currencies, and which people want to hold because it is expected to maintain or improve its value in terms of other currencies.

soft landing

The term is used for a successful stabilisation programme which restores price stability after a period of excess demand and inflation without provoking a recession in the process. The problem with achieving stabilisation is that if restrictive monetary and fiscal policy are not tight enough, the inflation will continue; whereas if restrictive policies are too strict, there will be a slump in demand before stability is restored.

soft loan

It is a loan on terms less strict than normal market rates. It may take various forms. For example, loan may carry a low rate of interest, the start of interest payments may be deferred, repayment may be spread over an unusually long period. It is easy to arrange deferment of interest or redemption payments, or the debtor may be allowed to make interest or redemption payments in soft currency.

sole proprietor

It denotes a person running a business, without partners or incorporation. The advantage of sole proprietorship is unity of control, as the owner and management are the same. The major drawback of sole proprietorship is that in many industries economies of scale cannot be availed.

Solow growth model

It is an exogenous growth model, also known

as neo-classical growth model. It studies the long-term growth. A common prediction of this model is that an economy will always converge towards a steady state rate of growth, which depends on the rate of technological growth progress and the rate of labour force growth.

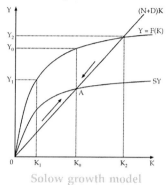

Solow growth model

solvency
It refers to possession of assets in excess of a firm's or a person's liabilities. Where the assets are either cash or marketable securities it is clear that a person or firm is solvent. It is illegal to trade knowing oneself to be insolvent, but if the assets are non-marketable solvency is largely a matter of judgement. Individuals and firms can and do obtain unsecured credit, which they rely on future earnings to repay.

sound money
It refers to money which preserves stable real purchasing power. It will only happen if the authorities issuing the money give priority in their policies to maintaining its value, and enjoy credibility for such policy priorities, which in turn leads to market expectations of price stability. A sound money policy is in conflict with the Keynesian view that the primary responsibility of the monetary authorities should be maintaining a stable level of effective demand.

sources of capital
These are the sources from which business, whether private, corporate, or state-owned, obtain their capital. One major source is the savings of the owners of private businesses, and the undistributed profits of companies. A second major source of borrowing, by selling bonds or by borrowing from banks and other financial intermediaries.

sovereign debt
It refers to debt of the governments of independent countries. With the debt of an individual or corporation, it is often possible to use legal procedures to compel them to pay the interest and redemption payment due, or to hand their assets over to the creditor if they do not pay. Such legal sanctions are not available against governments.

spare capacity
In economics, it implies capital equipment which is not currently needed for production. Manufacturing units like to have some spare capacity available, to meet sudden increases in demand for their products, and to be able to maintain production if equipment breaks down.

special deposits
These are additional deposits that other banks are required to make with the central bank. These may carry low or no interest. These deposits do not count towards any normal minimum reserve requirements.

specialisation
It denotes concentration on providing particular types of goods and services, and relying on others to provide what one does not produce. This takes place at all levels of production. Individuals acquire particular skills or professional qualifications, while marketing managers concentrate on specific firms concentrate on particular industries; districts, regions, or areas. Specialisation may be total or partial. With total specialisation, most activities are not carried on at all, and the goods and services concerned are entirely out-sourced through others. This is very common at the individual and the firm level.

specific tax
It refers to a tax levied at a fixed rate per physical unit of the good taxed, regardless of its price. It is in contrast to an ad valorem tax, where the tax is proportional to the price of the good. Specific taxes have administrative advantages where measuring quantities is simple, for example, in licensing cars or television sets, while the measurement of second-hand values would be very cumbersome.

speculation

The term is used for economic activity aimed at profiting from expected changes in the prices of goods, assets, or currencies. Due to inherent uncertainty, most transactions are capable of being interpreted as speculative, but the term speculation is reserved for transactions where expected capital gains provide a major motive. Speculators may buy assets like stocks of shares or commodities they do not want but whose prices they expect to rise, or buy call options on such assets. They can contract to buy assets they do not have the funds to pay for. Speculators may sell goods, assets, or currencies they do not really want to part with, but whose prices they expect to fall, so that they will be able to buy them back more cheaply in future; or they may buy put options on shares, etc. It is also possible to contract to sell assets one does not actually possess.

speculative motive

It refers to the effects of expectations of changes in interest rates on the demand for money. In Keynesian theory, such expectations are important. If it is believed that interest rates are likely to rise, and thus that bond prices are likely to fall, bonds will be less and money more attractive to hold. This gives an incentive to sell bonds and hold money, or to deter buying bonds and hold on to money which would otherwise have been put into bonds to earn interest.

spillover

It implies a connection between different parts of the economy. Spillovers may be either pecuniary or non-pecuniary. A pecuniary spillover occurs, when changes in one industry affect factor supplies to another, i.e. if a new factory bids up the wages of unskilled labour so that local people find cleaners or gardeners more expensive, this is a pecuniary spillover. Pecuniary spillovers produce their effects through markets. A non-pecuniary spillover occurs when one industry brings external diseconomies to the other: there is usually no market through which they can be paid not to do so.

spread

It is the difference between the bid and offer prices quoted by a market maker. The prices of securities at which market markers are willing to sell are higher than those at which they are willing to buy. The spread has to cover the operating costs of market markers and provide profits, and includes a premium against the risk that any particular customer has insider knowledge about some security.

stabilisation

It means alternating the behaviour of a system to induce it to return to equilibrium following disturbances, or to speed up the rate at which it does so. Where a system is affected by stochastic shocks, which cannot be anticipated or offset without a time lag, complete stabilisation is not possible.

stabilisation policy

It refers to the use of economic policies to reduce fluctuations. This may be applied at the macroeconomic level, to reduce fluctuations in real incomes, unemployment, inflation, or exchange rates, or at the microeconomic level, to reduce fluctuations in the prices of particular goods. Where a system is based on stochastic shocks, to the extent that these can be foretold, stabilisation policy can work by either preventing or offsetting them.

Stackelberg duopoly

It is defined as a duopoly in which one firm is the leader and the other is the follower. The leader is assumed to act strategically, choosing a strategy considering the follower's expected reactions. The follower is assumed to act non-strategically, reacting to the leader's strategy but not anticipating the leader's reactions.

stages of economic growth

It refers to the theory that countries develop through a series of modes of economic organisation, each leading to the next. Various such sequences have been proposed: for example, hunting-gathering-herding animals-Agriculture-industry-service-based economy or feudalism-capitalism-socialism.

stagnation

It is a situation in which there is little or no change in techniques or income levels. This is in contrast with development, when techniques are changing and income levels increasing.

stakeholder

It means anybody with some form of interest

in a business. This includes directors, managers, other employees, customers, subcontractors, shareholders and even the general public in cases where the firm's activities impact on the environment. A stake-holder is thus anybody who stands to lose if a business is not carried out properly.

stamp duty
It is a tax on transactions, levied by requiring that documents bear an official stamp to be legally valid.

Standard and Poor's (S&P)
It is one of the main US credit-rating agencies. It procures the S&P 500 stock price index, based on the prices of 500 principal shares traded on the New York Stock Exchange (NYSE). This covers about 80 per cent of the total value of stocks traded.

standard deviation
It is a commonly used measure of dispersion, defined as the square root of the mean of squared deviations of a variable from its mean.

standard error
It refers to the standard deviation of the estimates that would be arrived at by taking repeated random samples of a given size from the same population. It is a decreasing function of sample size; the lower the standard error, the more reliable is the estimate.

Standard International Trade Classification (SITC)
It refers to the system used to classify international visible trade. The main sections are denoted by single digits. For example, 0 is food and live animals, 1 is beverages and tobacco, etc.

standardised commodity
It refers to a commodity produced to uniform specifications, so that different units become interchangeable. Standardised goods make use of lower costs of production through economies of scale, but place some restriction on consumer choice.

standard of living
It can be defined as the economic component of people's welfare and is measured by consumption per head, or by consumption per equivalent adult, counting children as fractions of adults. It is not a perfect welfare measure as it ignores some important factors contributing to overall welfare; for example, it does not count services such as health care and education, which are sometimes provided free or at subsidised prices by governments, and at times have to be provided by consumers for themselves.

state enterprise
It refers to a firm founded on the initiative of the state and run by it. The state enterprises is undertaken because there are some activities which would be socially beneficial, but are not attractive to private entrepreneurs, and others which would be profitable but involve natural monopolies and are therefore not to be trusted to private owners.

statistics
The term refers to the following:
1. The numbers which are used to describe the functions fitted to data in summary form. Sufficient statistics constitute a set of parameters which contain or imply all available information about the functions they describe.
2. The collection of data and the mathematical methods used to draw inferences about the relations between different variables.

statutory monopoly
It is defined as a monopoly protected by law from entry by rivals. Such monopolies are sometimes set up as a quid pro quo for an obligation to provide a universal service.

steady state
It is a state of the economy where all aggregates are constant. This includes zero population growth, zero net investment, no technical progress and a constant level of GDP.

step function
A function a = f(b) where the value of the dependent variable, a, remains constant over ranges of the independent variable, b, then changes by discrete amounts at particular values of b. Step functions are extremely common in economic life, as they provide administrative simplicity.

sterilisation
In economics, it is the method by which a central bank prevents balance-of-payments surpluses or deficits from affecting the domestic money supply. If there is a surplus in

the balance of payments on current and capital account combined, it brings a rise in the foreign exchange reserves, and an increase in the money supply. If the central bank does not want the money supply to increase, it may have to sell securities so as to sterilise the cash inflow.

sterling, pound
It is the UK currency. The name originated from the pound Easterling, formerly used in trade with the Baltic. The sterling area was an arrangement under which a number of Commonwealth countries pegged their exchange rates to sterling and held their foreign exchange reserves in London.

Sterling, pound

sticky prices
These are prices which do not vary due to small changes in costs or demand conditions. These are common in many manufacturing and service industries. It is because changing prices is administratively costly, and because of uncertainty about which way costs or demand conditions will move next.

sticky wages
These are wage rates that are not readily changed due to changes in market conditions. It often expresses itself in the form of either nominal wage resistance - an unwillingness to accept lower money wages - or real wage resistance - an unwillingness to accept real wage cuts, i.e. wage increases less than the rate of inflation.

stochastic process
It describes a process in which what happens is not exactly predictable, as it is affected by apparently random factors. It is often not known whether the apparent randomness is actually so, or whether it is the result of the action of forces which are determinate, but so numerous that it is not practicable to model their effects.

stock
It refers to the following:
1. A collection of goods held by an enterprise. It has various connotations: Stock appreciation is an increase in the value of stocks held due to price changes, while a stockpile is a large holding of commodities, held for example by a government as a strategic reserve.
2. A synonym for shares. Here again it has various connotations : Common stock is ordinary share; government stock is government debt instruments. A stock exchange is an institution through which shares are traded, whereas a stock option is a right to buy shares at a fixed price.
3. The state of affairs at a point in time. For example, stock concepts which include: the money supply, the price level, the assets of a firm, or the level of employment while the national income, profits of a firm, etc. are flow concepts.

stock appreciation
It is the part of the change in the value of the stocks held by a business over any period which is due to price changes. Rising commodity prices cause this to be positive; falling commodity prices cause it to be negative.

stock exchange
It denotes an institution through which company shares and government stock are traded. Originally the exchange was a building, where trader would gather and trade proceeded either by individual negotiation or by 'open outcry', where prices bid and offer were announced out loud so as to inform all traders within earshot. However, modern stock exchanges are institutions with traders linked by computer networks and telephones.

stock exchange listing
It is the right of a company to have its shares traded on a stock exchange. Listing is conditional on the company providing a satisfactory level of information on its activities.

stock jobber
The term is used for an individual or a firm who deals in shares, buying and selling as a principal. Jobbers are distinct from stockbrokers, who act as agents for buyers and sellers of shares.

stock option
It is a right to buy shares in a company on

some future date at a pre-arranged price. Stock options are often granted as incentives by companies to their directors and top executives. The greater the rise in the company's shares by the time the option can be exercised, the more the holder will gain.

Stolper-Samuelson theorem
It refers to a theory concerning the income distribution effects of inter-industry trade. It shows the effects of trade in a two-good, two-factor model having constant returns to scale and incomplete specialisation. The theorem attempts to prove that trade raises the real income of a country's plentiful factor, which is used relatively heavily by the exportable industry.

stop-go cycle
It is a sequence of alternations of official policy between trying to expand and contract effective demand. If the economy, when left alone, tended to produce alternating spells of depressed and excessive demand, stop-go policies may be taken as stabilising.

store of value
It refers to one of the functions of money. If asset prices are stable, money is unattractive as a store of value, as it brings in no income, but if asset prices are not stable, it is better to hold some part of total assets in money, as a safeguard against risk.

straight-line depreciation
It is the system of accounting for depreciation on an asset by taking an assumed life, say x years, and charging depreciation at the rate of $(1/x)$ of its cost each year until it is fully written down.

strategic entry deterrence
These are actions undertaken by a firm to deter competitors from entering their markets. Such actions may include making large investments of sunk capital, which render it unlikely that rivals could drive it out, or offering long-term low-price contracts to customers.

strategic trade policy
It is a trade policy intended to influence the trade policies of other countries. A policy is said to be 'strategic' if it believes that while it would not be beneficial to adopt it if the policies of all other countries were taken as given, adopting it would in fact be beneficial

because it would cause other countries to change their trade policies.

strategy
It is a plan for dealing with uncertain future circumstances. This is a set of rules by which the actions to be taken depend on the circumstances, including natural events and the actions of other people.

structural transformation
It is a process of major change in a country's economy and can involve a large-scale transfer of resources from primary to industrial sector activity, as in many newly industrialised countries like China, India, Brazil, South Africa, etc.

structural unemployment
It refers to unemployment due to a lack of capital equipment which unemployed workers could use, or lack of the skills among unemployed workers required to produce anything for which there are buyers. This can occur because investment has failed to keep pace with growth in the labour force: this is common in the developing countries.

subcontracting
It is the practice of the principal suppliers of goods and services buying in some of their inputs from independent firms, rather than using employees to produce them in-house. Subcontracting is resorted to because the work concerned needs specialised skilled labour or equipment which the principal producer does not need full-time.

subsidiarity
In economics, it is the principle that decisions on policy should be taken at the most decentralised level. Decisions affecting the global atmosphere, e.g. restrictions on the use of chlorofluoro-carbons (CFCs) need to be taken at an international level. Decisions regarding safety standards for vehicles need to be taken at a national or even international level. There is a tendency in modern economies for an increasing proportion of policy decisions to be centralised, from local authorities to national governments, and from national governments to international bodies such as the European Union (EU), World Trade Organisations (WTO), etc.

subsidiary

It refers to a firm which is owned or controlled by another. There are wide variations in the extent to which subsidiary companies are allowed to make decentralised decisions about matters like investment projects, and choices between trading with other firms in the same group or with outsiders.

subsidised credit

It refers to the credit provided on terms below normal market rates. Subsidised credit may be granted to encourage particular forms of activity such as exports, provision of affordable rented housing by housing associations, or the growth of entrepreneurship among minority groups. Subsidised credit is also sometimes granted as a corrupt favour to people or firms with political influence. Credit may be subsidised by governments, or lending institutions. Subsidised credit is considered bad for economic efficiency in economies where the interest rate for favoured borrowers is below the rate of inflation, because they can borrow at negative real interest rates and make profit simply by holding unproductive assets.

subsistence level

It is the minimum level of consumption on which people can survive. This is an ambiguous concept and it refers to the level of consumption needed for an individual to survive for some limited period, such as a year.

substitute

It implies a good or service which can be used instead of another. Every good is thus a substitute for other goods in general. Two goods are said to be substitutes of each other if, holding the utility level constant, a rise in the price of one of them increases demand for the other.

substitution effect

It denotes the part of the effect of a price change on demand due to the change in relative prices, assuming that the consumer is compensated sufficiently to remain at the same level to utility. The substitution effect is distinct from the income effect, which is the effect on demand of the change in real income change in price.

sunk costs

These are parts of the costs of an enterprise which cannot be recovered if it ceases operations, even in the long run. These include items such as the construction costs of mines or tunnels, the development costs of industrial processes like assembly lines, marketing structure, etc.

superannuation

It refers to payments to retired employees. In some countries superannuation contributions are deductions from the pay of employees still working, to help to finance payments to those retired.

supply-side economics

It refers to the view that real growth in the economy depends to some extent in the short run, and almost completely in the long run, on factors affecting supply rather than on effective demand. Supply-side proposals to increase economic growth may include measures like the reform of tax systems to encourage investment and innovation, improvements in the infrastructure of transport and communications, better training facilities for newly employed workers, and reforming social security systems to encourage labour supply.

supply-side policy

A policy intended to increase the aggregate supply available in an economy. These policies could include reform of the social security system to encourage the supply of effort, reform of restrictive practices and restrictions on market entry to improve efficiency, etc.

surplus value

It implies the excess of what workers can produce over what they need to consume. As pointed out by Karl Marx, surplus value is essential if economies are to be able to afford either investment or unproductive workers, producing goods or services which are not part of essential consumption.

survey data

It refers to data collected by surveys of individuals or firms. Surveys may be total in their coverage, as with censuses, or may be based on samples of the relevant population. They may be conducted by authorities like government bodies speci- fically set up for the purpose. Surveys are also conducted by private commercial bodies like market research firms, by private bodies, etc.

sustained yield

It is a level of output which can be continued indefinitely, without impairing the future productivity of any natural resources used. It is distinct from over-cropping or resource mining, which reduces or destroys the productive capacity of the resources involved. For example, agricul- ture, where good practices can improve the soil while over-cropping or over-grazing damages it.

sweated labour

The term is used for workers employed for low pay and often for long hours under poor working conditions. In many poor countries, this is true of almost everybody who is employed at all.

syndicate

It is a group to provide insurance. Each member of a syndicate provides a stated amount of capital. If the syndicate makes a profit on the policies it has issued, all members of the syndicate gain in proportion to their share of the capital employed.

syndicated loan

It is a loan provided by a syndicate of banks or other lending institutions. Such loans, often to developing countries are normally arranged by one or a small group of leading banks negotiating the terms, and persuading a large number of other lenders to take up small parts of the loan.

synergy

It refers to benefits from combining different businesses. For example, if company X has a large stock of good ideas ripe for development but few production facilities or funds, and company Y has a large fund of accumulated reserves and factories whose products face declining markets, the two can both benefit by combining.

systematic risk

It refers to the risk arising from disturbances which affect all projects in a class. This type of risk cannot be reduced by diversification. It is distinct from non-systematic or idiosyncratic risk, where the disturbances affecting different projects are independent, so that the overall risk of a portfolio of assets can be reduced by dividing it between a number of projects.

T

take-off
In economics, it is development at which an economy becomes capable of sustained growth in per capita income. An economy which has not reached take-off has savings and investment inadequate to do more than keep pace with population increase, at stagnant levels of per capita income.

takeover
It refers to the acquisition of a company by new owners. The shares of the company are acquired by new owners, normally another company. They may be paid for in cash, or in the purchaser's shares.

talk down
The term is used to refer the attempt to bring down any economic variable through persuasion by the authorities. The variable concerned could be inflation or the exchange rate. Taking down works through policy announcements by influential people such as RBI governors or finance ministers of the country.

tangency equilibrium
It is an equilibrium which can be represented as a position of tangency between two curves. For example, consumer equilibrium is represented as the point where a budget line, which is usually a straight line, is tangential to an indifference curve, which normally has a positive second derivative.

target
It refers to an aim of policy. Economic policy targets include objectives such as high levels of employment and growth, low and stable levels of inflation, or maintenance of particular exchange rates. Policy targets are different from both instruments and indicators. For example, policy instruments are variables the government or central bank can control, or at least influence, such as tax rates or the money supply.

targeting
In economics, it is marking benefits available to particular groups rather than to the public at large. It is intended to keep down the total cost of attaining a policy objective. Targeting can be done in two ways:

(i) providing benefits in kind which appeal only to particular groups, and
(ii) administrative restriction of the availability of benefits in cash or in kind.

target zone
It is a range within which a country decides to keep its exchange rate. The range may be broad or narrow, and may be specified in terms of some single foreign currency or some suitable basket of foreign currencies. A target zone can be interpreted in a strict or relaxed manner.

tax base
It implies the set of incomes on which direct taxes, and transactions on which indirect taxes are charged. The tax base is lowered by all allowances and exemptions: for example, the tax base in some countries is lowered by excluding the investment in insurance, PF, etc. tax base for income tax.

tax burden
It is the total cost to the economy of having to pay taxes. It not only includes the actual amount collected in taxes, but also deadweight costs. Compliance costs include the costs of additional record keeping required because of liability towards tax, and the extra accounting costs of devising methods of tax avoidance.

tax credit
It is a procedure used in some countries whereby income tax on distributed profits is deducted at source. The shareholder receives dividends net of tax, and a tax credit equal to the amount of income tax deducted. The gross dividend including the tax deducted has to be reported, and is used in calculating the taxpayer's gross income and total tax payable.

tax expenditure
It implies the means by which the government can encourage particular activities without appearing to spend money. For example, if the government wants taxpayers, to take out private medical insurance, either it either make specific grants for the purpose, which will appear as government expenditure, or it can pay by giving a tax allowance which reduces net tax paid by an equal amount.

tax evasion
It is an act or a situation when a person deliberately pretends himself/herself to be not liable to tax by showing himself/herself not in possession of goods, services or income subject to tax. It is illegal as the evader cheats the government by concealing facts and the latter loses its due revenue. Tax evasion is, therefore, a cognisable offence.

tax haven
It is used for a country which provides foreign residents with opportunities to reduce their tax payments by doing business there. Tax havens can be used for tax avoidance, when tax liabilities can legally be reduced by using foreign financial intermediaries. They can also be used for tax evasion, for example, by using the confidential bank accounts to facilitate concealment of income and money laundering. Switzerland is a tax haven.

tax holiday
It is a limited period of tax-free operation, or of specially reduced taxation. It is used to induce foreign firms to invest in a country, or domestic firms to invest in an industry or area which the government especially wishes to encourage.

tax refund
It defines a repayment by the tax authorities of excess tax previously collected. This may occur because of mistakes in the original tax assessment which are corrected on appeal.

tax return
It implies a report by a taxpayer to the tax authorities of his or her income, and of any facts affecting their entitlement to tax allowances. Tax returns may be demanded by the tax authorities, with legal penalties for failing to make returns.

tax shelter
It refers to an arrangement by which part of a person's income is protected from taxes.

tax wedge
It is the difference, caused by taxes on employment and social security contributions, between the money benefit to an employee from additional work, and its cost to the employer.

technical efficiency
The term refers to those aspects of efficiency concerned with getting the largest possible outputs for given inputs, or the smallest possible inputs for given outputs. It brings efficiency in production. It is distinct from effi- ciency in exchange, which is concerned with the distribution of outputs between different users.

technological unemployment
It denotes unemployment due to technical progress. This applies to particular types of worker whose skill is made redundant because of changes in methods of production, generally by substituting machines for their services. However, technical progress does not necessarily lead to a rise in overall unemployment, and may even generate employment.

technology
It is the body of know-how about materials, techniques of production, and application of equipment, based on scientific knowledge. Technology requires the services of people who are literate, numerate, and computer-literate to acquire these skills which usually requires a high level of formal education.

technology gap
It is the difference between two countries in the techniques available for production. Technology gaps are based on differences in the education, training and motivation of the labour force, the availability and quality of infrastructure.

technology transfer
It refers to the transfer of techniques from countries where they are more advanced to other countries where they are less advanced. Technology transfer may involve foreign direct investment (FDI), transfers of skilled personnel from advanced countries, training of workers from developing countries like India, China, etc. or licensing of patents.

tender issue
It is an issue of treasury bills by inviting bids or tenders for a stated quantity, and accepting the bids from those offering the highest price.

terms of trade
It can be defined as the ratio of an index of a country's export prices to an index of its import prices. The terms of trade improve if this ratio increases, so that each unit of exports pays for more imports, and deteriorate if the ratio falls, so that each unit of exports buys fewer imports. However, it can be misleading if a country's terms of trade improve because of increased foreign demand for its exports; this is an improvement in its economic position.

test discount rate
It is the real rate of return required to justify investment projects undertaken for commercial reasons in the nationalised industries of some countries.

third-degree price discrimination
It can be defined as the price discrimination where sellers can identify different types of customers, and offer different contracts to different classes of customers. Special prices may be offered, for example, to students or pensioners. This type of discrimination is possible only when resale of goods or services is costly or impossible, otherwise every customer would buy through the groups offered the lowest price.

third world
The term is used for poor or less developed countries. It originated to cover countries which were neither part of the Organisation for Economic Cooperation and Development (OECD), the advanced capitalist bloc, nor of the former Soviet bloc including USSR and East Europe.

tied aid
It is assistance to other countries, normally the Less Developing Countries (LDCs), which has to be spent on goods and services from the donor. This is contrasted with untied aid, which can be spent in any way.

tied loan
It refers to a foreign loan, normally to a developed country, which has to be spent on goods and services from the lender. This is distinguished from an untied loan, which can be spent in any way. A tied loan may be of less value than an untied loan of equal size.

time consistency
It is the property of policies carried out over a period of time, so that the policy choices made at later dates are independent of any commitments made at earlier dates. Where the policy authorities have little credibility, a time-consistent policy is the only one available to them, as there is no point in making promises that others do not expect you to keep.

time discounting
It means placing a lower value on receipts or payments due than on equal payments occurring immediately. It may be on account of time preference, uncertainty as to whether one will survive to benefit from receipts or make payments.

time horizon
It is the most remote future period taken into account in making economic decisions, e.g. investment. While expectations about conditions in all future periods could affect present decisions, there are practical reasons for adopting a limited time horizon.

time inconsistency
It is the property of policies carried out over a period of time, emphasising that the policy choices which would be made at later dates if the authorities were starting afresh are not consistent with commitments made earlier. Where the authorities have credibility, they may choose time-inconsistent policies. Inflation, for example, this year can be reduced by promises to cut government spending or growth of the money supply next year.

time lag
The term refers to the delay, both in the real world economy and in economic models, of actions after the events which are believed to have triggered them. Time lag arises in several ways: (i) there are lags in the collection, collation, and dissemination of economic data. (ii) even where the data is available, economic decision-makers often defer action while they wait for more data to try to assess whether changes are temporary or permanent, or because of disagreement about what should be the response. (iii) when decisions have been taken, it takes time to put them into effect.

time preference

It is the tendency to prefer goods and services now to the same goods and services at a future date. This may be due to three causes: uncertainty, decreasing marginal utility, and impatience. Goods now may be preferred to goods in say 2030, because of uncertainty as to whether one will be alive to enjoy them; because one expects one's total income to be higher than at present so that the expected addition to utility from an equal addition to consumption is less.

time-series data

The term refers to data for the same variable at different times. The intervals may be of any length, ranging from decades or whole trade cycles for economic historians, two years or quarters for national income data, monthly for prices, and weekly, daily or even minute-by-minute for stock exchange prices.

total utility

It denotes a measure of the total welfare of an individual. It is only meaningful on the assumption that utility is cardinal, that is, measurable. Total utility is stated to be a function of the quantities of goods and services consumed and the quantities of various forms of work done.

trade barriers

These are laws, institutions, or practices which make trade between countries more difficult or expensive than trade within countries. Some are deliberately designed to discourage trade, e.g. tariffs, special taxes on imports, which come under this category. In many countries, tariffs have been reduced under the World Trade Organisation (WTO), and various groups of countries including the European Union (EU) and the North American Free Trade Agreement (NAFTA).

trade creation

It is the effect of a customs union in creating or increasing trade between member countries. This new trade results from the reduction in tariffs between the members and is generally welfare increasing. Trade creation is distinct from trade diversion, which is the replacement of trade with non-members by trade between members.

trade cycle

It is a tendency for alternating periods of upward and downward movements in the aggregate level of output and employment, relative to their long-term trends. These are also known as business cycles. In economic models, trade cycles tend to be repetitive in duration and magnitude. In the real world economy, trade cycles have been observed for as far back as statistical records go, but these have been of very varied duration and severity. The horizontal axis shows time; the vertical axis the level of GDP, on a logarithmic scale. ABCD is the ceiling, given by population increase, net investment, and technical progress, EFGHI is the floor, given by population increase, government policy on income support, and autonomous investment minus the maximum feasible rate of induced disinvestment.

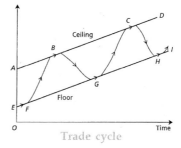

Trade cycle

trade liberalisation

It is the process of reducing or removing restrictions on international trade. It may include the reduction or removal of tariffs, abolition or enlargement of import quotas, abolition of multiple exchange rates, and removal or requirements for administrative permits for imports or allocations of foreign exchange.

trademark

It is a symbol, logo, or name used to enable the public to identify the supplier of goods. Trademarks can be registered, which gives the holder exclusive right to use them. Trademarks may be registered by manufacturers, distributors, or importers.

trade-off

It is the process of deciding whether to give up some of one good or one objective to obtain more of another. The need to trade off goods or objectives against one another is a sign of economic efficiency.

Trade-Related Investment Measures (TRIMS)

It implies an agreement reached in the Uruguay Round of GATT meetings to attempt to control national policies such as investment subsidies which have significant effects on international trade.

Trade-Related Intellectual Property Rights (TRIPS)

It refers to an agreement reached in 1995 as part of the Uruguay Round of GATT 's meetings concerning countries' respect for other countries' copyright, patents, and trademarks. The OECD countries, which own most of these, were very keen on TRIPS. However, many developing countries were very suspicious of it, but some of the NICs, which are developing their own patents, supported it.

trade sanctions

The term denotes a restriction or prohibition by one country of trade contacts with another country of whose actions or policies it disapproves. Sanctions may be general, or applied to particular goods, especially arms and oil. It is difficult to enforce sanctions completely, as trade can be conducted by smuggling or the use of indirect routes. Sanctions increase the costs involved in trade and so can bring some pressure on the countries on which such sanctions are imposed.

trade union

It refers to an organisation of employees, formed for the purpose of collective bargaining with employers over wages, hours, conditions of service, job security, and manning levels. They collect subscriptions to fund services for members such as legal advice about unfair dismissal, strike and pay during stoppages. Trade unions have in the past provided friendly society facilities for their members, including sick and unemployment pay, working conditions, hours of duty and may also negotiate price concessions for their members.

trading currency

It is a currency used to invoice international trade transactions. While the currency of either the buyer or seller is frequently used, in some cases transactions are invoiced in the currency of a third country. European countries use Euro as trading currency.

transfer earnings

It is the amount which a factor of production could expect to earn in its best alternative use. To obtain factor inputs, an industry needs to pay factors at least equal to their transfer earnings. If demand for factors is high, competition may force employers to pay factors more than their transfer earnings. The additional payments are an economic rent.

transfer payments

These are payments of income which are not a return for the provision of current factor services. In many countries, the state makes large-scale transfer payments, particularly to pensioners, the disabled, and the unemployed.

transfer pricing

It refers to the prices of goods and services provided by one part of any organisation to another. This applies particularly to transactions between firms and their branches, subsidiaries or affiliates in other countries. It is possible by using suitable transfer prices to shift overall profits between different parts of the same business.

transitional economy

It can be defined as an economy in the process of major changes in its mode of economic organisation. It may be from a centrally planned economy to a market-based economy, as in the erstwhile Soviet Union and many countries of Eastern Europe. It may also be from a highly dirigiste policy regime to a more liberalised one, as in many developing countries. Transitional economies face special microeconomic difficulties, as they may need to reform their institutions, for example, by creating clear property laws and introducing bankruptcy procedures.

transitional unemployment

It refers to unemployment due to a major change in the way an economy is organised. This could apply to conversion from wartime to a peacetime economy, industrialisation of a developing country, or a shift from central planning to a market economy.

transmission mechanism

It refers to the ways in which changes in prices, incomes, interest rates, etc. are spread between sectors, regions, or countries. It involves the working of both goods and capital markets, and the relation between them. A boom in industrial countries, for example, affects less developed countries through several channels: higher output increases the volume of exports of developing countries.

transplant

In economics, it refers to a product made within a country which was previously imported. Transplants are normally made either by foreign firms, or by domestic firms in association with foreign suppliers. They are common in the motor industry, with many European firms producing in Brazil and other developing countries, and Japanese firms producing in the US and Europe.

treasury

The term is used for the UK's ministry of finance, headed by the Chancellor of the Exchequer. It is responsible for collecting taxes, budgeting for and controlling government expenditure, and management of the national debt. Earlier, it was responsible for overall economic management of the economy, but this responsibility is now shared with the Bank of England, which was made more independent in 1997.

treasury bill

It is a short-dated UK government security. Treasury bills bear no formal interest, but are promises to pay in 91 days, issued at a discount on their redemption price. They are regarded as a highly liquid financial asset by banks and other financial institutions.

trend

It describes a long-term growth path of an economic variable, around which there may be short-term fluctuations. Trends may be calculated by various methods. One of the simplest trends is to regress the variable on time using ordinary least squares. If it is widely believed that there is a constant proportional long-run growth rate, the trend is found by regressing the logarithm of the variable on time.

triangle of loss

It implies a measure of the loss attributable to setting an output level so that marginal cost and marginal benefit are not equal. In a market with an upward-sloping supply curve and a downward-sloping demand curve, if output is below the equilibrium level, the triangle of loss is the area between actual and equilibrium output above the supply curve and below the demand curve.

trickle-down

It denotes the proposition that economic development benefits the poorest members of a society mainly through the effects of increased national income on the demand for labour, rather than through explicit measures to assist them.

trigonometric function

It is a function relating the properties of triangles to their angles. The sine of an angle a, written sin (a), is the ratio of the opposite side of an angle in a right-angled triangle to the hypotenuse (i.e., the longest side). a is the size of the angle measured in radians. The cosine, written cos (a), is the ratio of the adjacent side in the same triangle to the hypotenuse.

triple-A rating

It is the highest grading available from credit rating agencies. A triple-A rating (AAA) means that delay or default in payments of principal or interest on the security concerned is regarded as extremely unlikely.

trough

It refers to the lowest period for real incomes or activity in a trade cycle. In a severe cycle, the trough may be a minimum in absolute terms. In a mild cycle in an economy with a positive trend rate of growth of output, the trough may be minimum relative to trend rather than in absolute terms.

turnkey project

It is an investment project where a foreign firm contracts to build a factory, install equipment and train local labour, and hand it over as a going concern ready to start production. This system means that the supplier's experience of similar plants elsewhere is made available, and unexpected problems have to be sorted out before the host country takes over respon- sibility for the project.

turnover

It can be defined as the value of total sales of goods and services by any organisation during a given period, or the total value of transactions in a given market.

turnover tax

It is a tax proportional to a firm's turnover. This gives an incentive to vertical integration, as the tax may make it cheaper to produce an intermediate product within a firm than to buy a similar input produced more efficiently by an outside supplier.

two-gap model

It is the proposition that development of developing countries is constrained by two gaps: that between domestic savings and the investment required for take-off, and that between export revenues and the imports needed for development.

U

U-form enterprise
It refers to a company in which decision-making has been centralised around a top board of executives whose operational responsibilities are applicable to all company products.

unbundling
It is the sale of peripheral parts of a business to concentrate on its core activities. It may be attributed to the fact that the outlying parts of a business empire could operate more profitably if they are made independent.

uncompetitive
It means incapable to be sold at a profit. Goods or services may be uncompetitive because their prices are too high relative to alternative suppliers, or may be unsaleable because of defects in quality, where other suppliers offer better products. Inability to compete may also apply to a firm, a region or a country.

undated security
It is a security with no set redemption date. With such a security, the borrower has only the obligation to pay interest as agreed, and need not redeem it. An undated security may be irredeemable, when the borrower has no right to redeem it, or it may be redeemable at the borrower's discretion.

undercapitalised
It denotes having too little capital in relation to the business carried on or intended. If a business has insufficient capital, it may become insolvent too easily in the face of the risks normal in its line of activity, such as delays in payment by customers. It is risky to lend or extent credit to an undercapitalised business. Being charged premium rates or refused credit is bad for its profits.

underlying rate or inflation
It refers to the rate of inflation as measured by a retail price index (RPI) excluding mortgage interest payments. It is distinct from the 'headline' rate of inflation, which in some countries like the UK is the Retail Price Index (RPI), which includes mortgage interest payments.

undersubscription
It is the failure of applications for shares in a new issue to match the number on offer. It implies that some shares will be unsold, or bought by underwriters, which makes it probable that when the shares are listed, the issued shares will sell at a discount.

undervalued currency
It is a currency whose exchange rates with other currencies are lower than is necessary for external balance. Such currency tends to improve the country's balance of payments on current account, as relatively low prices make exports easy to sell and imports easy to compete with. It should also make it possible to borrow easily, if the market expects the exchange rate to rise.

underwriting
It is the provision by merchant banks of a guaranteed market for a new issue of shares. Firms making new issues cannot anticipate whether there will be sufficient demand for the shares they offer at the issue price, from the public or institutional investors. An underwriter removes the uncertainty whether shares will sell by promising to buy any the market does not take up.

undistributed profits
These are profits of a business which are neither paid out in taxes nor paid to the shareholders or owners. Undistributed profits are retained into the business. While they may be kept as cash balances or marketable securities, they are usually invested in buying physical equipment, acquiring other companies, or giving trade credit to customers.

unfair competition
It refers to business practices complained of by firms whose rivals offer prices or use methods with which they are unable to compete. For example, they may argue that foreign competitors receive help from their governments in the form of subsidies or cheap loans, which their own government may be unable to provide; or that rivals are unhampered by laws on health and safety which they have to obey.

unified budget
It is the system by which the Parliament is presented with a budget covering both gov-

ernment spending and tax plans to be considered together.

unitary taxation

It describes a system of taxing firms operating in several countries on the basis of a country's share in their total operations. If taxation of a multinational company (MNC) operating in a country is based purely on its profits made in that country, tax can be avoided by accounting procedures. Measures to shift apparent profits out of the country include transfer pricing, i.e. overvaluing purchases by branches of the firm from its branches in other countries, or undervaluing sales to them.

United Nations Conference on Trade & Development (UNCTAD)

It is a United Nations' (UN) organisation established in 1964. It is intended to represent the developing countries and acts as a pressure group for increased aid and an international regime for trade and investment more favourable to developing countries.

United Nations Development Programme (UNDP)

It is a United Nations' (UN) body formed to give technical assistance and make soft loans to underdeveloped countries.

universal benefit

It implies a benefit available to all citizens of a country regardless of income. Universal benefits may be conditional on other criteria, like age for pensions, or disability. Those who favour making benefits universal rather than conditional on a means test believe that means testing is expensive and open to abuse, and an invasion of privacy. Those who oppose the idea state that this is extremely expensive, and may involve most of the money going to people who are not in severe need.

unlimited liability

It refers to liability for the debts an individual or business has incurred, without limit. It is distinct from limited liability, where shareholders in a limited liability company are not liable for its debts provided they hold fully paid-up shares. Unlimited liability for the debts of a business makes it difficult to raise capital for large and complex ventures, as without the protection of limited liability small investors are not willing to put money into a business they do not fully understand.

unofficial economy

1. The term is used for economic activities which are not conducted through legally incorporated bodies and are not reported to the tax and social security authorities.
2. It is also referred to as the informal or unorganised sector. Such activities range from part-time domestic cleaning and gardening to large-scale organised crime and drug trafficking.

unregulated credit markets

It refers to a number of private credit agencies operating in every country. Unlike banks, their forms of organisation and methods of working are not standardised. There is rather great diversity in their organisation, methods, functional areas of operation, sources of funds, effective rates of interest charged on their loans, etc.

unsecured loan

It is a loan where the creditor has no claim on any particular asset of the debtor in the event of default. It is distinct from a secured loan, where the lender has a right to take over some particular asset if repayments are not made at the due dates. In case borrower becomes insolvent or goes bankrupt unsecured creditors normally rank below secured creditors for any available assets.

untied aid

It is the assistance to other countries, normally developing countries, which can be spent on goods and services from any country. This is distinguished from tied aid, which has to be spent on goods and services from the donor country.

urban economics

It is defined as the study of the economics of urban areas. This includes the factors making for the growth first of towns and then of metropolitan areas, including complementarity between industries and the advantage of proximity to markets.

U-shaped average cost curve

It is the shape that average cost curves are believed to take. The argument is that any productive process has some overheads or fixed costs which ensure that at low levels of output, average cost is high. There are bound to be some inputs which cannot be increased indefinitely, at least in the short run. When output is high, shortages of these restrict the efficiency with which such inputs as can be varied contribute to more output.

usury
It means charging excessive interest on loans. The term was formerly applied to charging any interest, but now refers to interest rates the writer regards as unreasonable.

utilitarianism
It implies the belief that rules and institutions should be judged by how good they are for people's welfare. 'The greatest good of the greatest number' was a slogan given by its inventor, Jeremy Bentham. A utilitarian attempts to tackle the question of how far the state should control and how far respect private property by considering its usefulness and defects as a framework for economic activity.

utility function
It refers to the following:
1. An expression showing utility as a function of income, assuming that this is optimally divided between the various goods available. This is usually assumed to show decreasing marginal utility of income.
2. An expression giving utility as a function of non-wage income, the price of each type of good, and the wage of each type of labour, assuming that the quantities of goods consumed and work performed are chosen optimally, so as to maximise utility.
3. An expression showing utility as a function of an individual's consumption of various goods and performance of various types of work.

utility maximisation
It is used for the device of explaining choice in consumption and labour markets by assuming that individuals have utility functions which they attempt to maximise. It made possible by choosing the quantities of all goods consumed so that their marginal utilities are proportional to their prices and choosing the amounts of various forms of work done so that their marginal disutilities are proportional to their wage rates.

V

value

The term denotes the following:
1. It can be deduced by multiplying price with quantity. For example, if between two years, prices quadruple in two years and quantities in the economy increase by 20 per cent, the money value of GDP will be four times its former level.
2. The size of a variable or parameter.
3. A synonym for price. Valuables are goods which sell for high prices. The stock of a shop or firm is transferred from one proprietor to the next 'at valuation', that is for an amount set by a valuer.
4. Also a general term of price. Value in this sense is alike price, but somehow more important, more permanent, and better. This usage is found in the definition of a cynic as 'one who knows the price of everything and the value of nothing'.

value index

It is an index number of the total value of any economic aggregate at current prices. For example, if p_t is the price and q_t the quantity concerned at time t, the value index is given by $V_t = (p_t q_t)/(p_0 q_0)$, where 0 is the base date. Where p_t and q_t are themselves index numbers, which usually is the case in dealing with aggregates, for example, consumption, the value index v_t can be found as the product of a price and a quantity index. One of these must be base-weighted and the other current-weighted.

value-subtracting industry

It implies an industry where the value of output is less than that of purchased inputs, so that value added is negative. Such a situation can arise in two ways: (i) the industry concerned may be heavily subsidised, either by the government or by cross-subsidisation from profitable parts of the same firms; and (ii) value subtraction may be apparent only if inputs and outputs are valued at prices other than those actually prevailing.

variable

It is a quantity which is liable to change. Variable may measure prices, interest rates, income levels, quantities of goods, etc. An exogenous variable is said to be one where the changes originate from causes outside the scope of a given model; an endogenous variable is determined within the model.

variable costs

These are the costs which vary with the level of output such as labour costs. In the short run, some costs will be fixed and some variable. In long run, all costs are likely to be variable.

Variable cost

variable factor proportions

The term denotes the ease with which one factor input can be substituted for another. Where factor proportions are variable, the elasticity of technical substitution between inputs is high. A small change in relative factor prices causes a costminimising firm to shift its use of factors strongly towards whichever has become relatively cheaper.

variance

It is a measure of dispersion. The variance of a set of n numbers is found by adding the squares of their deviations from their mean value, and dividing by n.

venture capital

It is the capital whose owners are willing to invest in new or small businesses, where the risk of losing it is high. Venture capital is necessary if people without sufficient capital of their own are to be able to start new businesses.

vertical equity

It implies the place of income distribution considerations in economic policies such as taxation. For example, if we take the question of how far taxation should be progressive, while there is fairly general agreement that it is necessary to exempt the very poor from income tax, so that some degree of progression is inevitable, the proper degree of progression is controversial.

vertical integration
It is the combination in one firm of two or more stages of production normally operated by separate firms. Vertical integration involves forward integration, for example, an oil company running filling stations; or backward integration, for example, an army running its own ordnance factories.

vertical merger
It is a merger between two firms where one is a major supplier of the other. Examples would be a brewery and a chain of public houses, or a publisher and a bookshop.

volatility
It simply means fluctuation in price, value, etc. over time. Fluctuations may be measured in absolute terms, or relative to trend. Most economic variables are volatile, but some are much more so than others. For example, share prices and primary commodity prices tend to be much more volatile than wage rates and the prices of manufactures.

voluntary exchange
It is the exchange between two parties where each is free to refuse to trade. Under these circumstances both parties will gain, or at least not lose, from the exchange: support for a market economy rests on this point.

voting share
It refers to an ordinary share in a company giving the owner the right to vote at the company's general meetings. This is distinguished from a non-voting share, which gives the holder equal rights to information about the company and to dividends, but no vote.

W

wage differential
It describes a difference in wage rates between two types of worker. Wage differentials may be on account of different levels of skill, different formal qualifications, between unionised and non-unionised firms, or between workers of different age, sex, or ethnic groups.

wage drift
It is the tendency for the average level of wages actually paid to rise faster than wage rates. It may be because of increases in overtime, increases in special allowances, the operation of age-based salary scales, or upgrading of job descriptions.

wage freeze
It refers to a prohibition on changes in wages, imposed as part of a price and income policy. As a temporary measure, a wage freeze may help to cut inflation. It is not very likely to be a practical long-term policy: the pattern of wage rates in force at the time the policy starts is unlikely to equilibrate labour markets even at the time.

wage-price spiral
It is the tendency during inflation for wage increases to lead to price increases and for price increases to lead to wage increases, thus creating an inflationary spiral. Wage increases tend to take prices higher in their own industry by increasing costs, and in other industries by increasing demand.

wage rate
It is the rate per hour paid for work of a given type. It applies where time rates are in force; some types of work are paid for at piece rates. The wage rate is taken as that applying to normal hours of working. Special rates, usually higher, tend to apply to overtime, or work at night, weekends, bank holidays, or other unsocial times.

wage resistance
It refers to difficulty in cutting wages. Real wage resistance applies to cuts in real wages, and nominal wage resistance to cuts in money wages. Both trade unions and those bargaining individually with employers tend to consider wage rises to be lower than the increase in the cost of living which are unacceptable. They also take nominal wage cuts as insulting. Most employers take the same view and are embarrassed even to suggest wage cuts unless their own economic survival seems to be at stake.

wage restraint
The term is used for decisions by trade unions not to demand wage increases, or to moderate their demands. Such restraint is often urged on unions by governments trying to restrain inflation. From the point of view of workers as a whole, there is an argument for wage restraint: if large demands are met, this is likely to lead to loss of jobs. If inflation continues, the authorities are likely to shift to restrictive monetary and fiscal policies, and even with given policies, higher money wages lead to higher prices, lower real balances and thus lower effective demand.

wage rigidity
It is the tendency of wage rates to be 'sticky' and not to adjust so as to clear the market in the short run. There are several reasons for this. Adjustment in the labour market involves the selection of suitable staff by employers and a search for suitable jobs by workers. However, this takes time, and at any moment, nobody has any idea what the market-clearing wage rate would be.

warrant
It denotes a security giving the holder the right but not an obligation to buy shares in a company on some future date at a prearranged price. A warrant will be valuable if, when the date arrives, the market price is above the exercise price.

warranted growth rate
It is the rate at which growth must occur in a Harrod-Domar model if it is to be sustainable. If national income is Y, savings are S, and investment is I, savings are assumed to be a constant proportion of income so that $S = IY$.

warranty
It refers to a guarantee by the provider of goods or services as to their quality. A manufacturer's warranty is only of value of customers if it goes beyond the minimum properties of the good or service required by law.